Reflections From The Golden Era of Hunting

By Fred S. Scott

Reflections From
The Golden Era of Hunting

By Fred S. Scott

Author of *"Memories of Hunting Idaho's Golden Era"*

FOREWORD BY MIKE LAPI NSKI

Copyright 2010 by Fred S. Scott

ISBN 1-931291-79-9

Library of Congress Control Number: 2010925489

First Edition

Published in the United States of America

STONEYDALE PRESS PUBLISHING COMPANY
523 Main Street • P.O. Box 188
Stevensville, Montana 59870
Phone: 406-777-2729
Website: www.stoneydale.com

DEDICATION

To my beautiful wife of forty-eight years; I will love you forever, Karen.

Also, my parents, LeRoy and Elva, for their devotion and love in raising me to be respectful of others regardless of their circumstances, and gaining the respect of my peers by living the golden rule: "Do Unto Others As You Would Have Them Do Unto You."

FOREWORD

The pace of today's life is crazy. Cyberspace and the Internet has made us all instant gratification junkies. It even extends to our sporting world, where TV hunting programs show a random succession of freakishly massive bucks, bulls and bears killed with all the excitement of a commercial slaughterhouse.

That's why I found Fred Scott's new book, "Reflections From The Golden Era of Hunting" so refreshing. It shows us the way we are supposed to view the land, the hunt and its precious wildlife, and should be required reading for all beginning hunters.

Some may say that Fred's philosophy of subsistence hunting as a way of life is a stubborn refusal to accept the reality that we don't actually need the game to live on nowadays, what with our grocery stores stuffed with pre-packaged foods. On the contrary, Fred's collection of hunting stories, ranging from the nostalgia of yesteryear to the present, serves a valuable purpose of reminding us hunters that it's the hunt, not the kill, that defines the true hunter.

Mike Lapinski
Superior, Montana
April 14, 2010

TABLE OF CONTENTS

Dedication 3

Foreword 4

Chapter 1 • The Clays – 1940's 8

Chapter 2 • Bear Hunting – 1951 12

Chapter 3 • Tommy's Bear – 1952 15

Chapter 4 • Claude's Bear – 1953 17

Chapter 5 • First Doe – 1953 20

Chapter 6 • Brothers and Bears – 1954 23

Chapter 7 • An Elk Encounter – 1955 25

Chapter 8 • Not Smart – 1956 27

Chapter 9 • Bears Galore – 1957 29

Chapter 10 • Instinctive Shooters – 1958 31

Chapter 11 • Challenged – 1959 33

Chapter 12 • Tramp – 1960 36

Chapter 13 • Teacher's Pet – 1960 39

Chapter 14 • Combination Hunts – 1961-1962-1963 41

Chapter 15 • Daniel Boone Gets His Elk – 1962 43

Chapter 16 • Clearwater River Goat Hunt – 1963 46

Chapter 17 • Elk Hunters Supreme – 1963 51

Chapter 18 • The White Bull of Pony Gulch – 1963 54

Chapter 19 • .308 Norma Magnum – 1965 58

Chapter 20 • Crazy Horse – 1965 61

Chapter 21 • An Elk Slaughter – 1966 64

Chapter 22 • Good Time Hunt – 1967 68

Chapter 23 • Legal Encounter – 1968 70

Chapter 24 • Picture Book Bull – 1968 74

Chapter 25 • Run-a-Way 76

Chapter 26 • Two Close Calls – 1969 79

Chapter 27 • Holiday Cold Camp – 1969 83

Chapter 28 • Family Abuse – 1970 87

Chapter 29 • Packer's Nightmare – 1970 90

Chapter 30 • Lost Mine – 1971 93

Chapter 31 • Two Bulls Instead of One – 1974 97

Chapter 32 • New Country – 1975 101

Chapter 33 • Old Pete The Pack Horse – 1976 103

Chapter 34 • Montana Bear – 1978 107

Chapter 35 • Lady Luck – 1978 109
Chapter 36 • Montana Deer – 1978 112
Chapter 37 • Dozen Day Bull – 1982 114
Chapter 38 • No Buck No. One – 1982 125
Chapter 39 • Some Funny Happenings 128
Chapter 40 • New Hunting Partner – 1983 132
Chapter 41 • Three For Three – 1984 135
Chapter 42 • Mallard Mountie – 1985 145
Chapter 43 • Twilight Bull – 1985 149
Chapter 44 • Rheumatoid, No Bull – 1987 154
Chapter 45 • Montana Bears – 1990 156
Chapter 46 • Replay Bull – 1990 159
Chapter 47 • Muzzleloader Mishaps – 1991 164
Chapter 48 • Borderline Guide – 1992 168
Chapter 49 • Guide's Intuition – 1992 172
Chapter 50 • No Buck No. Two – 1993 175
Chapter 51 • Salmon River Cow Elk Hunt – 1994 177
Chapter 52 • Brad's Buck – 1995 181
Chapter 53 • Perseverance Pays – 1997 186
Chapter 54 • Big Windy – 1998 189
Chapter 55 • Big Freeze – 2000 196
Chapter 56 • Last Antelope – 2006 203
Chapter 57 • Nevada Buck – 2006 207
Chapter 58 • Never Say Never – 2008 211
Chapter 59 • Close Encounters 218
Chapter 60 • Buck Fever 225
Chapter 61 • Just Reminiscing 228
Chapter 62 • I Don't Want to Shoot a Bear – 2009 245
Chapter 63 • A Lifetime In the Outdoors – 2009 248

INTRODUCTION

The following stories are truly right out of the "Golden Era of Hunting" – they have been told and retold for fifty-plus years over hunting campfires and tables in our homes. We told our tales without regard to correct English, or composition, so you will not find them either grammatically or politically correct.

My father tried to raise his family of five boys and two daughters to be passionate about the outdoor life, particularly fishing and hunting. We were taught to respect nature, and the wildlife therein – but not to be afraid of either one. We also used the simplest of equipment in our pursuit of fish and game, nor did we seek out recognition of harvesting the biggest, or the most; instead, we harvested for the subsistence lifestyle of a bygone era. Our goal was to enjoy to the fullest the camaraderie of friends and family.

I relate these stories in a common man's style and have tried to capture the history of a bygone era, as well as the mystery of new country, or a secret spot, as well as the humor shared among friends and family. Hopefully, this collection of stories will be enjoyed by all members of any family, regardless of whether they are hunters or non-hunters.

In closing, I would like to thank all of my friends that were so generous in sharing their knowledge, and labor, as we shared the pursuits recorded in the stories of this book. Also included is Dale Burk of Stoneydale Press Publishing Company, for his guidance in the publishing and marketing process. I also acknowledge the help of Jack Reneau, director of Big Game Records for the Boone & Crockett Club, for his tips on shipping and handling issues. I also thank photographer Jay Van Kuiken of Wallace, Idaho, for the loan of his photographs to illustrate some stories. I want to thank my nieces, Penny Michael and Toni Jones, for their assistance in selling books.

Fred S. Scott
Wallace, Idaho
March 29, 2010

7

Chapter One

THE CLAYS

Henry and Dora Clay were an Indian couple from Canada, I believe. Henry was the foreman at the Jack Waite Mine over the mill crew, the mine tailings impoundment crew, and also the sawmill and framing shed crews, which consisted of the same people on all these different crews. Dora was a housewife like 99.9 percent of the female population was at that time.

Henry was a man about five feet, nine inches tall, of medium build and I would guess weighed about 180 pounds.. But he was strong and wiry, make no mistake about that. Dora was a women about five feet, five inches tall, and just about as big around as she was tall, but all lady with a capital L. They were our next door neighbors during the 1940's and early 1950's at Duthie, Idaho, the mine camp for the Jack Waite Mine.

The Clays had a huge English Bulldog named "Jiggs, which must have weighed close to fifty pounds and was all head and shoulders. Every evening at 8:30 Jigg's would scratch at our front door, and my mother would go to the door and let my sister's big Persian cat outside. Jiggs and the cat, named Fuzzy, would go over to the Clay's house and the two would sleep together in a big overstuffed easy chair. Come morning the Clays would let the cat out and it would return home. I don't know what started this ritual, but it didn't end until the Clays moved away when Henry retired from work at the Jack Waite Mine.

This Jiggs dog would fight anything. However, Jiggs would get a dog by the throat and clamp down, and he didn't know how to let go! The only thing that would save the other dog's life was when Henry, who was always close by, would pull Jiggs big old bulldog lips back and kick him right in the gums with his calk boots. The blood would just fly, and Jiggs would let go. However the next time that dog or any dog that had ever experienced the Jiggs' treatment would meet Jiggs again, he would take the long route around old Jiggs. One treatment was enough!

Henry was a hunter from the old school, and whenever he got that old .30/40 Krag trapdoor magazine rifle off the deer horns and dropped a handful of Remington Kore-lokt* cartridges into the trap door magazine on the side of the rifle, you could start slicing the onions and potatoes for supper because there would be liver on the menu. Henry, always brought home a nice buck whole, no packboard. He would just rig it up over his shoulder and pack it in. Always, Henry's game would be head shot, no exceptions.

The only other big game he hunted was black bear. Every year he would go hunting twice, every year he got his buck and a bear. No one ever hunted with Henry, and he never told anyone where he went. The only advice I ever heard Henry give anyone was when he told my Brother Don and me, "Always wear calk boots when you're hunting, because you can't hunt if you are on the back of your neck all the time."

He also told us to be quiet, go slow, and see what is in front of you. My dad said Henry would just follow a buck, or bear, into their bedroom, and walk up and shoot them at point-blank range. Henry also told my brother and me to get close and make your first shot count, because you have to walk both ways, anyway, so make it count.

Dad said that one year old Henry went elk hunting over into the Lochsa River country with my dad and his friends. Every day Henry would stay in camp and do the cooking and domestic chores. Dad said about a mile from their camp were the Walton Lakes. Everyday Henry would take some fish line he had coiled in his hatband with a hook on it, and a piece of red cloth. When he got to the lakes he would cut a limber willow bush and go fishing, baiting his hook with a small piece of red cloth. Dad said the trout were ten to twelve inches long, and fat, and hard from that ice cold water – the best eating fish you could wrap a lip over.

Henry also had and old handmade slingshot, made from a forked bush, two rubbers cut from a car innertube, and a leather pocket between the rubbers to hold his projectile. This was usually a ball bearing taken out of old wheel bearings. Dad said that occasionally Henry would come in with five or six blue grouse that he had shot with his sling-shot. I don't think Henry even took a rifle on those trips. My dad said of Henry that he could walk through a cardboard box full of cornflakes, with calk boots on, quieter than most people could walk across a featherbed. I would have to believe it because no one ever proved any different.

Dora was a fisherwoman, she wore the old striped, blue and white, dairy type bib overalls rolled up to her knee, and custom made "White" calked boots on her feet, plus a big, wide leather belt around her waist, and then a big old Stetson hat square on her head. She made her own fly poles out of bamboo kits she got from "Monkey Ward's" – the catalog outfit. I'm sure she tied her own flies, too. But then, like Henry and his hunting, no one ever saw her fishing so there was no way to know what her secrets might be. I do know she caught fish by the stringer-full every time she went fishing. She also liked to fish for "Blueback" salmon when they were running in the Clark Fork river. She caught them by the wash-tub full right below the Cabinet Gorge Dam below Thompson Falls, Montana. They ate fish fresh and fried, smoked, and canned.

Now it was a treat to be invited for dinner at the Clay's. Again, this was something that only my brother Don and I were honored with. Old Jiggs would sit in the corner and wait for Henry to throw him the fish bones.

The Clays had this 1941 Studebaker four-door sedan that was the most elegant car I ever sat in. I don't remember the occasion that Don and I got to ride in this car, but I do remember that car. It had real deep, plush upholstery, elegant wood trim around the windows, and a wood trim dashboard. The steering wheel was white glass with a horn ring that went all the way around inside the steering wheel. This car was equipped with a manual transmission for which the shift lever came up out of the floorboards, and a big V/8 engine that you couldn't even hear running. It was like riding inside a church – not a sound penetrated the inside of the car.

I think it was about 1954 that Don and I had hunted elk from Maple Peak down to the mouth of Butte Gulch where we hit the road. We hiked the two miles down to Murray, Idaho, where we would go into Tester's Store and get something to eat while we waited for Dad to come pick us up. Even though we were teenagers we always had credit at Tester's Store; he was our friend and mentor. We didn't make it to the store because we had to pass in front of the Clay's home, and Dora was in the yard working. As we passed by she hollered at us and asked if we were the Scott boys from the Jack Waite Mine. We answered yes. Dora said get over here so I can fix you some lunch.

We entered the house and sat down to await our lunch. Henry was questioning us about where we had come from and what we were hunting. Then, of course, he had to get out his new rifle that his son had given him. It was a model 721 Remington in .270 caliber, with a four-power Weaver scope and a carrying strap. It was a nice gun, but then Dora pointed out the fact that when Henry went hunting he still used the old .30/40 Krag. Dora called us to the table and set out these Spam sandwiches on homemade bread with some kind of homemade spread on them. They were delicious, and it wasn't just because we were hungry either. We found out that there were only two sandwiches in a can of Spam at Dora's house, and then she set out these huge glasses of cow's milk, and a plate of homemade cookies. It was all we could do to eat all this stuff she put out. Old Henry was just having the time of his life as he watched us eat like it was our last meal, and he was telling us bear hunting stories.

When Dad showed up to pick us up we almost had to stay for supper because the old folks didn't want us to leave just yet. I have no clue why this old Indian couple took such a liking to two blond-headed country boys who could have been their grandchildren. Maybe that was the attraction, because their only son was single. Anyway, we loved them like grandparents, so it was a good relationship for all concerned.

Chapter Two

BEAR HUNTING

I was raised at Duthie, Idaho, which was a mining camp for the Jack Waite Mine. This mine was on Tributary Creek, which was a tributary of the East Fork of Eagle Creek. The Idaho-Montana border was only four miles up an old CCC road, or one and one half miles straight up the hillside. The latter was usually the route that my brothers and I took on our bear hunting expeditions.

This area was heavily hunted by all the local bear hunters as well as nonresident hunters, most of whom were from the state of Washington. So from the time we were five years old we tagged along with our Dad, LeRoy, or neighbors that would tolerate us. Our next door neighbor, Mr. Clay. who was and Indian and an authority on bear hunting; kept our undivided attention for hours with his bear hunting tales. When we got to be about ten years old, bear hunting was our passion, and we were sought out by the nonresident hunters as guides and packers. Nowadays kids that age would be considered unable to perform tasks of that kind; however, we roamed the hills year around, and were expected to do chores that required hard physical labor. So, we were mature for our age.

By age ten my brother Don and I had already acquired our own hunting rifles, paid for by our own labor doing chores for neighbors that were willing to pay us. Our dad had trained us well in handling firearms safely, and in woodcrafts, teaching us to respect all of nature and not to fear it. Even though there was grizzly bears around, and we saw them on occasion, our parents had no concern if we were gone daylight to dark, pursuing bears; it was just what boys did at that time.

There is nothing like living right in bear country, with bear sightings possible any day, June through November, to make boys want to become bear hunters. Another incentive was that all of our neighbors had been through the Depression of the 1930's, and they welcomed any additions to the meat larder. Plus, the rendered lard from bears could be sold to the big hotels in Spokane, Washington. At that time there was no limit on bears, and hunting made the bears very wary, and good at evading detection by hunters, especially young boys

Grizzly bears. (Photo courtesy Jay Van Kuiken)

At the time, there was and old bachelor, a Mr. Blackman, who lived at Murray, Idaho, with his pet bears. Several of Mr. Blackman's pet bears turned on him and mauled him, and the bears in turn were killed by neighbors. But he never quit having pet bears until he could no longer capture them. I remember the story of one big female black bear that he had, that would accompany him every place. In to the grocery store, the Post Office, even the tavern, and she wasn't under any restraint. I remember stories of how they would go to the tavern and drink beer, and they both had a great capacity for beer, until one or the other would fall off the bar stool. At that point they would go home and get into the same bed and sleep it off. Mr. Blackman had a standing order for bear meat with us. He would say, "Boys bring me a big old boar bear, they are the best ones." If you should want to research the story of Mr. Billie Blackman, go to the Kellogg Evening News paper office in Kellogg, Idaho. I think they printed an article on Mr. Blackman during the 1970's some time.

Another bear story of the mid 1950's regarded a local logger in the Murray, Idaho, area who had sawed into a hollow tree during the mid winter months, killing a female black bear that was hibernating in the root system of the tree. This bear had a little cub that only weighed about four or five pounds and wasn't very chipper. This logger took the cub bear into the Courthouse Tavern in Murray, Idaho, to show to his friends. They tried to get the cub to drink some warm cow's milk, but the cub just lay on the bar squirming around and crying for his mother. The cub was real listless so one of the bar patrons suggested giving it some whiskey to revive it. And eye dropper was produced and a few drops of whiskey were forced down the cub's throat. In minutes he started crawling around on the bar top so then some whiskey was poured into a saucer and the cub bear's nose was forced into it until he lapped it up. Now the cub really came to life and started doing handstands, and rollovers, all over the bar top. In minutes the little cub lay on the bar dead; his little heart must have just blown up from that whiskey that he drank. Unfortunate circumstances for both bears; however, that is just life.

Tommy's bear. (Photo courtesy Jay Van Kuiken)

Chapter Three

TOMMY'S BEAR

It was along in the early fifties I'm not sure of the exact year. Anyway, my cousin Tommy came to the Jack Waite Mine camp at Duthie to ask brother Don and me to accompany him on a bear hunt. If Don and I weren't cutting firewood, picking huckleberries, or doing some other chore, we were roaming the mountains. Folks knew our habits so we were pretty popular come hunting season.

It was mid-September and must have been a weekend or we would have been in school. Tommy had his brother Gene's car so we loaded some grub and gear into the car and took off for Murray, Idaho, where another friend of Tommy's, named Buddy, would join us. I think that first night we camped out on the old "Golden Chest" mine dump. There were several old buildings still standing that were quite dilapidated and were full of packrats, so we chose to sleep out in the open under the stars. However, that didn't stop us from lowering the rat population in those old buildings. Someone in the party had a 12 gauge shotgun, and the rest of us were armed with pistols, or our hunting rifles. We would walk into those old buildings and see rats scurrying across the floor, climbing the walls, or hear them running on the ceiling. When the smoke cleared there were rat entails dripping from the ceiling and walls, and those old buildings were well ventilated.

I don't remember sleeping much that night, but that usually doesn't bother young bear hunters much the first night out. We built up a big bonfire to warm up by and cook our breakfast. I don't recall what we had to eat but I'm sure we had a big pot of "camp coffee" because we boys at that time thought you had to be a pretty big man to drink the stuff.

Along about daybreak we started up the ridge on the southwest side of Paragon Gulch about four miles above the old gold camp of Murray, Idaho. We hiked up along this ridge without seeing any game, so about 9:30 a.m. we decided to drop off into the gulch. We were almost to the bottom when Tommy spotted a medium-sized black bear on the side of a finger ridge about 150 yards away.

The bear spotted us about the same time we saw it, and it started across the slope for the ridge-top. Ka-Boom! Tommy's Model 94 .30/30 caliber carbine roared, and the bear started spinning in circles, biting at its side. It was gut shot! I don't recall how many shots were fired or who hit what, but finally the bear crumpled and rolled into the bottom of the draw we were descending. It wasn't long and we had the bear field dressed and tied a rope around the neck and front legs and a half hitch around the bear's nose, before dragging it out to the road. In no time we had it draped over a front fender of the car and we headed for Murray to show it off.

That was the end of the hunting for that day, Buddy knew a couple of girls that lived on the west end of Murray that were pretty popular, and so they dropped Don and me off at our campsite. It was way late the next morning before they returned to camp, and they were in no shape to go hunting. Don and I loaded up our camp into the car, and headed on home, with Tommy and Buddy, both fast asleep in the back seat of the car.

Don and I were happy to just have the chance of going hunting, regardless of whether we got anything or not. I'm sure Tommy and his family were glad to get the nice fat bear. So everybody went away happy, and that's the way all outdoor adventures are supposed to end.

Chapter Four

CLAUDE'S BEAR

I think this story took place about 1953 if my memories are right. I know it was a long time ago.

I was living at Duthie, Idaho, which was the mine camp for the Jack Waite Mine where my father was the mine foreman. There were several bachelors working at this remote mine site right on the Montana-Idaho border at the head of Tributary Creek, a tributary of East Eagle Creek.

Anyway, these old bachelors just loved kids and were always entertaining us boys with stories about their life experiences. This one bachelor named Claude decided that he wanted to be my mentor and teach me the fine art of rifle shooting for marksmanship. Claude had and Marlin Model 336 carbine in .35 Remington caliber that he always wanted me to shoot to sharpen my skills. Claude and I would walk the road down Tributary Creek on most evenings to the forks where Tributary and Columbus Creek joined to form the East Fork of Eagle Creek, a distance of two miles.

Usually, our first stop would be at the camp garbage dump which was only one quarter mile below the camp. This dump had numerous squirrels, rats, mice, porcupine, or just plain cans and bottles that made good targets. If Claude thought something was a challenging target he would give me one shell, and then coach me through the shot. "Now be sure and set the front bead right down in the bottom of the rear sight half moon" that perfectly bracketed the front bead half way up, and then it was "Set your target on top of the bead and carefully squeeze the trigger when the sight picture is right." This little gun was extremely accurate and I would hit my target dead center. And whoever we met after that had to hear how I had made the perfect shot on a difficult target.

I think the most spectacular shot I ever made with Claude's gun was on a porcupine. We had just arrived at the dump site and Claude spotted a porcupine sitting alongside the creek, facing us at seventy-five yards at a steep angle down. He coached me through the shot and when that bullet hit the porcupine, it just exploded like a jug full of water. I don't think you could have destroyed it any better with a stick of dynamite.

Another evening we arrived at the dump late in the evening and were looking for a target to test my skill when a big cardboard box only fifteen feet away rose up out of the garbage pile. And when it fell back into the garbage heap, we were faced with a black bear not fifteen feet away waving his head back and forth trying to get our scent. Claude handed me a cartridge and I quietly inserted it into the gun and brought the sight to the bear's forehead. The bear knew we were there but we were in what I call "My Space" which is when you're close to an animal but they will not hurry to leave. It is like they will leave on their own terms, but will not give up their dignity in doing so.

The bear moved up onto the road and past us, but every couple of steps he would stop and look right at us before moving away. I know that if we had made one move towards the bear he would have attacked. Several minutes passed before the bear climbed up over the road bank and into the trees, but it seemed like forever. We weren't alarmed, just cautious. Even though it was only late July we could have shot the bear, because at the time bears were still just varmints or predators. With them not being classified as big game animals, there was no limit or legal hunting season on them.

About one and three quarter miles down Tributary Creek road there was a settling pond where the waste sand that came out of the mill where the ore from the mine was processed was stored. This sand had a cyanide residue in it as well as some salt, so most evenings if we went that far there would be deer licking the tailings just like a salt lick. Evidently there wasn't enough cyanide in it to harm the deer, or the people that killed and ate them in the late fall of the year. The deer weren't on the tailings pile during the deer hunting season, but every deer in the area had been licking those tailings all spring and summer.

Claude and I had been down to the tailings pile and were walking back towards the mine camp in the late evening, of a late September day. As we approached the garbage dump area in the twilight just before dark, a black bear jumped across the road and ran up the steep road bank, stopping on the edge of the trees. Claude handed me a cartridge and then coached me through the fifty-yard shot. "Hold right behind the foreleg and up one third on the body," he whispered. When the rifle went off the bear just collapsed and slid down the bank into the drainage ditch. Claude about knocked me down slapping me on the back in congratulations for making a perfect shot. This was my first ever bear, and to listen to Claude tell about it you would have thought the bear was

18

running through heavy brush at 300 yards. I think Claude was prouder than I was.

In all the time Claude and I made these late evening hikes, I don't think he ever fired his own gun. In fact, I don't recall that he ever shot that gun while I was with him. I was quite impressed with that old 35 Remington as a killer cartridge. I have always believed a quote made by the late Jack O'Connor, the hunting writer to the effect that, "It doesn't matter the cartridge an animal is hit with, it matters more where it is hit." Another quote of Jack's was that a gut-shot deer hit with a .300 magnum is still just a gut-shot deer.

Anyway, I made old Claude proud, even if it wasn't a big deal to shoot a bear standing still at fifty yards. It made me happy too!

Teepee Creek at the headwaters of the North Fork of the Coeur d'Alene River.

Chapter Five

FIRST DOE

Fall 1953. Brother Don and I were going to join our dad, Leroy, for a deer hunt. Of course dad had gotten us up at 5:30 a.m., his normal time to get up for work. It was a Saturday as dad was off work, and he worked a six-day week at the Jack Waite Mine. We lived at the mine camp about one-half mile from the mine at Duthie, Idaho. Dad fixed us a good big breakfast, and Don and I made us up a big lunch to take along on the hunt. Our family, consisting of five boys and two girls, we gave mom the morning off to sleep in, which was something she didn't get to do very often with a family of nine.

Our family was raised with a strong work ethic. My dad's philosophy was that the only thing you would ever get for free in life was your own labor. From the start all of us children had chores to do every day with no excuses for not getting them done . We learned what a day's work was early in life. Besides our daily chores, we would work out for neighbors or other people cutting firewood, picking berries, shoveling snow, putting up hay, you name it, and we did it for damn little pay. However, we had saved enough money to buy our own hunting rifles cutting firewood for one dollar a cord with a hand saw, shoveling snow for one dollar a building, where the snow would pile up fifteen feet deep over the course of a winter. We never ran out of jobs to do!

On this hunt we would take dad's 1952 GMC pickup down the main East Fork of Eagle Creek to the Cabin Creek drainage, which was five miles below Duthie, Idaho. We hunted up the Westside of Cabin Creek, looking back over towards the more open east side, hoping to see deer browsing along the slope. We had proceeded up the steep brushy slope for about two miles with out seeing or jumping any game. Of course this didn't bother dad any as he just kept on, always climbing higher. Now Don and me, being much younger, were getting bored with this hunt, and tired of climbing besides. So, when ever dad wasn't looking, we would pitch a rock over behind us and down the hill. It worked as dad started sneaking down the hill in pursuit of this deer that always seemed to stay out of sight and below us. However, lo and behold, when we came to the edge of the trees bordering a meadow an old gold placer camp had occupied; there on the far side of the meadow, standing broadside looking at us, was a big mule deer doe. Even though it wasn't dad's custom to shoot does, he said, "Get that deer boys!"

Don and I didn't waste any time getting into a good solid sitting position for the shot. This deer, only seventy-five yards away, was an easy target for us. Our rifles went off simultaneously, and the deer dropped like she'd been head-shot. Miraculously, there were two bullet holes through her ribs when we walked up to her, so there was no argument about who hit where. Don and I couldn't have been prouder if the deer had been a world record class buck. And when dad congratulated us on our shooting, it was like winning an award because he didn't pass out his praise unless it was earned.

Then dad stood back and walked Don and me through the field-dressing process, one step at a time. First we cut around the sex organs and the anus, and then tied them with a string so the fluids wouldn't contaminate our meat. We started our incision right up under the chin cutting towards the rear of the deer so that we were cutting with the lay of the hair. When we got to the rear of the rib cage we put two fingers down alongside the point of the knife so we wouldn't puncture any of the intestines. After the brisket was split open with a hatchet we removed all of the insides, starting with the windpipe, just cutting where necessary until we reached the pelvis. Then we pulled the anus and sex organs forward through the pelvic arch. After this was done we split the pelvis to separate the hindquarters so they could cool out. We also spread the rib cage open by inserting a stick between the ribs. Don and I grabbed the ears and dad got both hind legs and away we went to the truck. Once at the truck we went ahead and skinned the deer so it would cool better, and after separating the quarters we put them in meat sacks to keep them clean.

By this time it was 11:30 a.m. so we sat down next to one of the old prospector cabins to use for a back rest while we ate our lunch. The day had been a beautifully sunny under a bright blue, azure sky like you only see during the month of October after the fall rains have washed all the haze out of the air. As we visited during our lunch break, dad suggested that we take our deer down to Mister Tester's store in Murray, Idaho, where we could hang it in the cooler room.

Mister Tester's store was one of those old country stores where you could buy anything that might be needed, or wanted, by anyone. Don and I really liked Mister Tester because he always had time to show us the rifles that he had for sale, and explain the merits of each one. In fact, the rifles that Don and I were hunting with that day had been purchased from Tester's Store. Don had a Model 99 Savage in the .300 Savage caliber, and used 150 grain Winchester Western Bronze Point bullets in it. I had a model 70 Winchester feather-weight in the new .308 Winchester cartridge, and I used the Winchester Silvertip 180 grain bullet.

It seems to me looking back on that long ago time that people had a lot more patience and respect for one another than they do now. Everyone was willing to help out their fellow man no matter what the circumstance might be. Sure, there were people that didn't share this respect from others, but you had to be a real son-of-a-bitch to find yourself in that predicament. I guess that is why I always believed that you should do unto others as you would expect them to do unto you.

Chapter Six

BROTHERS AND BEARS

Early 1950's. I remember that the black bear hunting was phenomenal in our area of Idaho right up against the Idaho-Montana border. We lived at the Jack Waite Mine Camp at Duthie, Idaho, in the head of Tributary Creek a tributary, of East Eagle Creek.

As boys we always studied the Stoeger's Gun Catalog religiously, and our dad subscribed to all the popular hunting magazines of that era so we thought we were pretty much up to date on hunting equipment, and hunting strategies of the times. Also, at that time people didn't just hunt for trophies or the meat harvested; it was for sport with family and friends.

I also remember that people thought nothing of walking wherever they had to go. The family sedan was used only once or twice a month to make shopping trips to the towns of Wallace or Kellogg for groceries. I know that my brothers and I thought nothing of walking the four or five miles required to put us in hunting country. However, in hindsight, at that time hunting country was anyplace outside of populated areas. You could encounter big game within yards of leaving the house.

One of our favorite hunting areas for bear was in the Butte Gulch drainage, which we could hike to in one hour's time and then hunt the entire drainage from east to west by making a ten-mile circle. On this nice late September morning we had left home real early in the morning because we wanted to be in the head of Butte Gulch by first light. We had just settled in to watch when a medium-sized, black-colored black bear stepped out into an opening and Don spotted it.

I don't know why but it was our custom that on spotting game all members of the hunting party would be made aware of it and everyone would prepare to shoot on the count of three. However, this time Don said "There's a bear down there, one, two, three," and his .300 Savage Model 99 roared and the bear was rolling down the hillside by the time Ray and I were able to spot it.

It was a nice 200-pound fall fat bear that was coal black with one little white patch on the front of its throat. Don was so proud of his bear he even saved the $35 dollars required to have the head mounted. Nobody at that time had trophies mounted, especially teenage boys. It was a short drag of one fourth mile out to the road, no big deal for us.

It was still early so we continued the hunt out along the ridge on the north side of Butte Gulch to the west. We had just gotten into the first side drainage when we saw another bear hurrying around the hillside some 300 yards away. The bears in this area were hunted hard every year by local and nonresident hunters so were very wary. I guess Ray and I were feeling left out from not getting to shoot at the bear Don got, so we opened fire on this nice bear. Ray was shooting a big .375 H&H Magnum Model 70 Winchester so when he hit the bear it did a complete somersault down the mountain and then headed out for the bottom of the gulch. We both managed to hit the bear several times, just not where we should have.

As the bear went to cross the bottom of Butte Gulch it stopped and turned broadside for just a brief moment, and I was able to shoot it through the shoulders with my Model 721 Remington in .270 caliber to put it down. As we went down the hillside to the bear we could see that every time that big magnum had hit it through the guts there was a big splash of blood and guts on the ground. We would find that Ray had hit the bear three times with that big magnum, and I had hit it once too far back and through the shoulder. Five hits on a 250 -pound bear before putting it down! I guess this proves the late Jack O'Connor's statement that a gut-shot animal with a big magnum rifle is still just a gut-shot animal.

It has always amazed me how much damage wild animals can sustain without expiring if not hit properly with the first shot. This brings to mind another statement made by the late Ted Trueblood, another outdoor writer of the 1950's: "Take the time to make the first shot hit where you intend it to because it will be your best opportunity."

In no time we had field dressed the bear and were ready to drag it the one and one half miles up the Butte Gulch trail to the Maple Peak road. It was early afternoon when we finally hung our bear on a pole between two trees next to Don's bear. We hiked back to the Jack Waite mine camp at Duthie and got dad's pickup truck to haul our bears the four miles home.

Hunting for most hunters today will never be the relaxed no pressure experience that we enjoyed. But if you just enjoy the experience, and leave out the quest for the recognition of being the best, or getting the biggest trophy, it can still be the rewarding pastime that we experienced. Whatever, just enjoy every hunt like it was your last.

Chapter Seven

AN ELK ENCOUNTER

Fall 1955. This elk hunt was just a weekend hunt in Butte Gulch, which is a tributary of Prichard Creek, north of Murray, Idaho, in Shoshone County. My brothers Ray and Don would be my companions on this hunt. Don and I were high school students in Wallace, Idaho, and brother Ray was employed as an underground miner at the Jack Waite Mine.

I'm sure this hunt was in October, because we were still enjoying those crispy cold nights and sunny warm days so prevalent at that time of year.

We parked Ray's 1951 Pontiac two-door coupe on the northeast side of Butte Gulch before first light as we wanted to be out on the ridge on the north side of Butte Gulch before another morning was born. We all went as a group because this was an exploratory trip out to Axe Gulch. It was decided that we would just traverse along about one-third of the way down on the hillside so that we could look into all of the little side drainages coming up onto this main dividing ridge.

We were only a mile out the ridge watching down into one of these little drainages when right on the upper edge of the pocket Don spotted a big trophy mule deer buck laying in front of an old grey log, with its antlers right in front of the root system. Don didn't bother to tell Ray and me about the deer; he just shot it with his Model 99 Savage in .300 caliber before Ray or I even knew the deer was there only 100 yards away. The buck was a real trophy with a thirty-three-inch spread, but since our family wasn't trophy hunters the buck was never scored or mounted; we just nailed the antlers up on the side of the woodshed.

Ray and I decided that since Don hadn't bothered to make us aware of the deer we would just continue our elk hunt while he took care of the deer by himself. Elk weren't real plentiful in this area, but just by luck we spotted a herd in Sheridan Gulch when we came over the hogback ridge on the eastside of this gulch. The elk also had spotted us so they were vacating the scene like a pack of Greyhounds. Our butts hit the bear grass and we commenced shooting as the elk lunged across the open basin. On my second shot I saw a cow elk I was shooting at do a complete forward somersault, and then she came up on her feet running. We had both managed to empty the magazines on our rifles before the elk disappeared over the far ridge.

Ray and I spent the rest of the morning trying to find some blood, or other sign that would indicate that I had scored a hit on the cow elk that had fallen head over heels. We couldn't come up with anything, so then we decided that maybe the cow elk had tripped over something in her path. In hindsight I guess we weren't very ethical in our decision to shoot at these running elk, but I guess you could say hindsight is 20-20.

After we gave up on finding the elk we went back to help Don pack his deer the mile back to the car. We didn't have any packboards with us but we were young and tough, so we just put the halves over our shoulders and went to the car. With me being the youngest, I got to pack the three rifles.

We all got our deer before the season was over that year. However, good old Dad was the only one to score on elk. It was a nice 5X5 bull elk, and we tough boys got to pack it out too. However, that is just part of the total hunting experience.

Chapter Eight

NOT SMART

Fall 1956. In early March of 1956 Brother Don quit school and joined the Navy, so I lost my hunting partner. When school let out in the spring I decided that I didn't need to go to school any longer. I had been getting into too much trouble at school by getting into fist fights between classes; I even punched one of my shop teachers for slapping me across the face like a goddamn woman. Mom was very disappointed in us boys, so she said you're not going to lie around and get into trouble, so you can just go to South Dakota and work for your grandfather. And what mom said was what the law was at our house.

I had worked all the previous winter again setting pins at Albi's Alibi Alley's in Wallace, Idaho, so I purchased a 1950 Chevrolet two door coupe for $400. My old 1941 Plymouth had given up the ghost after 120,000 miles and I had sold it for junk for $75 dollars, only $25 dollars less than I had paid for it in 1954.

Anyway, I took off for South Dakota to work on Grandpa's cattle ranch. Grandpa raised Hereford/Durham cross cattle, not the purebred compact Herefords that were so popular at that time. Grandpa's cows were big rangy 1,200 pound animals that could have a big calf without any trouble and gave more milk than the purebred Herefords. Grandpa's cows were open range cows, and were never brought in around the ranch buildings. Calving, branding and vaccinating were all done on the open range. Grandpa always said he didn't want any cows that were looking for ways to get hurt or sick and that the less fooling around with them that you do the better off you are. He must have been right because his cattle always topped the market, and Iowa cattle buyers would come right to the ranch to get them.

I guess that I wasn't cut out to be a ranch hand, and grandpa wasn't a strict enough disciplinary person to get along with an arrogant kid. We just didn't get along, so in late August I quit and went back to Wallace. When I got home a friend got me a job as the lot boy at Robinson's Motors Pontiac-Cadillac dealership in Kellogg, Idaho. There I was paid one dollar per hour for six eight-hour days per week, forty eight dollars a week. Anyway, I was back under mom's watchful eye, and besides with my work schedule I didn't have much time to look for trouble.

That fall my hunting was pretty limited because of the six day work week. However, every Saturday evening I would go back up to Duthie, Idaho, and stay with dad for a day. Along in mid-October, a friend, Bert, and I went hunting up on the Butte Gulch-Bear Gulch divide out by Maple Peak. We hunted up along the divide where we could watch down into the drainages on both sides until about noon without seeing any animals, so we dropped down onto the Maple Peak road and were walking back along the road towards my car. I just happened to be looking down over the road bank onto a ridge breaking down into Bear Gulch when I spotted a mule deer buck standing on the edge of the trees watching me. I sat down on the road bank and got into a good solid sitting position and shot the buck through the heart with my .308 Winchester model 70 feather-weight rifle. The little 3X3 buck just melted to the ground in slow motion. It was only about 200 yards to the road so Bert and I just grabbed an antler and dragged the deer up to the road.

This hunt was no big deal but did bring some closure to a year I wasn't very proud of. As I look back on that year of being a real pain in the butt for a lot of people, I can't believe that my dad hadn't kicked my butt. And believe me, even though he was only five foot six inches tall and 140 pounds he could have done the job. I guess he thought I just needed some time to get over being a boy and try to become a man.

Chapter Nine

BEARS GALORE

1957 was another year when I was working six days a week, ten hours a day, so I didn't get to hunt as much as I would have liked to.

However, a friend, Bert, and my brothers and I had purchased a Model 70 Winchester with a twenty-six inch barrel in .220 Swift caliber. This gun was equipped with a twelve power Weaver scope, with a three minute dot reticule, and let me tell you we were very proficient shooting it. When that Swift went off, something was going to heaven.

Early in the spring when I was on my way up to the Jack Waite Mine camp for my day off, a friend, Vern, and I jumped a pack of five wolves in the forks of Eagle Creek. There were five pure black timber wolves after Mr. Tester's dairy cows in the pasture. I got three of them before the rest of them got out of sight in the brush bordering the pasture. And during the winter of 1957, another friend, Ron, had run down a big gray wolf with his pickup truck on the plowed road on East Eagle Creek. These were not the only wolves that were seen in that area, just the only ones killed.

My friend Bert that we had purchased the gun in partnership with, and I made some spectacular shots with that gun on black bear. We were hunting off of the Maple Peak road, in Bear Gulch, which is a tributary of Prichard Creek in Shoshone County Idaho.

We would spot a bear in the huckleberry patches on the north side of Bear Gulch below the road, and then move into position for a shot. Usually, due to the steepness of the slope and the many ravines, it was not possible to get closer than 400 yards. With that .220 Swift we could hit small targets at 500 yards consistently, so 400 yards was a cakewalk. We both harvested our bears with shots into the spine for one shot kills. It was only after the shot that we wondered what had possessed us to shoot bears one half mile down that steep slope. By the time the bears were packed out of there, we were promising ourselves that we wouldn't do that again.

Later that fall I was hunting with a friend up on the state line above the Jack Waite Mine. This area was our favorite bear hunting spot because the northwesterly ridge would catch the wind in winter time and pile snow drifts forty feet deep on the east facing slope. It was always late summer before these drifts melted, so there were always huckleberries along this ridge to attract the bears in late September. This area was adopted by the locals as part of our territory that we referred to as Lapland (where Idaho lapped over into Montana). There were big alpine basins all along the state line on both sides of the border, and it was in one of these basins that I saw a big blond grizzly sow with two yearling cubs that were perfect replicas of their mother. This sow and cubs were chocolate brown about two thirds of the way up on their sides, and their heads were dark chocolate also. I would see this same family of bears three times that fall, and no one ever bothered them. Because we felt privileged to be able to observe them just being bears in their own habitat.

This same area made me question the statement made by many people that were supposed to know bears from years of study, and that was that bears have poor eye sight. These big basins were all east-facing, so we always hunted them in the evenings when the air thermals were rising, and we had the setting sun at our back. Most of these basins went down pretty steep for about one fourth mile and then benched out fairly flat for another one fourth mile before dropping off into the main canyons. The bears would go down into the creek bottoms during the day to lay up in the water and shade to keep cool, which is quite a problem when you're as fat as a fall bear. Anyway, the bears would come up to feed on the huckleberries on the upper slopes during the night. When these bears came up over the brink of the bench area you would see them climb up onto a log, or rock, and scan the slope above for hunters. And I'm telling you if you weren't concealed in front of, or behind cover, they would spot you every time from a half mile away. Now these bear were hunted hard and were very wary, but I don't think there was anything wrong with their eyesight. If they saw anyone along that ridge they went right back into the bottoms until after darkness fell.

You might not agree with my assessment of a black bears seeing ability, or their natural wariness when hunted hard. But those bears didn't get to be big bears by being stupid. I'll never forget that wonderful area as long as I live. It was as close to heaven on earth, as any place I've ever had the pleasure of living.

Chapter Ten

INSTINCTIVE SHOOTERS

I'm not sure if instinctive shooter is the right word to describe the people I'm trying to identify. What I mean is someone who just throws a gun up, points it at the target and fires without looking through the sights.

The first fellow I ever saw that could do this was a fellow who lived in the mouth of Tiger Gulch right beside the Murray Cemetery. This fellow's name was Clarence and he had an old Winchester carbine in .25/35 caliber and he claimed he could shoot the little metal ball off the end of a car aerial going by on the road in front of his house. This was a distance of about seventy-five yards. I never witnessed this maneuver, but I did witness him shooting quarters thrown into the air. The ding from the bullet might not be dead center, but it did indicate that he had hit the quarter, sending it spinning off across the lot behind Roby's Tavern in Prichard, Idaho.

There was another family that lived just across the road from the mouth of Pony Gulch on Beaver Creek by the name of Brittons The dad was the head sawyer at the Burns Yak Lumber mill in the mouth of Eagle Creek. The youngest boy, nicknamed "Tub," was a reckless, rowdy kid about eighteen years old. His younger sister was a blue-eyed blonde with an angel face with those bee-stung lips that just begged to be kissed. All of her other assets were in the right places, too. I guess you would describe her as being stacked. This little gal was called "Babe," short for daddy's baby.

I was keeping pretty close company with this doll, so Tub asked me if I wanted to go bear hunting. I said sure, and Babe can ride along too because then I won't have to do any hiking. We took my old 1948 Chevy (five window cab, a deluxe model) pickup and drove up the Coeur d'Alene River to Lost Creek and took off up this road to Taylor Saddle. We didn't see any bears on this drive so we turned off on to the road that would take us up over Bloom Peak.

We were just approaching Noseller Saddle on our way off the peak, when a black bear jumped up into the road and went running right down

31

the middle of the road. Tub grabbed my old Model 94 Winchester in .32 Special caliber and bailed out of the truck and went running down the road after the bear. Just before he passed from sight around a bend in the road, he threw the gun up and fired off a shot while still running down the road. When we pulled up to him I was surprised to hear him say he had gotten the bear, and it was just over the road bank. And then he said I shot him right in the back of the head. I said, "Yea Right," but when we dragged the bear up into the road he was hit right in the back of the head.

Later in the fall I brought Babe home in the wee hours of the morning and when we went in the house, Tub says, "Lets go elk hunting up Pony Gulch". I always had that old Model 94 Winchester .32 Special wrapped in a blanket behind the seat of my old pickup, so I said. "Why not." At first light we drove off up Pony Gulch road. We weren't a quarter of a mile up the Pony Gulch road when right by the first meadow a big 6X6 bull elk jumped off the upper road bank and lit in the middle of the road. In about five more big lunging bounds he was across the meadow and splashing across a beaver dam. Before it even registered on my sleep-deprived mind, Tub grabbed the rifle and jumped out and dropped that bull right in the middle of that beaver pond. We managed to get the truck down into the meadow and get close enough to tie a chain to the bull elk's hind legs and pull him up into the meadow. I couldn't believe it when I saw that he was hit right in the back of the head. Tub said, "That's the only place I shoot an animal because it doesn't waste any meat."

Now, you figure either one of these deals anyway you want to, but I would just call it INSTINCTIVE SHOOTING! You just couldn't call it "BLIND LUCK" because they were consistent at it. This Tub kid didn't even own a gun.

Chapter Eleven

CHALLENGED

1959 was a pretty hectic year for me as I had worked all over the Northwest, and part of the Southwest, chasing rainbows. As usual, I never did find the pot of gold at the end of the rainbow.

When October came around my oldest brother, Lawrence, and I took our vacations from the uranium mines that we were working in down in New Mexico and returned to Shoshone County Idaho, for an elk hunt. I was successful getting my deer on this trip, but was unsuccessful on elk.

When we got back to New Mexico I decided that I could always get another job, but maybe I should quit my job and go back to Idaho and try to get my elk. In a matter of just a few days I was successful at getting my elk, but I still wasn't ready to quit hunting and go find a job.

Bear season was still open so that gave me and excuse to keep hunting. I was headquartered at the Jack Waite Mine camp at Duthie, Idaho, where I was staying with my dad, LeRoy, and brother Ray. Now this area is awful good bear country and the fall had been extra mild so the bears were still out foraging for food.

I went up to the pass going into Montana and then drove out the Maple Peak road to Butte Gulch. Now that all of the brush had dropped their leaves and the golden tamarack trees had shed their needles, the country had lost that beautiful array of fall colors. Everything was a drab, denuded, a mixture of dull grays, browns and greens. The only bear food available was the sour, bright orange mountain ash berries, which bear like to feed on just before going into their winter dens.

The watershed for the mine and camp was the perfect spot to find the mountain ash berries. This drainage had the logical name of Water Tank Basin because of the big wooden storage tank located above the mine dump. So I climbed out onto and rock outcropping where I could glass this basin with my binoculars.

I had been watching for about one hour when I happened to look back over towards the road I had drove in on and saw a bear cross the road and go into the brush below the road. At least now I knew there

33

Photo courtesy Jay Van Kuiken.

was still one bear around so I was watching intently trying to spot it again. About forty-five minutes later I saw a brown-colored bear stand up on its hind legs and pull the branches of a mountain ash bush down and strip the berries off with its mouth. I was sure this was the bear that had crossed the road because it had been brown, too. The bear was only about 100 yards down the slope from where I sat on the outcropping of rock. And I had my model 721 Remington rifle in .270 Winchester caliber, with a four power Weaver scope, and a three minute lee dot reticule. I had worked up a reloaded cartridge with 150 grain Nosler Partition bullets at a velocity of 3,000 feet per second that was extremely accurate in this rifle, so I had no doubts about making the shot on this bear.

I very carefully aimed to hit the bear in the neck as that was all that cleared the brush. When the rifle shot shattered the stillness, the bear just disappeared. I was sure my shot had been true so I worked my way down through the brush to where the bear had been standing. When I parted the brush where the bear had been standing I found the bear, but there was a large cub lying across her body, snarling and popping its teeth together.

I didn't want to kill the cub so I threw a stick at him to scare him off. That little sucker didn't scare at all. Instead, he made a false charge

34

at me. At this time he was between me and his mother, jumping up and down on his front feet and popping those teeth together like pistol shots going off. I had a .22 caliber pistol on my hip so I shot three times right between his front feet, kicking dirt and rocks up into his belly. That cub never gave an inch, he just growled louder, and snapped his jaws together harder. At this point I decided the only way I was going to claim my bear was to kill the cub too. He was such a courageous little warrior I almost couldn't do it.

When I field dressed the bear I discovered that she was still nursing her cub, so the little guy probably wouldn't have made it anyway on his own. It was and easy job to drag the two bear about one fourth mile down through the brush to a road going below. However, the climb back up to my car took way over and hour.

It hadn't been my intention to kill a sow bear with a young cub, because no one would want to do that. I don't know if the cub had already crossed the road when I saw the sow cross, or if he crossed after I turned my attention away from the road. I do know I can still see that little guy ready to defend his mother, or be killed trying. And to this day, it is not a pleasant memory.

Fred Scott on State Line above Loop Creek.

35

Chapter Twelve

TRAMP

Fall 1960. This had been a very busy year for me because I was just tramping all over looking for work. And when I found a job it never seemed to satisfy me no matter how much it paid.

In April I quit my job at the Jack Waite Mine and went to work for Diamond International out of Superior, Montana. This job consisted of opening up logging roads into the Clearwater River Country. When we broke through the snow drifts on top of HooDoo Pass the snow measured twenty-two feet deep.

As soon as we got as far as the Cedars Logging Camp, it was opened for the season and the camp became our headquarters. We had opened all the logging roads, cleaned out the road culverts, and fixed any road damage we found by the end of May. So I quit again and went to work for Russell Oliver Logging Co. out of Superior, Montana. My first job was hooking logs and loading log trucks, on a single line heelboom on Sunrise Creek east of Superior. About the first of July I went to work on a Forest Service road building job doing the same thing as the Sunrise job, only on this job we were clearing right-of-way for the road.

About the middle of August everything had dried out and there was very low humidity, and then we had a fire. This was on a south facing slope with big mature yellow pine timber, with fir thickets in the draws. The exhaust off of the heelboom engine blowing on the slope caused the fire. The ground under the trees just started turning black, but there was no smoke or fire visible. Then, before you could say Jack Robinson, we had a crown fire burning up the slope. I was put right in the middle of this fire, using a chainsaw to fall snags that were burning and the sparks just showered down on us. When the snag would start to fall, the top would break off and come flying back towards us. I decided right then, I didn't want to be a forest fire fighter, and ever since then, if some one tells me they like fire fighting, I figure they have never been on a fire or they're stupid.

The Forest Service fire crews just stood in the road watching everything burn. I guess the contractor had to pay for any stumpage that burnt. The job was on Ward Creek, a tributary of the St Regis River. Right after this fire they closed the woods because of the extreme fire danger, so I headed down to Grants, New Mexico, to work in the uranium mines with my oldest brother, Lawrence.

This was my first contract mining job. I worked at the Dog Mine a small operation. At first I worked mining in the ore stopes that were flat veins of high grade uranium ore, using a pillar system. We drove multiple tunnels through the ore body to the back of the vein, and then pulled the pillars as we came back out towards the main drift. Finally, they put me mucking the ore out of draw holes that came down into muck bays off the main haulage drift, from there we hauled it by rail car to the main shaft pocket and dumped it directly into the ore skip to be raised to the surface. This ore was in a Sandstone Formation and was so fine that, when broken, it would hang up in an ore pocket or chute if left there. We made big money doing this extremely dangerous work; we were making $2,000 dollars a month. Most mines paid from $5,000 to $7,000 dollars per year.

Anyway, when the elk season opened in Idaho we decided we needed to go elk hunting. Lawrence had vacation coming, but I didn't, but the boss said, "Go anyway. We'll hold your job for you." We went to the Jack Waite Mine camp and stayed with our dad, and then hunted from there. We didn't have any luck elk hunting, so one day I went deer hunting with my Brother Ray. We were headed to Bob Tail Peak, once there we made a big circle around the base of the peak which was all good deer habitat. It was about 10:30 a.m. on a bright sunny fall day and we were almost down to the saddle where the road came up from the North Fork of the Coeur d'Alene River. We were walking along an old brushed in logging spur road when I spotted a nice mule deer buck about 200 yards below the road.

I had a Model 721 Remington in .270 Winchester caliber, loaded with 150 grain Norma Partition bullets at 3,000 feet per second velocity. There was an old stump on the edge of the old road that made the perfect rifle rest. I very carefully aligned the dot reticule in my four power Weaver scope tight behind the buck's shoulder, and low on the rib cage because of the steep downhill angle. Boom! My buck never moved out of his tracks. When we got the deer field-dressed, we just wadded it up on my packboard, head, hide, the whole works. Ray had to help me to my feet, and then hang onto the corner of the packboard to help balance the load. This was a nice 5X5 mule deer buck with eye-guards, or first points whichever you choose to call them. After the buck was skinned and quartered it weighed in at the locker plant on state certified scales at 160 pounds. No wonder it had been such a load!

The following day we made a hunt off the top of Dobson Pass, following the ridge trail going out towards Two Mile Saddle. We were only out the trail about a mile when as we came down into a saddle in the ridge, and there was a mule deer buck crossing the saddle. Brother Ray got into a steady position alongside of a tree and made the easy shot to harvest his buck. This buck was almost a twin to the buck we already had, only this one was a 4X4 typical that didn't have any eye-guards, and he weighed 150 pounds at the locker plant in the quarters.

While we were up elk hunting I read and ad in the newspaper where they had a 1959 Chevy ½ ton pickup for sale at an estate sale over at Hayden Lake, Idaho. So, I went over to look at it, and it only had 1,700 miles on it, and they wanted $1,700 dollars for it. I gave the man seventeen one hundred dollar bills, and he gave me the title. I needed a new truck anyway.

When we got back to Grants, New Mexico, I decided that I wasn't done elk hunting yet, so I quit my job and went back to Idaho. I did manage to get my elk all right but that is another story. You will have to get my first book, *"Memories of Hunting Idaho's Golden Era"* to read about that elk hunt.

After I was done hunting I got a job at the Jack Waite Mine again. I was just learning to be a drift and raise miner so this was another good experience for me. I had spent about six weeks hunting so now I was ready to go back to work.

Chapter Thirteen

TEACHER'S PET

Fall 1960. My brothers, Bob and Ray, came to ask me to help them pack out a cow elk they had harvested the day before. They had been successful on Hammond Creek, a tributary of the North Fork St. Joe River, which is a tributary of the famous St. Joe River in Shoshone County, Idaho.

Bob and Ray had hunted up the Hammond Creek Trail almost to the head of the creek, and then climbed up onto the south slope so they could observe the south facing slope on the north ridge, a perfect place to spot an elk feeding or bedded down. After much glassing with their binoculars, they were able to spot a cow elk bedded in the heavy alder brush, away, and away, across the canyon in a place that was un-approachable. Even though the range was an estimated 1,000 yards, Bob thought that his .375 H&H Magnum was up to making the shot if he did his part and squeezed off the perfect shot. Bob had a rock solid rest over a log so he went ahead and shot. At the shot the cow elk jumped to her feet, and then threw herself over backwards into the brush. After finding the elk, and field dressing it, the boys determined that Bob had luckily hit the cow elk in the heart.

We had a friend who rented his packhorses out for ten dollars per day for each head of stock, so we approached him for the use of a horse and instructions on how to pack elk quarters onto the horse. Our friend gave us every thing we needed, and then gave us a twenty-eight-year-old horse that had packed many an elk. This would be just the horse we needed because we were greenhorns when it came to packing horses.

We arrived at Hammond Creek with old Buck, the packhorse, and I would take Buck up the north ridge following the trail flagged out by my brothers. Suddenly, the flagged trail turned off into a wall of brush that was chest high on my six-foot frame. I dropped Buck's lead rope and fetched the pole-axe off the packsaddle, and then rolled up my sleeves to start chopping a trail through the thicket. I had only started when I heard a noise behind me and, to my amazement, here came Buck with his head off to the side to keep the lead rope from under his feet. When Buck got to me he just stepped around me and continued down the hillside following the flagging ribbon. I followed Buck right to the elk that the guys had skinned and quartered already. It less time than you would imagine I had Buck loaded with two hindquarters and was headed back for the truck. It was a five mile round trip to the truck so Buck and I was both ready for a break when we got back to the kill site.

The guys had a nice cheery fire going so we just cut some thin strips of meat off the loin and roasted our meat over the fire. We had no seasoning, but we didn't need any as we were hungry, and besides that, the roasted meat was delicious. This was the first time we had ever tried this deal, but it surely wouldn't be the last.

Just as we started out with our last two quarters of elk meat packed on old Buck's packsaddle, a big rainstorm came rolling over the ridge from the southwest. In no time we were drenched to the skin. When we arrived at the truck we hurried to unload the elk quarters off the horse, and get the elk quarters secured to the inside of the pickup rack. I fetched an old army wool blanket from behind the truck seat and then wrapped it around Buck and topped it off with a canvas pack cover to keep him warm and dry during the ride home in the open pickup box.

After thirty dripping wet miles we arrived back at the ranch and unloaded Buck, and he was completely dry under his blanket and canvas wrap. We rewarded Buck with a double serving of hard earned oats, and then turned him out into the pasture. It had been an easy day for old Buck, a piece of cake so to speak. We came away with some experience about packing horses, from an old horse that was sure a pro at his job. I think our friend gave us this horse for that reason; he knew that old horse wouldn't let us hurt him, and that the horse wouldn't hurt us either. We learned that if you use well trained horses your problems will be few, and your back will feel better at the end of the day.

My advice is to take care of your horses and they will take care of you. I wish you the best of luck in your packing classes, and may all your hunts be successful.

Chapter Fourteen

COMBINATION HUNTS

The year of 1961 was spent tramping all over the country working. In the early spring of 1961 I got laid off at the Jack Waite Mine and went back to Superior, Montana, to work at logging for Russell Oliver Logging Co. About June of 1961 we went on a Forest Service road contract job, building road down the main Clearwater River below Cold Springs Logging Camp.

By mid-July we were in the middle of another dry, bad fire year. Whenever you worked on a Forest Service road contract if they asked you to fight fire you had to go, even if it wasn't on your job. Anyway, there were big fires all over Idaho, and they told us we would probably have to go to Lost Trail Pass to fight the Saddle Mountain fire. So I quit and went back to New Mexico to work in the uranium mines out of Grants. I went to work at the Kermac Metals section seventeen mine driving drift on a contract. It wasn't long and I had a falling out with the boss so I quit and went to work at the Sandstone Mine, which was a Kermac Metals mine also. This, too, was a drift contract. The whole idea of contract mining is to develop a system where you could get the most footage, or tonnage production, with the most efficient use of time, material, and labor. I stayed with this job until about December, and then the boss tried to slip one of his friends in on my contract so I quit.

I ended the year working back in Montana, hooking and loading logs for Russell Oliver Logging Co. In 1961 I had a bad accident and totaled my 1959 Chevy pickup so I bought a 1961 Chevy Corvair SS new for $2,100. I also started buying old 1950-1952 Chevy cars and trucks for work vehicles because it cost too much to license new cars in Montana. That fall I managed to get my buck but I never did have time to do any serious hunting because of all the tramping around.

In 1962 I worked at logging until the spring break-up and then quit and went back to the Coeur d'Alene Mining District, where I worked in the mines doing contract work. I also got married in June of 1962. Later in the fall that year I was hunting with my brother-in-law, Bob, up in

Butte Gulch east of Murray, Idaho. We were hunting in Dry Butte Creek, a small tributary of Butte Gulch. I shot a running 3X3 mule deer buck with my .270 Winchester through the lungs at 100 yards. Bob got a little forked horn buck the same day.

1963, I was hunting with my brother-in-law, Frank, up by "Tankers Refill" – a spring on the ridge above Bob Tail Peak. We had hunted up onto the divide looking down into West Eagle Creek. That morning we followed a herd of elk up an old fire trail to the divide, but we never did catch up to them. About 11:00 a.m. I was coming back down this fire trail when I saw another hunter coming up the trail, so I just stepped off the trail behind a big tamarack snag. When this hunter walked by I saw that he was packing a Winchester Model 94 Carbine on full cock, and he was looking down at those elk tracks in the trail, and he was ready if one of them jumped out from under his foot. I just slipped around that snag and waited until this nut had gone out of sight for about twenty minutes before I hurried on down the trail. When I cut back over a low ridge to get to the pickup I jumped a 3X4 mule deer buck and shot him in the neck as he bounced down the hill in front of me. This was with the .375 H&H Magnum with 270 grain bullets. That poor old deer did a complete forward somersault down the mountain, which wasn't hard to believe when I saw that that big bullet had almost severed his head from his neck.

None of these deer hunts had been that exciting but that is the way it goes sometimes. However, I did better on elk but those are stories for another time.

Chapter Fifteen

DANIEL BOONE GETS HIS ELK

Fall of 1962. I was working on the Clearwater River, in Clearwater County, Idaho. My oldest brother, Lawrence, was my partner on a log skidding crew, working out of the Cedars Logging Camp

I had gotten married on June 2nd, 1962, so my elk hunting on weekends was kind of restricted. Lawrence and I would hunt after work in the evenings, returning home on weekends to be with our families in Wallace, Idaho.

It was a beautiful early October evening, as we motored up the Birchridge road to Birchridge Lookout. I was going to make a short hunt down the trail following Birchridge towards the river. After about one hour I came out onto the road where it crossed the ridge trail. Lawrence was parked in the turnout with the hood up on his old "Ford" military jeep. He was fooling around with the motor so I sat down on the road bank to watch for game.

All of a sudden, just like in a mirage, a big cow elk stepped out into a meadow below the road. The elk was about 200 yards away at a steep angle downhill. I was packing an old Model 94 Winchester in .32 Special caliber that evening. However, I decided that I could make the shot, so I just set the front sight bead on top of the cow elk's shoulder and touched off a shot. To my complete amazement I missed that cow elk three times, without even making her move. Lawrence then started giving me crap about not being able to hit the elk

It finally came to me that I was shooting over the elk's back because of the steep angle downhill. It works the same on a steep angle uphill, the true distance being only the distance measured on a horizontal line out to meet a line vertical from the animal. I adjusted my aim lower on the cow elk's shoulder and shot again. This time the elk collapsed like she had been struck by lightning.

Darkness was descending into the canyon bottom so we had to hurry down to the elk without delay. Just a short seventy five yards from the elk we had to cross a deep ravine, and when we came up onto the flat where the cow elk had fallen, she was gone. We found some hair and a spot or two of blood but were unable to follow the elk in the falling darkness with out a light.

There was a hunting camp down on the river by the steel bridge. This camp consisted of six railroad executives from South Dakota, being guided by their friend from Sandpoint, Idaho. We stopped at this camp and explained the situation to these fellows, in hopes that maybe they could retrieve the wounded elk the next morning. The next afternoon, after we had supper we rushed up to the river camp to see if they had had any luck finding the wounded elk. They told us they had hunted the area all day without seeing any sign of the wounded elk, or any others for that matter. We still had two hours before it would be black dark, so I had Lawrence drop me off on the road where I had shot from the night before. I took off down the hill towards the river. I hated having a wounded elk on my conscience.

I had only gone maybe 150 yards down the hill when right in front of me was a spike bull elk's head sticking up out of the grass. At first I thought some hunter had set it there to fool other hunters, but then I saw an eyelash blink. I instantly put a bullet right at the butt of the spike bull's ear. I then hurried back up the hill to stop Lawrence before he left me. We hurried down and field-dressed the little bull, and then discovered that we didn't have an elk tag with us. I had evidently left my elk tag pinned inside the pocket of my wool hunting shirt at home. We returned to the river camp to see if we could get one of the hunters to tag the elk and accept it as a gift. The leader of this group said he would tag the elk and take it. So we loaded a horse onto their truck and rushed back up the road to the turnout

These hunters had heard me shoot from their camp, and could not believe that I had killed an elk right where they had hunted all day. This bunch of guys said if I was trying to make them look bad I was having great success. They had been in camp for two weeks, and had only succeeded in killing a little black bear that came into camp to raid their garbage. These fellows were under the impression that I was a regular Daniel Boone type. Two shots at two different elk in two evenings! They were ready to hire me for a guide. However, love being a stronger urge than hunting I would return to my beautiful wife for the weekend.

Now we had to get back to the task of getting the elk packed to the road before darkness blotted out the trail. I was not a real experienced packer, but the horse they gave us was dog gentle so he allowed us to get the whole elk loaded on him, and up to the road without incident. A very rude game warden greeted us when the horse lunged up onto the road with the whole spike bull elk on the packsaddle. Mister game warden started reading us the riot act. Let's see some hunting license and tags, and who shot this elk? This fool was right in the middle of everything as we tried to get the horse over next to the truck where we could unload the elk off his back.

The head hunter from the river camp that had agreed to tag the elk grabbed this warden by the arm and bodily threw him out of our way. He exclaimed, "Get the hell out of the way here so these boys can unload that elk, and then I will show you my license, and the damn tag is on the elk." Now the chief warden deflated pretty fast when this old boy from Dakota got in his face. After all the legal beagle stuff was taken care of our warden tucked his tail between his legs and left.

We stopped at the river camp for a drink, and more hunting tales before taking off for home for the weekend. We finally came to the conclusion that I had probably only creased the cow elk over the spine, knocking her unconscious. The elk had probably awakened none the worse for wear, just a lot smarter about standing around while someone shot at her.

Our intention were honorable, we just made a few mistakes in our rush to get an elk. This would kind of be like forgetting your knife or rifle. Just make sure you have all your gear and tags, and enjoy a good hunt. Take your time and be successful, good luck!

Chapter Sixteen

CLEARWATER RIVER MOUNTAIN GOAT HUNT

Fall 1963. This hunt would take place on the North Fork of the Clearwater River, in Clearwater County, Idaho. This would be a general season hunt for mountain goat; the tag cost ten dollars and there were no restrictions. If my memory serves me right, the hunt opened in mid-September.

My brother, Don, and I went into the "Black Canyon" of the North Fork of the Clearwater River on the weekend prior to the goat season opener to scout out the Elizabeth Mountain country that towered over the cliffs lining the river through the Black Canyon. We climbed up through the breaks in the cliffs, following the drainages to access the goat habitat on Elizabeth Mountain. After six hard miles straight up the mountain we could finally see the walnut-shell-shaped solid rock cap of Elizabeth Mountain.

It had been a hard nine hours of climbing to reach the top from the river. All along our route there were signs of goats. The trees and brush had goat wool hanging on them, and there were blocky goat tracks every where, as well as goat beds. Even more surprising was all of the elk sign up there in those hanging goat pastures. We never saw any elk on our climb, and the only goat we would see was a lone billy goat bedded just under the top of Elizabeth Mountain.

This old goat watched us climb up that steep cliffy hillside until we were about one-fourth mile below him, and then he got to his feet and ambled around the mountain on that eighty degree slope like he was on a main trail. When we got to where the goat had been bedded we found the goat trail he had followed around the mountain, about four inches wide and that is no exaggeration.

Don and I, being young fools, just followed the goat trail to see where it went. We were too far out onto this slope before we finally saw what we were getting into, but we couldn't turn back. The slope went down about one hundred feet and then broke over a cliff about fifty feet high, and then there was a ledge about thirty to forty feet wide covered with rocks that had broken off the cliffs above. The only thing we could see below this ledge was thin, clear air all the way to the river six miles below. When we finally got around the mountain we hit a Forest Service trail going up to the crest of Elizabeth Mountain. At this point we were sweating rivers, and it wasn't from the climb up here, it was from pure fear from looking down into that empty "eagle" thoroughfare beneath our precarious perch on that goat trail on the side of the cliff.

It was getting late in the afternoon so we thought we would just follow the Forest Service trail down to the river. We surely didn't want to be on that mountainside we came up if it got dark on us. When we hit the river we discovered we had walked out the Elizabeth Creek trail, and it was nine miles to Elizabeth Mountain.

It was black dark when we arrived back at our truck. This was a one day scout so we headed for home, and it would be early morning of the next day when we arrived home. We found out that this goat hunting was going to be hard work no matter what kind of shape you were in, or how young you might be. And this realization came to two guys that thought they were about as rough and tough as a man could get.

The following Friday we had our camping gear loaded up and ready to head for the Clearwater River country by early morning. A friend, Bill, would join us, and he had a brand new 1962 Ford 4X4 pickup. We hooked Bill's single horse trailer behind the pickup with his horse "Stormy" aboard.

Our hunt plan was to set up our camp in the mouth of Elizabeth Creek, and then Bill could ride his horse to the top of the mountain and Don and I would hike up there. That way we would be above the goats from the get-go. Now I need to add some facts right here. At the time, I had only been married to my wife, Karen, for one year and three months, and we had a son that was only six months old. So let me tell you, I had to do some serious talking to get to go on this trip, but of course after five months of sweet talk I got my wife's blessings.

When we had arrived late in the evening at the mouth of Elizabeth Creek, we spotted goats right in the cliffs about one mile up the mountain, before we had even unloaded Bill's horse, Stormy, from the trailer. After our camp was set up the goats were still there at dusk, so that made a change in our hunt plan, because now we could access the goat's right from the river road.

We were up early, had our breakfast, and were waiting where we would climb the mountain before daylight. We started the climb with

47

high expectations, the wind was in our favor, and the goats didn't appear to be that spooky, so we were anticipating being successful on this first day of the hunt. After all, the goats had watched us all evening while we set up our camp without showing anything but curiosity.

It was only about 7:00 a.m. when we climbed up out of a brush-choked gully onto a hogback ridge at the top of a cliff. And that was when I spotted a lone billy goat laying on a rock ledge at the top of the gully we had just climbed out of. The goat didn't show any alarm as I got into position to make the 200 yard shot, but then Don said to hold up a minute. There were more goats in the brush at the head of the gully under the billy goat. Looking through our binoculars, we were able to spot twelve nanny goats and several kid goats in the herd that was already brushed up.

Don and Bill each picked out big dry nanny goats, and got ready to shoot. I had my .30-06 Winchester with 180 grain pointed Remington Kore-Lok bullets, and Don had his .300 Weatherby Magnum with 180 grain Nosler bullets. Bill was shooting a Feather-weight .30-06 Winchester with 150 grain Remington factory loads.

We all got ready to shoot and on the count of three we were to start shooting. I aligned my scopes crosshair right under the billy goat's chin and touched off my shot when Don said three. When my .30/06 recoiled there was a puff of white smoke as my bullet slammed into the cliff face right between my goat's horns, and with a rearward lunge the goat disappeared from sight. When I looked into the gully there were two goats tumbling down the mountain. The nannies finally stopped rolling, lodging in the brush right below us. I hiked up to where my billy goat had been bedded down to search for any sign of a hit and then I found that, luckily, I had missed completely.

Finally, I returned to where Bill and Don were working on their nanny goats and told them about my misfortune. Don said, "Why don't you go kill one of the other goats." They were only about a half a mile away on the next hogback ridge down river. I hadn't figured out that the reason for my high shot had been the seventy degree slope, and not my rifle being out of line.

The goats had started coming back our direction, only angling up the slope for some cliffs about 400 yards above us. Don said here take my .300 Weatherby and shoot that big goat in the lead. So that is what I did. The goat was slammed back against the cliff from the shock of the bullet, and then it did a head first-flip off the cliff face. He fell about 400 feet and hit on the slope and bounced thirty feet into the air and came flopping down the mountain almost to where the other billy had been laying. My shot had hit the goat right in the shoulder, but in the fall off the cliff face he had broken off one horn. I was lucky enough to find the horn just below where the goat had hit the ground the first time, several anxious minutes later.

We all had packboards so we just field-dressed the goats. Don and Bill wadded their goats up on their packboards and packed them down the mountain. I tied all three rifles onto my packboard, and then, taking the burlap sacks I had tied there, I put my goat into the sacks and tied everything together real tight and just kicked my goat down the mountain. I would only dislodge him about three times before he landed in the road.

When we got back to our camp and had the goats taken care of we measured the goats' horns. Don's nanny had eleven and one-half inch horns, and Bill's nanny had eleven and one-fourth inch horns, and my Billy only had nine inch horns. Don was the only one to have his goat trophy mounted. I kept the skull and horns off my billy for several years, but ended up giving them away.

Bill (left) and Don with Fred's goat. Fred is standing in the background.

We were early back in camp so just had lunch and some cold beer, before loading up our camp and heading up the river for home. It had started raining about the time we started up the river, and that Clearwater country has lots of clay in the soil so the road was slicker than hell. The horse trailer was fish-tailing on the curves, so I told Bill to slow down before he put the trailer over the road-bank, and tipped the horse out on the ground. His reply was, "If that son-of-a-bitch falls out of the trailer, I will kill him myself." I said, "That's enough of this shit, you stop this truck before I have to kick your ass for being stupid!" Bill slid to a stop right in the middle of the road, and then hopped out the driver's side door. I come flying out of the passenger side door and started around the front of the pickup, and that is when Bill said, "If that's the way you feel about it you can drive the goddamn truck."

That suited me just fine. It was awful quiet in the truck cab until we hit the highway at Superior, Montana, but by then there were three sober, much wiser hunters in that truck cab, so I turned the driving back over to Bill. Too much beer can cause reasonable men to do stupid things, so be cautious with your drinking before things go to hell in a hurry.

When we arrived home we were greeted by very happy wives, and my son wanted his daddy. I guess you could say that this hunt was more just plain stupid luck than any degree of skill or hunting knowledge. The smartest thing that Don and I had done was to wear calk boots so we could keep our feet under us on the steep hillsides and smooth rocks. We had learned this habit from an old Indian neighbor, who told us you can't hunt if you are on the back of your neck all the time.

Chapter Seventeen

ELK HUNTERS SUPREME

Fall 1963. My brother Don, cousin Tom, and a friend, Jack, all joined me for an elk hunt into the Murray Peak area. Murray Peak is north and east of the legendary gold camp of Murray, Idaho, in Shoshone County, Idaho.

It had been a warm fall so the elk rut didn't start in earnest until about the first week in October. This just happened to be the elk hunting season opener for this area that year.

Daybreak found Don and me hunkered down in the beargrass on top of the ridge to the north of Saw Gulch. Somewhere below us an elk shattered the morning quiet with his frenzied bugling. Then the whole basin started vibrating with elk bugles. We were in the right spot.

We broke off the backside of a dividing hogback ridge, and then got down on the same level as the elk to stay downwind of them. Then we started our stalk to get in on the first bull we had heard as he was staying in the same area, indicating he was a herd bull.

In just a little bit it seemed we were right on top of this bull but we couldn't spot him. The bull had quit bugling, and would just kind of chuckle every few minutes. We were being very cautious as we didn't want to bump him, or give him our scent as we were real close. I came up off my butt in a crouch to step over a windfall blocking our advance when, only fifteen yards below and to our left, a big 6X6 bull elk exploded out of a little group of bushy fir trees and crashed off down the mountain. We could hear the bull and his cows crashing brush as they crossed Saw Gulch and went up onto the opposite ridge. Then the bull started bugling again! We were half way to his new location when rifle shots started echoing all along the ridge the elk were on. Someone else had beaten us to the herd.

Finally, we walked up on our brother-in-law Bill dressing out a huge 6X6 bull elk. Four bullets through the ribs with a .30-30 Winchester carbine put the bull down in his tracks. Bill's hunting partners, Ron and Darrel, came along to inform us that they had a 5X5 bull elk and a cow elk down also.

51

Tom and Jack arrived just in time to load their packboards with an elk quarter. Don and I would pack the other two quarters, and Bill had the big trophy rack and three rifles to pack. We had decided to pack down to the East Eagle Creek road in the bottom of the canyon. This turned into a torturous, steep, brushy, route across rockslides and around cliffs. Ron and Darrell had taken the other two rifles and went back to the vehicles to bring them around to pick us up.

When they arrived we tied the big trophy antlers to the front bumper of my 1959 Jeep pickup. The end of the main beams almost touched the windshield, and the spread went right around the hood. The antlers were later scored at 363 Boone & Crockett points. 1963 was the year that Boone & Crockett raised their minimum score to 375 B&C for entry in the all time record book. The bull was not entered into the "Awards Book" which still had the old 360 minimum score.

We made a bee-line right down to the tavern in Prichard, Idaho, to show off that big trophy rack. Before we got out of the beer joint that afternoon it was agreed that I would return the next morning with a pack horse to pack out the other two elk. Old Buck, a thirty-one-year-old horse got the job. Buck would turn out to be a wise choice.

The next morning real early I met the fellows at the end of the road in Alder Gulch. I had gone ahead picking a trail through the wind-fallen timber. Ron hollered that the horse wouldn't come down the steep hillside, so I climbed back up to find old Buck sitting on his butt like a big dog. Ron was hanging on the end of the halter rope pulling for all he was worth, but Buck wouldn't budge! I pulled my pocket knife out and walked over to a clump of alder bushes, and started to whittle me a switch. Old Buck jumped up and started down the hill, following Ron. As I passed Ron and Buck I handed the switch to Ron with the instructions to just show it to Buck every little bit. We made it to the elk without any further delays.

The elk were both laying out in the middle of a big rockslide. Both of them only hog-dressed. When I sat down on the side of the 5X5 bull elk, blood came boiling up out of the wound in the shoulder. This was followed by a stench that would run flies off a gut wagon. The cow was soured also. I was elected to pack the whole smaller cow on the horse, and the guys would pack the bull on pack-boards.

Buck and I hadn't gotten far when we ended up in a jackpot of windfalls about hip high off the ground. I dropped Buck's halter rope, and then started looking for a route through this maze of wind-fallen trees. As I jumped off the last windfall about 100 yards up the hill I heard a ruckus back where Buck was. Here came old Buck, head off to one side to keep the halter rope out from under his feet. He was jumping over windfalls like a deer, and all that with a whole cow elk on his back. When Buck came up beside me I just took the rope off the halter and let him follow me back to the truck. Buck and I were back at the kill-site before the guys had gotten 100 yards up the hill. I loaded the front quarters off the bull onto Buck's packsaddle. The four guys would alternate the other two quarters. Buck and I were back at the ranch for dinner.

It turned out to be a hell of a job trying to get that awful smell out of my pack manties. However, after several soakings, washings, and air dryings the manties came clean and sweet smelling once more. I don't believe that I could have eaten one mouthful of that meat from the small cow or bull either, not even if you threatened me with a gun! Any time that you hunt this moist northwest country you had better plan on skinning, quartering, and hanging your kill so it can cool out. You need to get that body heat out as soon as possible. If you don't you are probably not going to like that "wild" meat. Well good luck, and take care of what you kill to keep it sweet, and tasty.

This would not be the only bull elk that Bill would harvest in Saw Gulch. It was just the biggest!

Chapter Eighteen

THE WHITE BULL OF PONY GULCH

Fall of 1963. This hunt would take place in Pony Gulch, a tributary of the beautiful North Fork of Coeur d'Alene River, in Shoshone County, Idaho.

It was late fall and the alders had shed their leaves and the tamarack had shed their needles; everything was kind of drab, and dead looking. Then it snowed about eight inches, putting a beautiful white mantle over everything.

Brother Don and a friend, Jack, joined me for a last hunt into Pony Gulch to see if we could get a shot at that big trophy bull referred to as the "White Bull of Pony Gulch." This bull was so old, and big, that his sun-faded coat made him appear stark white. He looked like a great big quartz boulder when viewed from a distance. A long distance away and way across a deep canyon was where most hunters seen him.

We were going to pull a trick on this old bull. We would go up the old dozer trail in Pioneer Gulch and drop over the saddle where this

A perfect replica of the White Bull of Pony Gulch.

54

road ended, into the head of Pony Gulch. Come in the back door, so to speak.

Don was driving my 1959 Jeep pickup; on each switchback we would have to back up three times because they were tight. And on the very first switchback it happened! Reverse gear was right next to first gear, and we were perched right on the edge of the road bank, and then Don got into reverse instead of first gear; and over the edge we went backwards. Crash! We smacked a big red fir tree on the slope below the road. Before Jack or I could say a word, Don found first gear and let in the clutch; that old jeep went digging and roaring right up over the road-bank and back into the road. Just as we lurched up into the road and made a tight right turn there was a loud bang up in the front-end of the jeep

We could move but we couldn't steer. The worm gear in the steering box had broken. We were afoot now, but we decided to continue the hunt and worry about getting the jeep out later. (We went back the next day and retrieved the jeep by tying ropes to the steering rod and guiding it by hand. It was quite a job but the weather didn't leave us any alternatives.)

When we topped out on the dividing ridge between Pony Gulch, and Pioneer Gulch it was time for a well-earned rest. As we sat watching away over across the canyon on the south facing slope, we spotted some elk moving through the timber. The elk were moving up towards the saddle between Pony and Potosi Gulches. When the elk crossed an open hogback ridge single file; we counted twenty cows and calves, and that great "White Bull" bringing up the rear. It was now about 8:30 a.m. and the elk still had about one and a half miles to go to their bedding ground.

Our problem was we had to go two and one half miles to get to where the elk were, and this was through a steep, deep canyon. It was 11:00 a.m. when we came pussy-footing up onto the flat ridge where we expected to find the elk bedded down.

However, the elk hadn't followed our plan. They went on down into Potosi Gulch. We didn't know where we could expect to find the elk, and it was another five miles out to the road in Pony Gulch, so we headed on down the main dividing ridge to the road.

When we hit the bottom of Pony Gulch, we were ready for a rest and a cold drink of water from the crystal clear stream running down the canyon. It just so happened that we came out at Bob's cabin (Bob was an old prospector who had some mining claims in the area.). Old Bob had told us where he hid the key to the cabin, and had said we could use the cabin any time we wanted. After getting a fire going in the stove I went out to fetch a pail of water to make some coffee. Bob had put a small dam in the creek so that he could dip water with out getting a bunch of sticks and dirt in his bucket. Lying across this pool was two three by twelve inch boards. When I knelt down to get my water, I happened to look back under these boards, and there was about a case of beer, some canned fruit, and canned tomatoes back under the boards. I fetched up three of those cold beers and headed for the cabin; I forgot about the coffee water. We just sat around the fire and drank beer until it was gone. After the beer was all drank up we left a note for Bob, telling him what had happened to his beer, and then headed down the road to Beaver Creek.

When we hit the main Beaver Creek road we were right at a little cluster of homes called "Beaver Flats". We knocked on the door of one of these homes and asked to use the telephone. This man, a retired cop, invited us in; we made our call and contacted a friend Frank to come pick us up. Now we had about two hours to kill while we waited for Frank.

Now this old cop was kind of curious as to how we had gotten about half drunk up the creek, and how in hell had we got up there. The cop said there were no tracks going up from this end. We told him our story about our jeep troubles, the elk, and Bob's cabin and the beer. This old cop is dying for company so he wants us to stay at his place to wait for our ride. He didn't know it but we wanted some company, too, while we waited in that nice warm house. The old cop made some coffee and then he fried up some steak and potatoes. Now you couldn't buy this kind of service most places; and this old man is giving us this royal hospitality just for our company. There just aren't any people of this caliber left any more.

We sure hadn't had much luck hunting but we sure used up a bunch in our travels. We couldn't have had it any better if we had planned it ourselves.

I know that you are wondering what ever became of the "White Bull of Pony Gulch". Well, in 1965 a fellow found him winter-killed in the head of Unknown Gulch. The bull had a 7X8 point rack of antlers that scored in the high 380's Boone & Crockett. However, this bull was never entered into the records book. People that should have known said that this was not his biggest set of antlers. No matter what happened to this great old bull or how big he was; he still left his genetics in the many calves that he sired in his life time as the "King" of Pony Gulch.

Well, happy hunting and May all your luck be good and your shots true. Good hunting partner.

Don Scott and Nig at elk camp at the heliport, Bloom Peak, fall of 1981.

Chapter Nineteen

.308 NORMA MAGNUM

Fall 1965. We were back in the head of Butte Gulch camped on the ridge going down between Butte-Bear Gulches. We had set up my big 14X16 wall tent right on the ridge-top, which would turn out to be a mistake.

I had bought my son, Jeff, a puppy that he named after the "Little Joe" character in the "Bonanza" western series on TV. My son called his dog "Joe Poke" and this dog was a character, too. He was a Beagle-Terrier cross and like all Terriers thought he was tough. That little dog would fight a buzz saw and give it the first three turns, so we thought maybe he would make a bear dog.

My brother Don, wife Karen, and my son Jeff, and the dog, were my companions on this trip. The first night we found out that we were camped right in the middle of a deer crossing. We had just turned off the lantern, and my wife, being one of those people that was scared of the dark, was just beside herself listening to the night sounds. Pretty soon we could hear something coming, and then we could hear it coming down the side of the tent, making these snuffing sounds. About the time that my wife was ready to pass out from the suspense, Joe Poke the dog crawled under the tent wall right by Karen's head. She made me go lock the dog in the truck cab, and things had just gotten quiet when the deer started walking by, tripping over the tent ropes. Their hoofbeats on that frozen ground sounded like someone beating on a drum, and it would be almost daylight before they stopped coming by. Between the deer stumbling by and my wife asking, "What's that" we hardly got any sleep at all.

The next morning we had a good camp breakfast, and then hiked out along the divide ridge stopping on different lookouts to watch for bears. We must have seen at least twenty different bears that morning but they were all away down in the bottoms. Even though the ground was white with frost every morning, by 10:00 a.m. it would be 60 degrees, and would get up into the high seventies by 4:00 in the afternoon.

We had hunted several different drainages and had seen bears in every one of them without seeing one bear that we would want to pack out of those deep canyons. It was Sunday evening and the next day we would have to go home, so we changed our strategy. I had Don take Karen and Jeff out along the ridge-top on the Stateline Ridge, and I took Joe Poke, the dog, and went down into the bench area to see if I couldn't scare a bear up onto the ridge-top.

The dog and I had crossed the first two basins coming from the southeast and we hadn't jumped an animal. Usually these basins were full of deer, grouse, bears, and even occasionally a wolverine or grizzly bear. When we got around into the last basin the dog started getting gamey, so I said, "Get-um out, Joe Poke." The dog took off with his nose to the ground like he knew what he was doing, so I took out after him. We were in huckleberry brush about waist high on my six-foot two-inch body when ole Joe Poke started picking up the pace. We were getting up onto the sidewall of the basin where it started up steep for the ridge, and that was when I saw a bear rushing through the brush ahead of us about 250 yards away.

I had just had this new rifle built that fall. It was a Model 70 Winchester in .30/06 caliber that I had re-chambered for the new .308 Norma Magnum cartridge. This was my first bear hunt with this rifle but I had shot it at targets until it was right where I wanted it to shoot. I didn't have any trouble getting my scope onto the bear, and then he stopped. And that was just what I had waited for, and when my rifle shot split the evening peacefulness wide open I had my bear. My new rifle had made its first one-shot kill, and it would make a name for itself in the future doing it many times over.

This turned out to be that once in a lifetime rifle, one that was both accurate and lucky for me in the years to come.

That crazy dog ran up to the bear just seconds after my shot knocked it down, and he never waited one second. He just grabbed a mouthful of bear and hung on. The bear would roll down the mountain and throw the dog down the hill, and then roll right over the top of him, and that dog never did let go. By the time I got up to the bear the dog had made up his mind that he had killed that bear all by himself, and he wasn't going to let me have it. After several attempts of trying to talk him into giving me the bear, I would finally have to resort to kicking him in the butt before he gave up.

The bear wasn't that big so Don and I just grabbed a paw apiece and pulled him the 200 yards up to the ridge-top. From there it was all downhill to the Maple Peak road. We didn't hurt the bear population any but we sure had a good camp out, and would have lots of stories for future bear hunts. Joe Poke's reputation would keep building for several years to come.

Any hunt can be fun if you just let things happen, and don't worry about the small stuff. Just hang loose and be happy!

When the passes get blocked by snow.

Chapter Twenty

CRAZY HORSE

Fall 1965. Brother Ray, and brother-in-law Randy came to me with a success story. Ray had been lucky on an elk hunt and harvested a nice cow elk. Now they needed a pack horse.

My horse Nig was the only horse available, as all of the others horses along with the pack saddles were already on another packing assignment. However, Nig wasn't a real good choice as a friend had had a real rodeo with him trying to pack an elk the previous fall. We decided that we would give it a try anyway.

The next morning I loaded Nig onto my 1951 Chevy stock truck along with my riding saddle. It was only about an hour drive to the trailhead at Sunset Peak. We took the trail out along the ridge to Pony Peak, but we turned off short of Pony Peak, and went down the ridge between Idaho and Vendetta Gulches to the elk. What a ridge it is, knife blade thin along its spine, rocky, and as steep as a church steeple down both slopes.

We found the elk, skinned and quartered it and then put it into game bags to keep the meat clean. However, we didn't have any pack covers or, 'manties' to wrap the elk quarters in. My helpers had heard the packing story of the previous fall, so were not looking forward to helping me pack the elk quarters onto the horse. There wasn't even a big stout tree to tie Nig to. I finally convinced Ray that he could hold Nig on a little flat spot in the ridge while I packed him.

I had one elk quarter up on my saddle and was pulling the slack out of the cargo rope when Nig turned his head back and sniffed the quarter of elk, and then he turned his head back around and blew snot right into Ray's face. His eyes were all bugged out, his nostrils flared open, he looked like he was about to blow up. Then he did!

Ray, jumped back to the end of the halter rope, and that is when old Nig jumped right over his head, and went bucking and bawling down over the side onto the steep slope. I was still right alongside him, hanging onto that cargo rope. Sometimes I was on my feet, other times I was dragging on the ground alongside the horse, getting the hell kicked out of me. Finally, Nig stopped and turned to go back up the slope, and that is when I made a lunge and caught hold of the halter. I had a good hold of the throat latch with my right hand and the halter ring with my left hand. Now the quarter of meat was hanging down on Nig's side, and he was doing his best to kick it away from him. After he got rid of the quarter of meat he stood on his hind legs, striking at me with his front hooves. He would whirl first one way, and then the other and this would throw me out away from him to where he couldn't strike me with his front feet. I just can't explain what kept us both on our feet on that steep hillside during this struggle. The fight must have lasted at least thirty minutes before Nig finally give up the fight. I wasn't far from give out myself. I finally got Nig calmed down and back up onto the ridge-top. While Nig rested and relaxed, I retrieved the elk quarter and packed it back up to where Nig was standing. I was ready to give it another try but Ray and Randy were not about to get near that crazy horse.

I can't explain why Nig went berserk like he did. He was just plain scared to death of that meat on his back. Nig wasn't trying to get out of packing it. He had packed bear, deer, and elk many times before this without any problems. I believe that he must have had a cougar or something jump him in the pasture or something like that. We were able to get him over his fear some what in later years. Nig packed lots of cargo and wild meat in the years following this incident.

The guys decided that it would be a lot easier to go ahead and back pack the meat down to the road below. So I mounted old Nig and headed out for Sunset Peak. I took Nig back to the ranch, and then got the packboards and drove around to the mouth of Idaho Gulch. At this point I started hollering, trying to locate the guys. No answer! Finally, some fellows came by and informed me that they had seen two guys packing half an elk, swinging on a rope in the middle of a pole. Now if you want to experience the ultimate hardest way to pack something, just try that stupid trick! I was unable to make contact with them so I returned to the truck. About black dark they came splashing down the main Prichard Creek. They had gotten on the wrong ridge, and given up the packing chore and came out two miles upstream from where I was parked.

It took another day to get the elk packed out, and it was a work day too! So now that elk meat was getting pretty "DEAR" before it was in the locker plant. If I would have known that they would have all this trouble, I would have built a "Squaw Boat" and taken the elk down the mountain myself.

Now if you find yourself in this kind of situation, get the right pack horse and equipment and your pack trip will work out fine. Keep those cinches tight and good luck.

Splash packs a bull elk out of the rough Selway River country in the fall of 1984. (Photo courtesy Joe Anderson)

Chapter Twenty-one

AN ELK SLAUGHTER

Fall of 1966. My workmate at the Star Mine in Burke, Idaho, would accompany me on this mid-November elk hunt. His name was Chuck. This hunt would be in Butte Gulch east of the old Gold Camp of Murray, Idaho.

On our way to the hunting ground we were driving through a forlorn moonscape, created by a bright harvest moon shining down through a heavy fog bank in the creek bottoms. Up high the moon was both full and bright, and the stars flickered and danced across the sky so close it appeared that you could reach up and grab a handful.

On our arrival at the trailhead we still had time for another cup of hot refreshing black coffee as we planned our day's hunt. In no time at all the approaching dawn accented the ridge-tops to the east in a faint pink glow. Our hunt plan was that I would hunt up the Dry Butte drainage until I intersected the ridge between Reeder Gulch and Butte Gulch. Then I was to await the warming air thermals before descending down the ridge to a flat saddle where the elk liked to bed down after crossing this saddle. This saddle broke off into a little blind drainage formed by the main dividing ridge splitting. Chuck would come up this blind drainage from the bottom, hoping to intercept any elk I chased off the saddle above. This was a favored bedding area for the elk after feeding on the grassy ridges of Dry Butte. This site also had multiple escape routes off the saddle.

As soon as we had good light we took off. I hurried right along as the ground was frozen hard as flint, and the dry leaves crackling and crunching underfoot made any attempt to be quiet impossible. It was too cold to sit and watch as there was a mean cold drift of air coming down from the Arctic. The only thing blocking this wind was a couple of barbed-wire fences in Canada, or maybe Montana.

As I approached the saddle from above I slowed down and tried to make a more stealthy approach. The sun was shining on the ridge-top, making everything appear beautiful in the crystal clear air. This was a beautiful place; mature red fir trees with an under-story of grass, and low bush huckleberry only six inches high covering the ground.

The sun shining on the tree trunks had fooled me; an elk exploded up off the ground right at my feet, I was almost bowled over. There were elk bedded all around me. With the elk surprising me so, I was in a confused state and failed to get my gun up, let alone a shot off at an elk. The elk plunged down into the blind gulch that Chuck was coming up. Our plan was working. I listened for Chuck to shoot. However, fifteen minutes later he came up the hillside with a sheepish grin on his face. The elk had outflanked both of us.

The warming air rising into a bright azure sky assaulted our nostrils with the pungent odor of damp earth, rotting leaves, and other odors of a damp northwest forest in late fall. Our ears were assaulted also by the joyous chirping and chattering as the little critters came alive, scurrying, and flitting through the forest gathering their breakfast.

Chuck and I decided that we were also ready for a sandwich and an ice cold beer. On our arrival back at the truck we were off to "Sag's" beer joint in the old railroad and logging town of Prichard, Idaho. Sag's beer joint didn't have a TV set, or need one with Grandpa Sagdal in attendance. He kept everyone entertained with his ribald stories of the good old days on the "North Fork".

After a hearty lunch and a couple of beers, Chuck and I decided to go upriver about five miles to the Lost Creek drainage for our afternoon hunt. The Hat Creek drainage a tributary of Lost Creek would be our afternoon hunt. The Lost Creek area was one of the first drainages stocked with elk from Yellowstone Park by the Shoshone County Sportsman Association in the mid-nineteen thirties. It has those grassy south facing slopes and jackpine thickets along the ridge tops that elk like so well.

We were only about a mile up the creek when I spotted a herd of elk on a side ridge 500 yards up the creek. I pointed the elk out to Chuck, and then sat down to look at them through my binoculars. Holy Cow! Chuck started shooting at the elk from the off-hand position. I asked Chuck what in the hell he thought he was doing; it would have been a difficult shot from a dead rest. He replied that he thought I was going to shoot when I sat down. After the elk went out of sight up the creek, I told Chuck I thought I knew where they would cross a saddle in the head of the canyon, but we would have to hurry up the creek two miles before they got over that saddle. When we panted into view of the saddle, the elk were strung out single file behind a big cow headed across an open slope, in that ground-eating lope that they use when they are changing country.

Just as I had predicted they were going to cross that saddle into the next drainage. Our buns hit the ground as we hurried to get into position to shoot before the elk were gone from sight. It was a strong 450-500 yards to the elk but with the open slope behind the elk we could track our hits by the dust kicked up when the bullets hit. In three shots I had the range figured out and hit the big cow elk leading the herd. Maybe not where I wanted to hit her, but three shots later I was out of ammo, and there were two gutshot elk humped up on the hillside. Finally, I got Chuck focused on the wounded elk and he managed to kill one cow before he ran out of ammo also. I had my .22 caliber pistol on my hip so I took off after the remaining cow. I was able to corner the big cow down in a little narrow steep draw, and shot her six times in the forehead, putting her down.

Chuck and I both walked up to the big cow I had head shot with the pistol. We rolled her on her back to position her for field-dressing, Chuck was holding her on her back by her front legs. When I inserted my knife into the elk to start the incision to remove her intestines, her hind legs started kicking. I stepped back, and looked down at her head, her eyes were all bulged out, and she was trying to bite Chuck's leg. In dumbfounded amazement we realized that she was still alive. Chuck sat down on her head, and I was able to cut her throat and end her struggles before she committed mayhem on us.

We were well into the shank of the evening before we had the two elk hanging in the trees ready to pack out on our return. We had built a nice cheery fire to chase away the gloom, and warm our hands by as we worked on our elk. It would be a clear moonlit night as soon as the moon got high enough in the sky to light our way back to the truck. To kill some time while we waited on the moon we roasted some thin slices of loin meat over the fire, on forked sticks for our dinner. Really, mountain men didn't have it so tough; our meat was delicious.

Our arrival back at the truck was well after midnight. We were in and exhausted state but were content that our winter's meat was hanging in the tree's awaiting our return to pack it out.

We returned four days later on Thanksgiving Day with four big strong gelding packhorses to pack the elk quarters out. It was only a matter of a few hours and we had the elk quarters secured to the stock rack, and were ready to load our horses and head for home. We were very fortunate to have good sturdy packhorses at our disposal. Horses sure take the stress out of packing in your elk.

In retrospection, we could have made a planned stalk on this elk herd the first time we spotted them and killed an elk apiece with one well directed shot instead of the ammo-wasting slaughter that ensued. The memory of those elk humped up on that hillside is not a fond one. I am also haunted by the image, that for that one instant, filled my binoculars on our initial contact with the elk, and that was the image of a very large six point royal bull elk following in the dust of the herd as it passed from sight. Oh how I would like to have collected that regal bull elk.

Now you don't have to follow our lead just slow down and do it right the first time in a thoughtful planned manner. Good luck in your pursuit of the wily bull elk, and maybe some day we will meet up on a steep Idaho mountain.

Joe Anderson and stepson Jeremy packing out my elk in 1986.

Chapter Twenty-two

GOOD TIME HUNT

Fall 1967. This weekend hunt was in Pony Gulch, a tributary of Beaver Creek, which drains into the North Fork of the Couer d' Alene River at Babin's Ranch in Shoshone County, Idaho.

My friends Bill and Alva had horse-packed camp up into the saddle between Pioneer Gulch and Pony Gulch. I had driven my 1959 Jeep pickup up the old dozer trail, via Pioneer Gulch, to the camp site. This camp was located on a high alpine ridge with dark green forest spilling down both flanks, harboring all of the beautiful colors of fall in a northwest forest. We would be hunting the wily elk that inhabit this area.

We had staked the horses out along the ridge on good grass. That is all except, Skeeter, Bill's pet. He just wandered around being a pest. Every time you sat down, or bent over, Skeeter had to stick his nose right in your face. Bill had encouraged this behavior by always having "horse pellets" in his pockets to feed him. I was setting on a block of wood enjoying a sandwich, when here comes old Skeeter and sticks his nose right on my sandwich, so I just offered him a smell. He was snuffing so hard that he sucked a big gob of mayonnaise right up his nose. He curled his lip up and starting backing up with his nose pointed at the sky, and then he fell over a log and went tumbling down the hill. Of course Bill thought that I had set his pet up someway, but honest to god it just happened that way.

The weather was nice and fallish, cool nights, and warm sunny days. We hadn't even bothered to set up a tent; we just stretched a fly over our cooking area. We would sleep out under the stars, just using pack manties for a ground cloth. A man can sure get some quality sleep under the bright night sky that is if you don't have a loose horse wandering around all night.

The next morning we hurried through breakfast because Bill and Alva were anxious to get started. They had heard a bull elk bugling all night on the north ridge in Pony Gulch. They just took off straight down the mountain to cross the canyon onto the opposite ridge. It goes with out saying that a straight line is the shortest route between two points. I had decided to traverse around into the elk wallows in the head of Pony Gulch. I figured that might be a good place to find a big old bull elk trying to cool off after a full night of lovemaking.

I spent the whole morning on stand by the elk wallows without any luck. So about 10:30 a.m., I just started up a game trail that would take me right to a bedding area that the elk preferred this time of year. This would also put me in the area where the bull elk had been bugling during the night. This was no time to get in a hurry so I just sneaked along at a snail's pace, looking, listening, and taking in everything around me. I was just approaching this flat hog-back ridge where the elk like to bed for the day, and then I heard something on the hill-side above me. I had the wind right in my face so that was of no concern, and then I spotted something moving through the trees, and huckleberry brush. For just one short instant, I saw three different cow elk moving up the mountain. I never really had a good opportunity, so I didn't take a shot. That is just the breaks of elk hunting; you cannot take a chance of wounding one of these precious elk and wasting it by not recovering a wounded animal.

Bill and Alva had not seen any animals at all, so I had better luck than they did. The hunting was good; it was success that wasn't very plentiful. We spent the whole day on Sunday with out any luck that day either. We enjoyed a good camping trip and hunt even without the thrill of the kill. Good friends, horses, and delicious food cooked over an open fire. I think you would have to agree that this is a hard combination to beat. We are all blessed to be able to share these good things in life.

Chapter Twenty-three

LEGAL ENCOUNTER

Fall 1968. It was the first weekend in October, which was opening day of the general elk season in Unit 4. Brother Don and a kid named Joe were going elk hunting with me. We would hunt in Butte Gulch right up against the Idaho-Montana state line. Butte Gulch is a tributary of Prichard Creek in Shoshone County, Idaho.

Right at 4:00 a.m., I picked the guys up in my 1951 Chevy stock truck with three saddle horses on board. I had my horse, Nig, Don's horse, Rusty, and Joe's horse, Smokey. We drove north out of Wallace, Idaho, to our designation, the old Jack Waite Mine camp. At the Jack Waite Mine camp the road changed to an old CCC one track road built in the 1930's by the Civilian Conservation Corps. About two miles up this road you cross a little one lane bridge right on a curve. As I swung the truck out to the right to make my approach to this bridge, Don screamed, "Get over." I turned hard to the left almost missing the bridge. After we got the truck stopped, Don said, "You almost ran over someone lying alone side the road back there."

We got out of the truck, and walked back across the bridge to find two "OWL-EYED" boys sitting up in their sleeping bags. They had no fire, and no vehicle; just their sleeping bags and packs. The tire tracks through the frost across the bottom of their sleeping bags told the whole story. We had missed running over their legs by mere inches! Man, what a way to start the day.

As soon as we found a place where we could get the truck into the road bank we unloaded the horses. This is also when Joe tells me he doesn't have an elk tag. He said he couldn't buy one in Wallace, Idaho, and Don had told him not to worry about it we would get one in Prichard, Idaho, on our way back to town.

Our hunt plan was to hunt out along the north side of Butte Gulch going to the west. This would allow us to look down into all the little hidden pockets on both sides of the ridge. This is a good way to hunt on horseback. You just tie your horse back out of sight as you approach each new pocket, and then sneak around the point of the ridge and have a look-see.

Noon found us stretched out in the beargrass enjoying a bright warm October sun. After our lunch break in the head of Axe Gulch, we started plan B with high expectations. We tied our horses back in the timber so some great elk hunter wouldn't mistake them for an elk. I would bird dog down around the points of flat benches breaking down into Butte Gulch trying to jump any elk that might be bedded there. Don and Joe would stay up on the main ridge watching the saddles for elk crossing the ridge. After a full afternoon of bird dogging, I arrived back at the horses about 3:30 p.m. to find a note tied to my saddle. The note said that Joe had shot an elk, and that they were tracking it.

I was standing by a cheery warm up fire about 5:30 p.m. when the boys returned. The grin splitting their faces told me that they had been successful, and found the elk. Joe was proud to announce that it was a five-point bull elk. Don said it was skinned, quartered, and ready to pack on our return with and elk tag for Joe. We stopped at Sag's Bar in Prichard for a beer and elk tag for Joe. Sagdal told us he was sold out of tags same as everyone else that he had called trying to get some more. Don informs Joe not to worry about it because he would tag the elk if he had to. Isn't that the way it always happens, you try to help someone be successful, and it turns out that something wants to foul up the process. Like not being able to purchase the proper tag.

Early the next morning we loaded two extra horses to pack the elk. We had old Buck, and a little Welsh pony named Sparky. We would go up the old Chapin assessment road that morning because the elk was just off this old brushed-in cat trail. It was only a one and one half hour ride into where the elk quarters were hanging in a tree, all cooled out, firmed up, and ready to pack. Having good, strong and experienced horses we were back at the truck before noon.

We made a beer stop at Sag's and then headed out for town. The Y at Babin's ranch never had a check station so we thought we had it made. However, at the King's Pass intersection was the official sign: "Stop! Idaho Fish & Game hunter-check station." Don had his elk tag in his shirt pocket but needed some time to punch out the proper information. My old truck had vacuum boosted brakes on it, and if you just applied a little pressure they would squall and screech like you were really riding the brake hard. After knocking down a couple of stop signs and running over several reflectors we got stopped about 100 yards past the check station. I started backing up just as a little smooth-faced checker jumped up onto the running board of the truck. "Have any luck?" he says. "We sure did," Don answered as he handed him the elk tag. "Where is the meat?" our man asked. "Tied up on the side of the rack," was our reply. "You fellows know that the tag is supposed to be on the meat," our checker informs us. "We were just trying to make it easy on everybody," Don told the checker, "As you can see it is wrapped in mantles to keep it clean."

"Well, you will have to pull over into the turnout and show it to me," said the checker. I pulled over and jumped out like I was madder than heck. Poor little Joe looked like he had seen a ghost. I told him in a whisper to just stay in the truck. Don climbed up into the truck bed and untied a hind quarter off the inside of the rack. I was on the outside of the rack where Don could just boost the quarter over to me. I took the quarter in one hand and climbed down off the side of the truck, and when I hit the ground I slammed the meat down on the checkers pickup tailgate about breaking it off. I was doing my best to intimidate this kid so he would forget all this legal stuff. This kid jumps back like you had slapped him in the face, and he was all owl-eyed as I unwrapped the meat so he could look at it. Now I'm sure this kid couldn't have told us if the meat was elk, or camel. But he did his duty, and then tells me I can put it back in the truck. Now our kid tells Don that he will have to call his supervisor. In about an hour here comes mister top warden with his blue lights flashing, and slides to a stop in a big cloud of dust. When he jumps out of his pickup it is easy to see that he is of high authority. The kid tries to explain the situation to the top warden.

Where is the meat our top warden wants to know? In the truck there our checker tells him. Get it out here said top warden. I tell top warden that the kid just inspected the meat and it hasn't changed any since. I want to see it anyway says top warden. I said mister warden if you just crawl up into the back of the truck, and untie a quarter off the rack and get it down here where you can untie the mantle to look at it, and then you retie the mantle and get the S.O.B. back up there where you got it, and if you get your head kicked off in the process so be it. You guys were trying to sneak this elk through without tagging it exclaims mister warden. Yea right, that is why we tied it up on the side of the rack with the antlers where everyone could see it I tell the warden. Now top warden calls Don off to the side and tells Don that I can't talk to him like that. Well, Don said you'll have to take that up with him.

We had been there for about two and one half hours by then, so told the warden, "You make up your mind and either write a ticket, or whatever, because we are about to leave." Top warden walks over to talk to his kid warden again, and then rubs his head and kicks his toe in the dirt. In a little bit he comes back and hands Don a courtesy ticket. Wow, that was close!

Now we didn't completely corrupt little Joe. I can tell you for a fact that Joe went on to become a good hunter, packer, and all around guy. You don't have to follow our example. Just do it by the book and keep your nose clean. The top warden turned out to be a good fellow and a friend in the years following this incident. Keep it legal, and good luck hunting.

A good way to pack elk quarters on a riding saddle. Joe Anderson, packer extra-ordinary.

Chapter Twenty-four

PICTURE BOOK BULL, NO KILL

Fall 1968. This was a day hunt into Pony Gulch via the old dozer track up Pioneer Gulch. Pony Gulch is a tributary of Beaver Creek, which drains into the North Fork of the Coeur d'Alene River, at Babin's ranch in beautiful Shoshone County, Idaho.

Friends Jack and Punky were my hunting companions on that beautiful October morning. We had put my old 1959 Jeep pickup to the test by navigating up that terrible trail called the Pioneer Gulch dozer track road. This trail, or road as some folks preferred to call it, had switchbacks so tight that you had to back up three times even after climbing the bank as far as the back bumper would allow. We arrived up on top just as a new day was breaking promising another bright sunny October day. This was encouraging because the headlights on the pickup had revealed a frost encrusted landscape.

Jack and Punky decided that they would drop straight down the south canyon wall, and then hunt on the opposite south facing slope, because this was where you would normally encounter elk feeding in the early morning. I would traverse up around the head of the gulch to check out the elk wallows, and springs, that the elk liked to visit before bedding down for the day. After spending two hours on stand by the wallows, I took a big game trail leading west that went up onto a flat bench where the elk liked to bed down for the day.

I was just taking it nice and easy, take a few steps, then stop and look everything over good before proceeding on. I had hunted at this snail pace for about one hour with the wind out of the west, right in my face, and it was getting up in the day, about 11:00 a.m., so I really wasn't expecting to see any animals. Just like it always happens, a big six-point bull elk stepped across the trail and stopped behind a bushy fir tree. All that I could see was the bull's big broad butt on one side of the tree, and his nose and big ivory tipped brow tines on the other side. On this day I was hunting with a .375 H&H Magnum that I had wanted to try on elk. I thought to myself that I could punch one of those 270

74

grain bullets right through the tree limbs into the elk's lungs. However, on second thought I decided to wait until he moved off down the hill. I put my crosshairs in the center of the opening where the bull's nose was sticking out. I waited, and waited some more, and then the bull finally moved. When the bull moved I only had a micro-second to shoot before he disappeared, and then, like a damned dude, I just froze up. I think I might have had that old "bull fever" that grabs a-hold of all elk hunters sooner or later. But I didn't let it bother me too much because being the good elk hunter that I am; I would just follow the bull until he gave me another opportunity. I pussyfooted along tracking this bull down into the canyon bottom and up the other canyon wall until he crossed into Unknown Gulch. At this point it was getting late in the afternoon and I suspected that the bull knew that I was following him. So I just gave it up and headed up the ridge to where the Jeep was parked. Jack, and Punky were at the Jeep waiting, and they hadn't seen a thing all day.

There were two other friends that had parked right beside us that had a lot worse luck than us. When they had come back to their Scout 4X4 one of the fellows had leaned his rifle on the front bumper, and then they went around to the back of the Scout, and let the tailgate down so they could eat their lunch before going down the mountain. When they got done eating they got in the Scout and drove off, forgetting the rifle leaning on the front bumper. They drove right over the rifle, breaking the stock at the pistol grip and also breaking the scope. It was a very unfortunate accident. I would say their luck was a lot worse than ours. The only thing damaged with us was our egos!

I sure would have liked to have gotten that royal bull elk. He had those picture perfect ivory tipped antlers that all elk hunters lust after. This bull was without a doubt one of the nicest bulls that I ever encountered. But then that is the way elk hunting goes, you win some, but lose most encounters with the wily bull elk. However, that is the way it was intended to be by a higher authority than us hunters. Anyway I wish you the best of luck in your hunting endeavors, because like most of us you will need it to out maneuver the wily bull elk. Good luck and good hunting.

Chapter Twenty-five

RUN-A-WAY

Fall 1968. I was hunting by myself on a Friday, even though it was a work day. I was, at the time, working at the Crescent Mine, sinking shaft for the Bunker Hill Company on the swing shift.

I had parked my pickup at Slate Creek Saddle and followed the St Joe Divide trail out to Bad Tom Mountain. I had hunted across the head of Red Top Creek to the south and looked down into Murray Creek. After watching there unsuccessfully for over one hour I went back around onto the northwest side of Bad Tom Mountain and watched down into a drainage coming up from Elbow Creek. No luck there either, so I picked up the trail and went back to the east to the saddle between Experimental Gulch, and the head of Red Top Creek.

It was a bright clear sunny day after a late October snowfall of about six inches. The sun reflecting off of the mantle of fresh white snow was very hard on my eyes. I needed some dark glasses, but would just have to get used to squinting. No wonder old outdoor people have that squinty eyed look.

I decided that I would hike out along the ridge and look down into the Dry Creek basin on my way back to my truck. I had just started out when I looked down onto the slope below the ridge on the Experimental Gulch side, and there on the edge of the tree line was a big mule deer doe going along the slope with a 3X3 mule deer buck following her. These deer were only about 125 yards away and didn't have a clue anyone was around. So I just threw my big Stetson hat down in the snow, and got into a prone position with my rifle resting over my hat. I aligned the dot reticule in my scope on that buck's neck and touched off a shot from my .308 Norma Magnum rifle. When my rifle went off there was a big cloud of snow flew into the air from the muzzle blast of that big magnum. There had just been a dull thud when my rifle went off; the snow had absorbed the sound completely. The buck went down in his tracks, and the doe walked on, she hadn't heard the rifle go off either. I hurried down and field-dressed the deer and propped him open to cool out, and then took off for my truck. I still had to go to work at 3:00 p.m.

76

I had left word for my brother, Don, that I would need some help getting the deer packed out the next day. I met Don at the Sweet's Café in Wallace for breakfast, and then we took Don's 1967 Ford pickup and went up to the ranch after some packhorses. I don't recall the reason but the only horses available were my horse, Nig, and a Thoroughbred cross gelding named Brownie. Don had stock racks on his pickup so we jumped the horses into the pickup box. It had snowed most of the night leaving about a foot of snow in the valleys. Don's Ford was a 4X4 so we didn't expect any problems from the snow.

However, just to be on the safe side we went to the top of Moon Pass and then turned west out to Slate Creek Saddle along the St Joe Divide.

When we unloaded the horses we had to rig some stirrups on the Decker pack saddles so we could ride out to the deer. We just adjusted the sling ropes off of the front bars for stirrups, and then laid our mantle pack covers up over the bars front and back for a comfortable seat. Don said he would ride Nig, so that left me with Brownie. Brownie was a spoiled, flighty bugger that wasn't very steady. When I went to put my bridle bit into his mouth he started rearing up and striking at me with his front feet. I had a fifteen foot halter rope on his halter that had been hanging down in the snow and was frozen solid on the end, so after I whacked him across the shins with that frozen rope a few times he settled down and I just flipped a half hitch over his nose with the halter rope, and then went up over his neck and tied the end back to the halter shank. That snorty bugger stood right there while I got my foot into my makeshift stirrup and swung aboard. Don took the lead so that kind of restrained Brownie from trying to run off with me.

When we got out to where the deer was the snow was eighteen inches deep and drifted. Don asked, "Where is the deer?" I said, "Right by a snag." But now there were probably fifteen snags to choose from. So I dismounted from Brownie and just put my hand on the halter shank and led him down onto the slope and started along the tree-line. Pretty soon I saw where a small animal had come down the hill and went into a hole in the snow. About that time this white ermine's head popped out of the hole, and he started hissing at me with his face covered with blood. The ermine went back down the hole so I started kicking around in the snow and found the mule deer buck. I told Don, "Why don't we just tie a sling rope to the deer and pull him up to the ridge-top where we would have better footing."

After tying the sling rope around the buck's neck I stepped up beside Brownie and patted him on the shoulder so he would move up and take the slack out of the rope. When that sling rope came tight alongside his flank, Brownie lunged ahead and looked back to see that deer come hurtling out of the snow. That was all she wrote, he was going up the hill side in twenty foot bounds. When Brownie lunged ahead he knocked me down, so when that deer went by on the end of that sling rope I grabbed a hold of a back leg and went flying up the hill with the deer. Just as we cleared the ridge-top I lost my footing and had to let go of the deer. Now old Brownie was headed for the truck with the devil on his trail. The sling ropes on this Decker saddle were five/eights inch hemp rope so when Brownie headed out the trail towards the truck that deer was on the end of that forty foot sling rope bouncing along through the snow. When Brownie got into the jackpine trees, which were about ten feet tall, that deer would get hung up on a tree and then came flying up over the top in a big cloud of snow. I was laughing so hard Don must have thought I had gone off the deep end.

Finally, we took off following Brownie's tracks. I figured he would be at the truck, and we would find the deer with its head torn off along the trail. But, finally, we came up to Brownie standing in the trail, shaking like a leaf, and the steam was just poring off his wet, sweaty body. The deer had finally gotten behind a tree that Brownie couldn't pull it over and the sling rope held. But you could see that Brownie had sure tried, he had dug all the way down into the dirt trying to jerk that deer over that tree. I slipped around him and came up to his head and got him quieted down and let him rest and cool down. I didn't think there was any way in hell we were going to put that deer on Brownie's back, but he had shot his wad and just stood still as a statue while we got it lashed to the saddle.

The deer was frozen solid when we pulled him out of the snow, but after being dragged for half a mile through and over trees he was pretty limber. That old horse was as meek as a lamb all the way to the truck; he never even looked back once. I think he was afraid too!

I think old Brownie learned not to get so excited from this deal. But what a hell of a way to train a horse. I was just thankful that he hadn't gotten hurt, or hurt one of us. Now, tell me somebody isn't looking out for us fools. The 3X3 buck weighed in at 140 pounds on state certified scales at the locker plant. Minus his hide and legs.

Chapter Twenty-six

TWO CLOSE CALLS

Fall 1969. It was getting up about the middle of the elk season when I heard through the rumor mill that a friend, Rich, had harvested a 5X5 bull elk on the ridge between Vendetta and Idaho Gulch. Also, the story was that the 5X5 bull had a 6X6 bull traveling with him. It was several years later that Rich told me the real story of shooting his bull in the head as it ran across the slope. Rich said it was about 10.30 a.m. when he got sleepy, so he just leaned back against the hillside above a red fir tree and went to sleep. Rich said he woke up about noon and when he looked over to the open slope coming up out of Vendetta Gulch there was a 5X5 bull elk followed by a 6X6 bull elk trotting up the hill for the ridge-top. Rich said, "I just grabbed my rifle that was leaning against the tree, pointed it in the general direction of the two elk and jerked the trigger" and to his complete amazement the 5X5 bull went over backwards and rolled into the trees. Rich found that he had hit the bull right behind the ear, a very deadly hit.

Idaho and Vendetta gulches both drain into Prichard Creek about two miles east of the old gold camp of Murray, Idaho, in Shoshone County, Idaho.

It must have been about the third week in October for these bull elk to be buddies after the rut. However, I remember it as sunny but cold weather. My friend, Jack, and I had hauled our horses in my old 1951 Chevy stock truck up to Sunset Peak Lookout. I had my good horse, Nig, and Jack was riding a big red roan horse that was about as useless as anything could be. We rode down off of Sunset Peak on the Pony Peak trail. About one mile down the trail we turned off to the north on Vendetta Ridge. This ridge is a high alpine area with timber down both flanks, with Idaho Gulch to the west and Vendetta Gulch to the east. This ridge-top is knife blade thin, rocky, and steep as a church steeple on both slopes.

It was real early in the morning when we rode over a little rise, and there on the edge of the trees on the Vendetta Gulch side of the ridge stood a big 6X6 bull elk. Right next to this bull was his buddy hanging in a tree, all quartered up. Now that is what I call loyalty! I just stepped off my horse and told Jack there was a bull elk just below the ridge-top. I yanked my rifle from the scabbard on my saddle, and then flopped down prone on the ridge-top. The elk was only about 100 yards away when he started for the timber, coming directly at us. I don't like a front-on shot unless I can shoot at the neck, but the bull had his head down, sneaking away so the only shot I had was that big chest. I held low on the brisket for a heart shot. When my .308 Norma Magnum went off the bull did a forward flip down the mountain, and then rolled head over heels from view, in a big cloud of dust, into the trees.

When I turned to see what Jack was up to, I saw that he was hanging head down off of his horse. He was wearing a pair of logger type boots with a heavy lug sole, and his boot sole had hung up in the off stirrup, throwing Jack off balance. Jack was hanging head down on the near side of his horse with his head right at the heels of my horse. Jack hadn't said anything or struggled because he didn't want to excite either horse for fear of getting kicked or dragged behind his horse. I moved Nig over to a tree and tied him up, and then helped Jack back up on his horse. It was no easy chore with a man that weighed 235 pounds naked! This was one time Jack could be thankful that he was riding a dead-headed horse.

After getting Jack untangled, we went down to see about the elk. It was gone! We followed it for about 200 yards, and then it crossed a rocky area and we lost the track and the micro drops of blood. You have probably seen the little low bush huckleberry that grows along these high alpine ridges. As you know the leaves turn yellow with little red splotches on them. You can imagine trying to follow a blood trail through that stuff. Before long your eyes will start to tear, and then you go cross-eyed, get dizzy, you'll know the feeling if you have ever been there and done that. We tried every trick we could think of to try and find this wounded bull elk for two hours without uncovering one clue as to where he had gone off to. I had been sure that he was dead on the shot.

After a leisurely lunch break under the warm October sun, we decided we would go over into Pony Gulch for the afternoon hunt. We hadn't gone back up the ridge 300 yards when I looked over on the Vendetta side of the ridge and spotted a deer standing in an avalanche chute. It was a little three point mule deer buck, and Jack wanted a deer so he got into a good rest alongside a red fir tree and took the easy 100 yard shot. His shot was true and the little buck tumbled down the mountain, out of sight. We dismounted and started down that steep slope, leading our horses in a switchback pattern. I was in the lead about fifty yards ahead of Jack, when Jack screamed, "Look out!" I looked up to see Jack's horse rolling down the hill right at me. I was able to get out of the way, and then lucky enough to grab the halter rope as he tumbled past me in slow motion.

When the horse hit the end of the halter rope I was braced enough to give the horse enough purchase to get his feet under him and stop rolling. The horse just laid there with his eyes closed, his body trembling, hurting like hell. Finally, the horse got to his feet and I was right beside him to steady his balance. When it seemed like he was going to be all right we coaxed him over to a flat spot above a big tree. We left him tied to that tree to try and recuperate as he acted like he had ruptured himself. He was all hunched up anyhow so we left him while we went to see about Jack's deer.

We found the deer in the creek at the bottom of the canyon. In no time we had it field dressed and ready to pack on my horse, Nig. This was not going to be and easy chore as several years before a friend, Rich, had trouble packing an elk on Nig, and Nig hadn't gotten completely over that experience. Rich told me that Nig had gone nuts at the time, bucked the meat off, and kicked the saddle off his back.

I led Nig over to a little flat spot above the deer, and had Jack get a good hold of the cheek pieces on the halter so he could hold on tight. However, I really wasn't expecting any trouble as Nig had been smelling the deer and had his nose in my face the whole time I was dressing the deer out. I got the deer up on my saddle and cut a slit in the belly skin to button hook it over the saddle horn. I was just pulling the slack out of the hitch when Nig turned his head back and smelled the deer, and then let a bellow out of him and started bucking down the creek bottom. He had managed to stomp Jack on the foot, and jerk me off my feet, and then throw the deer off his back into the creek. Nig turned around and came running up to me to protect him from that nasty old deer that had jumped on his back. I got him calmed down and got the deer back in the saddle only this time I got my hitches thrown and my knots tied, and ready to ride. I swung up behind the cantle of my saddle and Jack threw me the halter rope and we were off up that steep mountainside.

Now old Nig had rollers in his nose, and a lot of white showing in his eyes as he painted the trees with snot all the way to the ridge-top. Once on top we headed out for Sunset Peak in a fair hurry. I sure knew

81

I was a horseback, that's for sure.

As we came busting around a corner in the trail we ran into Rich coming in with his pack string to get his elk. We almost scared them to death. I got Nig stopped and his chest was just covered with deer blood and foam where the lather worked out from under the breast strap on my saddle. Rich says, "I wouldn't believe this if I hadn't seen it with my own eyes." His horses were all as far off the trail as they could get, so before Nig blew the plug again we headed up the trail again. I know that you're thinking that I was crazy to let Nig push himself up that steep mountain. However, Nig was setting the pace. I never encouraged him at all. It has always been my habit to just let a horse be everything that he can be. I know I have been surprised at some of the things horses have done for me on their own intuition, and you will be too if you just give them the chance.

I was at the truck for a long time before Jack came in, leading his crippled horse up the trail. Jack never did take the horse to a vet, but the horse had injured his back, his hind end would just flop from side to side. The poor old horse I really felt bad about his accident even though I didn't like him to start with. I would have never made him walk back to that peak injured like he was. A bullet would have been the right thing to do, a mercy killing if you will.

We hadn't gotten the bull elk, but the way things turned out I thought we were lucky to escape with our lives. I went back the next day and spent the whole day looking for that bull elk. I found not one clue as to what had happened. It must have just been a marginal hit that I made. I want to think that the elk recovered from his wound wherever it was. Good luck now and be careful!

Chapter Twenty-seven

HOLIDAY COLD CAMP

Fall 1969. This was a Thanksgiving Day holiday hunt into the famous Lost Creek drainage. Lost Creek is a tributary of the North Fork of the Coeur d'Alene River in Shoshone County, Idaho. Lost Creek is a very unique area encompassing terrain nine miles long and seven miles wide, with no roads. However, it is accessible by several good Forest Service trails – the East-fork trail, the East-fork Ridge trail, the Hat Creek trail, and the main Lost Creek trail. All of these trails merge or end on the high alpine ridge separating Idaho and Montana at Bloom Peak. This wonderful elk habitat was created by forest fires in 1910, the teens, twenties, and thirties This was one of the first habitats stocked with elk from Yellowstone Park in the 1930's through the 1940's by the Shoshone County Sportsmen Club.

This would be a couple's hunt; we all had our wives along, Bob and Kathy, Frank and Norma, Skip and Darla, and myself and wife Karen. Everyone had a camper trailer which was a good thing as it was single digits above zero in the day time, and down to five below zero at night. The trailer windows were frosted over solid and the walls sweat gallons, so someone was kept busy wiping and swiping.

The first evening everyone gathered in my trailer for cards and conversation. The highlight of the evening, to Kathy's embarrassment, was when she (Kathy) decided she needed to use the outside toilet. When she opened the door and that below zero cold came rushing in, she just wet her pants right where she was standing. Now Bob was all red -faced with embarrassment as he hurried to get Kathy over to their trailer and get a change of clothes.

When we had gotten into camp that afternoon we had decided that we had better put all of the horses in my covered stock truck out of that cruel cold wind. When Frank went to unload the young horse that he had borrowed from a friend the horse came scrambling out of the pickup, and stepped down between the four-inch pipe bumper and the pickup box. Luckily I was standing right there and was able to get my shoulder under the horse's butt before he slipped down, and give him the old heave-ho back into the pickup box. It's a wonder he didn't injure his leg. I had Frank turn the horse around so he could see what he was doing and he stepped right out on the ground.

The next morning I told the guys to be sure and warm up their bridle bits before putting them in their horse's mouth because during cold conditions like this the metal bit can adhere to the horse's mouth, tearing the skin when removed – not a good thing to have happen to your favorite horse. We were all ready to ride off when there was a delay in our departure. The young horse Frank was riding decided he needed to buck a little to warm up and get the kinks out. Frank was able to stay on him, but I don't think that would have been the case if the horse could have gotten its footing on that slick, ice-covered road. Frank unfortunately was warmer than the horse, from grabbing at the saddle horn. Skip had Jack's horse, Blue, Bob was riding our horse, Rusty, and I had my favorite horse, Nig.

We rode up the East-Fork Ridge Trail on this cold, clear, morning in a silent white world. The forest birds were all hunkered down sitting on tree limbs with their feathers all puffed up to ward off the sub zero cold. The Pine Squirrels had their tails up over their backs, and didn't even scold us as we rode by. Our horses had their hair all standing on end with a rind of frost on the end of each hair, giving them a frosted look. Their faces and chest were frost covered also, from their breath vapor freezing on them. Everything looked to have gained weight with their blown up appearance. The trees complained with cracking and popping sounds as their sap froze, causing some trees to burst open.

We were in that big brush-field just before you intercept the main Lost Creek Trail, coming up on to the ridge, when I looked off to the east where a north-south ridge juts out into the East-Fork of Lost Creek, and there on the edge of the trees was a big old black-faced bull elk watching us ride by his bed.. I turned to Frank and pointed the elk out to him. Frank grabbed his rifle and tried to jerk it out of the saddle scabbard as he was dismounting. The young horse wasn't about to put up with this nonsense so he dropped his head back under his chest, and started bucking, and this time he had good footing. About the third jump Frank went airborne, and landed about ten feet out in the brush in two feet of fluffy cold snow. Frank wasn't hurt but the horse still had his gun hanging about half out of the scabbard, slapping him in the flank each jump. Frank hollered for me to shoot the son-of-a-bitch. As the horse bucked past me, he kicked at my horse, just missing my leg. After this close call I was able to catch the horse without committing any violence on him. I got the rifle secured back in the scabbard and then returned to the others. Everyone had been so busy watching the bronco ride that the elk had escaped without a shot being fired at him. Evidently the elk wasn't a rodeo fan like the rest of us.

Before we could get going again Frank discovered that he had lost his rifle ammo out of his coat pocket during his bronco ride. This caused quite a delay as we searched for Frank's ammo. Thankfully, it was in a bright red plastic box, or we never would have found it in the deep snow.

After all this excitement we decided we would build a fire and eat our lunch while things settled down. After lunch we left our horses and started up along the ridge in a line, with Frank leading on the left side and the rest of us spread out behind and across from him about 100 yards back on his flanks. If we jumped any elk somebody should get a shot as the elk tried to circle into the wind to get our scent.

We hadn't gone far when there was a shot off to my right, and that was where Bob was supposed to be. I stood still as death watching and listening for any animal that might try to get around me. After about fifteen minutes I thought I had better check to see if Bob had had any luck. One shot usually means meat down! When I came up to Bob he was so excited he could hardly talk. I ask what he had shot at. "It was an elk," he blurted out, "a bull elk!" When I ask if he thought he had hit it, his reply was, "I don't know I couldn't see it in my scope because it was clogged with snow." We went over and found the lone track and followed it for about a mile. It had been a bull all right as the drag marks in the snow indicated but it wasn't bleeding, and the bull knew we were following him. After circling into the wind for about a mile he headed out in a bee-line for the bottom of the East-Fork Canyon.

When we returned to the horses it was to find that there had been a near disaster! We had built our warm-up fire right at the base of an old rotten snag. While we were gone hunting, the fire had burned out the rotten center of the snag, making it into a chimney. Finally, it had burnt the snag off at the stump, and the snag came crashing down amongst the horses. Man-o man, the snow was melted down in a fifty foot circle, and all of our horses had their eyes all bugged out, and white, as they danced around the trees they were tied to. We would have all been walking back to camp if we hadn't had the sense to tie our halter ropes in a bow line knot around the horse's necks. It was just a miracle that we didn't have some badly burnt horse's to doctor. I guess we owe somebody for looking out for us after we acted so stupidly.

When we got back to our campsite we all pitched in and got the horses fed and watered, and what ever you do don't forget the water when it is cold. Our wives were actually glad to see us, I think; they had prepared a big turkey dinner to celebrate the holiday. Us guys were so hungry that we just bolted our food down like a pack of wolves. After the dinner mess was cleaned up it was cards again until midnight. The next morning the thermometer showed a frosty seven degrees below zero. It was just too cold to enjoy the hunt so we just fed our horses and prepared to break camp. The women also pointed out the fact that we were the only fools out in this cold anyway.

This trip would not be remembered for the good food, camaraderie, or the companionship of good horses. But for all the strange occurrences that turned out so well, with the help of you know who, so give thanks to your god. Well anyway be careful and good luck hunting.

Notice the "bench" built to cool out elk quarters where no trees were available.

Chapter Twenty-eight

FAMILY ABUSE

Fall 1970. We had attended the Plains, Montana, rodeo and fair so we had missed our annual bear hunt up by the Jack Waite Mine. However, it was raining cats and dogs so we probably wouldn't have gone hunting anyway. The rodeo arena was just a sea of mud so when it came time for the bull riding event, the rodeo clown couldn't even stand up let alone get a bull off a bucked-off rider. But there was a local rancher that saved the day when he volunteered to rope the bulls if a rider got bucked off. Now I know that you're thinking there is no way that a man on foot can hold a big old bucking bull on a rope. But this old boy didn't rope the bulls around the neck; no, he would rope their front feet and stand them right on their nose in the mud. By the time the bull came to it senses the rider was safely on the fence. Everybody in the stands would stand up and cheer every time that old cowboy roped a bull. A local rancher sitting next to me said, "Now there is a real cowboy, not just somebody dressed up like one." I don't think anyone could dispute that. I was impressed.

It was the middle of September and a nice sunny Sunday, so we had decided to go to Murray, Idaho, to visit friends. I had my wife, Karen, along, and my son, Jeff, as well as two nephews, Mike and Ray. Of course, because there was an open hunting season for bear, I had put the old Model 94 Winchester .32 Special in the car. This old rifle was an heirloom that had been in our family since 1937 when my dad bought it new for thirty seven dollars.

As we were proceeding down the Beaver Creek side of Dobson Pass, two bears went flashing across the road. I stopped the car and grabbed the gun, and then started walking down along the road looking up onto the slope the bears had gone up. I was standing in the road where the bears had crossed when down below the road I heard the awfullest wailing you ever heard. And then I spotted two cub bears in the top of a pine tree about eye level with me, and that was when I heard rocks rolling down the road bank behind me. As I turned to see what had made the noise, there in the middle of the road was a bear with its hair standing on end. I turned towards the bear just as her ears went flat; then she dropped her head and charged! I didn't have time to even think, I just reacted. When the gun came to my shoulder just by instinct the bear was in the sights and I fired, and then the bear swerved and went over the road bank. I hadn't even consciously aimed or even had a thought about where to aim I had just reacted to the situation.

When I cautiously looked over the road bank all I could see was glimpses of black fur about fifty yards down the steep bank in the heavy underbrush. We were right where and drainage came up the hillside, so I decided to get across the drainage and see what I could see from there.

At this time my wife was screeching at me to do something, and all of the kids were crying because those cub bears had changed from squalling to pitiful screams. I told the wife and kids to get into the car and stay there, and then I walked down the road until I could look back across the drainage. I still couldn't see anything that I could positively identify, so then I got down on the slope and started stalking along the hillside. Finally, I could see that the sow bear was evidently dead and the two little cubs were laying across her body, screaming like banshees. The cubs were so small that I didn't have any alternatives other than killing them, because they would never survive without their mother.

After field dressing the three bears I grabbed the cubs and climbed up to the road. I would need some help with the sow bear. The whole family was still distraught from listening to those cubs cry, but I couldn't get the sow bear up that steep bank by myself, so I told the three boys to get their butts over that bank before I threw them over it. They changed their minds and came to help me and we finally hunched the sow bear up into the road.

That was when a Washington car pulled up alongside us and this fellow stepped out and said, "I see you got my bear." When I turned around this fool has a fifty dollar bill in his hand and a big grin on his face. I said, "Mister, there are no bears for sale here, so I suggest that you get the hell out of here." I can't imagine what he thought when he saw the wife and kids with tear-streaked faces and me in such a foul mood.

I'm not sure what was happening with this bear family when we drove up, but I think there must have been some kind of dispute between the mother bear and the bear she chased across the road in front of us. I know I wasn't very popular for the rest of that day, or the week that followed either. It wasn't a case of knowing what I was getting into, because I just reacted as the thing developed. Looking back on this incident I don't think I would have intentionally shot the sow bear, but as it turned out I wasn't the one making the choices. On the plus side I had a bear tag, and I always had orders from people that wanted a bear if I happened to get one. So I tagged the sow bear and then took the two cubs to some friends in Prichard, Idaho, who loved bear meat.

I hope that you never get caught up in a situation like this, but if you do I hope you are lucky enough to come out of it unscathed like I did. I believe in the old saying, that all is well, that ends well. Somebody up there was looking out for old Number One.

Motorcycle packer extra-ordinary Rick Eichinger with a nice bear he shot in Placer Creek.

Chapter Twenty-nine

A PACKER'S NIGHTMARE

Fall 1970. My brothers-in-law, Bob and Jim, came to me to pack out an elk for them. The elk was away up in the head of Hat Creek, a tributary of Lost Creek, which is a tributary of the North Fork of the Coeur d'Alene River in Shoshone County, Idaho.

Earlier in the fall I had quoted Bob a special price of $35 per elk. Now here it was the middle of November and a cold front had come roaring down out of Alaska, freezing everything solid as iron. And to add insult to injury, I had hurt my knee at work that week and it was sore and stiff. Now that $35 sure didn't look like a gold mine when you consider it would be a fourteen-mile round trip, not even counting packing the elk up out of the head of Hat Creek. It would be a hellish trip down into Hat Creek from the main Hat Creek ridge trail. It is a steep, brushy, rocky area that is almost impossible to penetrate. However, the elk get through this jungle so I guess my good horses could make it too.

By 4:30 a.m. the following morning I had loaded my old standbys, Nig and Rusty, onto my 1969 Chevy 4X4 pickup and headed out for the trailhead fifty miles away. I had Nig saddled with my riding saddle, and Rusty was outfitted with a Decker pack saddle. When I arrived at the trailhead Bob's car was already there with a note under the windshield wiper blade. The note told me that Bob and his boys had gone up to the elk. I tightened my cinches and rode off up the ridge trail at a brisk trot. I wasn't the only one that wanted to get this deal over with. Both Nig and Rusty were trotting right along without any encouragement from me. That is their way of doing things "get it done and get back to the ranch" where they will get their reward of oats.

When I got up where I expected to find Bob no one was around so I let out a bellow to let them know where I was. Very faintly, from away and away down in the bottom of the canyon, I thought I heard an answer. To heck with this! I had told Bob there was no way I could make two trips in and out of that canyon bottom. I just headed back down the ridge for the truck. I hadn't gotten far when one of Bob's boys ran up behind me and asked where I was going. When I told him he said that what I had heard was a raven calling. He told me the elk was just another half mile up the ridge and about 500 yards down the sidehill.

When we got back up to where we had to go down off the ridge I tied Nig to a tree just off the trail. I had lots of flagging ribbon tied in his mane and tail so some great sportsmen wouldn't come along and mistake him for a black elk. I took Rusty's lead rope and we followed our guide down the steep hillside. Even with heel and toe caulks on his shoes, Rusty was just like he was on ice skates. Straight down was our only option as we could not sidehill at all. I had to run to stay out of Rusty's way as he slid down the hill with all four feet bunched under him like a roping horse stopping a calf. Rusty would just bull-doze through the small clumps of brush with sticks and rocks flying out and around on both sides. Whenever we hit a clump of brush big enough to stop Rusty, he would get a well earned rest. It was during one of these rest periods that Rusty blew snot all over the back of my neck and head. When I looked to see what his problem was, he was dancing around like he was standing on hot coals. Looking down I saw an elk's ear sticking out of the dirt and a big old bear track imprinted in the soft dirt. We were standing on top of a bear's dinner cache! We bailed out of there in a fair hurry.

When we came up to Bob he had a nice little four-point bull elk all butchered and ready to pack out. He also had a nice, cheery fire going with a coffee pot sitting alongside. I poured a cup of coffee and started warming my cold, stiff hands by the fire. Bob asked if I wanted some cream for my coffee. When I looked up, Bob had a big smile on his face and was holding a bottle of good whiskey out to me. For the next three hours we worked on getting both halves of the elk to the ridge-top. At this point my knee was so stiff and sore I could hardly stand on it. In fact the last trip up the hill I had rode astraddle the packs, and it turned out to be our best trip as all that weight gave Rusty better traction on that hard, frozen ground.

I decided that I was going to need a saddle horse to pack me the slick seven miles back to the truck. That left old Rusty to pack a whole elk off that mountain. Now don't go to feeling sorry for Rusty. He is 1,250 pounds of solid muscle. His mama was a Quarterhorse mare bred to a Shetland pony stallion. Rusty was built like a rhinoceros, short legged, broad and deep through the chest that holds big lungs; plus, he has a big heart that will never stop. It didn't take long to rearrange the packs into

91

two equal halves. Each hind quarter was fitted inside the front quarter with the leg coming out of the neck channel making a good solid pack when it was wrapped in a canvas mantle, and tied up tight. Bob's boys were getting pretty tired so they would take turns riding behind me on Nig.

When we came out onto the road in Lost Creek, a pickup with three guys in it pulled up and they started grilling us. "Where did you get that elk?" the driver wanted to know. Looking down at their car license I saw it had a 7B (Bonner County), so I answered: "We had killed it up by Sandpoint, Idaho, and were just packing it all over the country for the exercise." "That's one hell of a load you have on that horse," retorted the driver. I said, "The only one whining is you," and then rode off up the road to the truck.

Jim was waiting for us with a big bonfire, and had a pot of chili bubbling away alongside the fire. We were all tired and hungry so that chili sure hit the spot. We didn't show very good eating manners so someone driving by probably thought we were kind of an uncouth group. I was loading my horses onto the truck when I heard Bob tell Jim that he owed me $17.50 for packing his half of the elk out. Jim got all bristled up and said, "I wouldn't have let him pack it for that much, because I could have backpacked it out." I told Jim that if he wanted to backpack it out on his back, I would sure pack his half back up where I got it so he could have that experience. Bob says to me, "Here is your thirty-five dollars. If Jim don't want to pay he won't get any meat, because I am the one that shot the the elk, butchered it, and helped get it packed out so it is my damn elk."

If you should need a packer's services and make an agreement before he loads his horses onto his truck, then don't try to weasel out of the bargain after the job is done. Those horses have to be trained and equipped with tack, fed and watered, and given shelter. So take all of this into consideration, and those old ponies will save you lots of sore muscles and grief. Good luck and goodbye I hope I can be of service to you some day.

Chapter Thirty

LOST MINE

Early fall of 1971. Friends Jack and Bob would join me for an elk hunt off of Sunset Peak in Shoshone County, Idaho. Sunset Peak has been the trailhead for many of our hunts in the past because the area is inhabited by all species of big game found in the State of Idaho.

This frosty fall morning we arrived on top of the peak way before daylight so we had plenty of time to discuss our strategy for the day. Deer, black bear and elk were all legal game so we had a good chance of being successful. As we drank coffee while we waited for shooting light, Bob mentioned that if we had an opportunity at shooting game he would like to have first shot as Jack or I usually beat him to the shot. We assured Bob that he had first shot on anything we saw while we were together.

Finally the stars winked out and a pink glow highlighted the ridge line to the east. We headed down the trail and as soon as we could see the open ridge going to the north between Granite Gulch and Pioneer Gulch we stopped to watch for game. We were just about cold enough to move when I spotted a herd of elk climbing up out of Granite Creek to cross the sharp notch saddle on the East Ridge between Vendetta Gulch and Granite Gulch. The herd consisted of three large cow elk with three new calves as well as three yearling cows that were probably their calves from the year before. We waited for forty-five minutes to make sure that there were no bull elk following this herd.

We had just gotten down the steep part of the trail and out onto the sunny alpine ridge when we saw two 3X3 mule deer bucks grazing along, unaware, only seventy-five yards away. We got Bob into a good rest over a stump right above the trail and he missed the bucks three times before they became aware that he was shooting at them. As they bounced down the hillside Bob was hollering for Jack or I to shoot. Even though it was probably in the low twenties, Bob had sweat running down his face and was shaking like he was having a heart attack. I guess you could call it "Buck Fever". We all had a good laugh about it and decided to go after the elk herd that we had seen.

A foggy morning on the St. Joe River.

Jack would go out almost to Pony Peak and then drop down into Idaho Gulch and hunt back towards the lower saddle on the Vendetta Ridge. Bob was to go on stand above the saddle, and I would go down to the saddle that the elk crossed on that morning and hunt back towards Bob. Somebody should get some shooting as we tried to get this elk herd between us.

I found the tracks of the elk herd in the saddle and started following them into Vendetta Gulch. This was my first time hunting this particular part of Vendetta Gulch. However, it was nice open timber with hardly any underbrush, so I had good visibility for 100 yards or better. I just eased along as it appeared that the elk were browsing mushrooms off the damp forest floor.

As I came into the crease of the headwaters of the gulch I found an old caved-in log cabin with only the base logs not rotted back into the ground. Some one had leveled off a place about twenty feet square and built a cabin ten by sixteen feet. A trail led off into the main draw about fifty yards away where a spring gurgled out of the mountain. From the spring I could see an opening down the gulch about one hundred yards, so I moved down the hillside to check that out. I came onto the tracks of my elk herd where they had slid down a steep bank into the creek bottom, and I could see where they had climbed out the other side, going

94

towards the saddle Bob was waiting on. The sun was shining onto the slope with mature red fir trees with the openings between the bigger trees having a scattering of smaller fir saplings. Overall it was quite open so I just sat down to watch for awhile and use my binoculars to try and spot an animal. After watching for about one hour I slid down into the creek where I discovered some steel mine rails coming out of the rubble of the creek bottom and twisting down the creek bottom for another thirty feet. There was no evidence of a dump or portal, just the mine rail coming out of the creek bottom. (Later looking at an old Metsker's Map of Shoshone County I could see two claims straddling the creek bottom. The claim on the west side of the creek was the Ocean and on the east side was the Moscow).

Evidently when they leveled off a spot to portal into the mountain the headwall of the cut in later years had sloughed down, taking out the dump, and had washed away all evidence that there had ever been a mine tunnel there. On closer inspection I found the dump body off of an old mine car buried in the gravel of the creek bottom. This tunnel site had to be at least two miles from any road and there wasn't even any indication of a trail leading into the area. I just wonder if some old prospector hadn't skidded that mine car and rail right up the creek bottom with a mule or horse. Those old prospectors were tough old guys; you just never knew where you might find a tunnel that had been driven into some outcropping using hand-mining methods. More than likely the work had been done for a grubstake back in the late 1800's, from some business owner just trying to rid himself of a miner down on his luck. And don't think that there weren't lots of millionaires made from these grubstakes, like old Nora Kellogg who discovered the great Bunker Hill Mine on the South Fork of the Coeur d'Alene River.

Getting back to the elk hunt, I just followed the elk tracks up the far bank until I came up against a root wad about two feet thick capping the steep creek bank. I laid my rifle up above this obstacle and reached up over the root wad to get a handhold to pull my self up over the top of the bank. I had a hold of some huckleberry brush and when I pulled myself up over the bank just as a cow elk exploded up off the ground from behind a little three-foot-high fir tree. She kicked dirt right in my face as she sped off across the hillside, flushing the rest of the herd as she ran. By the time I got my wits about me there wasn't an elk in sight. These elk headed across the slope like they would go into the blind drainage formed by Vendetta- Idaho Gulch Ridge that forked to send finger ridges to the west and east.

So I decided to just hike on up to meet Jack and Bob at the saddle because it was past noon already. When I got to the saddle Jack was waiting for me but Bob was nowhere around. Jack and I hiked back up the ridge towards the main divide, hoping to find Bob somewhere along the way. We were past the top saddle when Bob came crawling out of a brush pile back in the timber, shaking so bad he could hardly talk. At first we thought he had seen some game, but he was just cold from sitting on the frost-covered ground back in that brush pile. We got him out into the bright sunlight and built a fire to toast our sandwiches while Bob warmed up.

Bob was the only one to get any shooting, but then any day spent in elk country is a successful day as far as I'm concerned. I still can't believe that I watched that hillside those elk were bedded on for an hour and never saw them. That just goes to show you that we don't always see what is right in front of us. I can't believe that those elk let me fool around there that long because they had to have heard me fooling around in the creek bottom. Maybe they were asleep like I must have been to have not spotted them, but in hindsight I don't think I was looking that close because I wasn't expecting them to bed down on that partially open hillside.

Chapter Thirty-one

TWO BULLS INSTEAD OF ONE

Fall 1974. A friend, Jack, and I backed my 1969 Chevy 4X4 pickup into the road-bank and unloaded our horses. We were going into the Hat Creek drainage for an elk hunt. Hat Creek is a tributary of Lost Creek, which is a tributary of the North Fork of the Coeur d'Alene River in Shoshone County, Idaho.

On this fine fall morning there was a high overcast, making it one of those gray, dreary and cold days that are so common in mid-November. The horses were dancing around stomping there feet, and blowing great clouds of vapor from their nostrils into the cold morning air. They were ready to be off up the mountain and work some warmth into their cold bodies. It felt good to be astraddle a big strong horse as we followed the open grassy ridge up the north-side of Hat Creek. We would go all the way to the forks of the creek, and then cross over onto the middle ridge where we would have both forks of the creek under observation as we climbed to the top. This is a good area to conduct an elk hunt because there are Forest Service trails bordering both sides of Hat Creek, and those trails are where most of the other hunters would be accessing upper Lost Creek. All of this activity pushes the elk into Hat Creek from both forks of Lost Creek.

It was still early in the morning when we arrived at the spot where we wanted to watch from. We got our horses tied back in a group of trees where they would be out of sight, and out of that cold wind blowing up the ridge. Jack and I moved out onto a flat spot on the open ridge and then built a small fire to warm our cold stiff hands. We had been on this stand for about two hours when we spotted two 5X5 bull elk coming over the ridge out of the East Fork of Lost Creek. It is not that unusual for young bulls to buddy up after the rut like this. Lots of times these young bulls will have a big old trophy bull elk hanging back in the shadows letting them check things out before he shows himself. The two bulls were about 500 yards away across the draw from us, but Jack wanted to try for them as we hadn't been enjoying very good luck so far this elk season. I said okay, and then started looking for a rest for my rifle to steady my aim on such a long, difficult shot.

Boom, boom, Jack started shooting from an offhand position at the elk. Of course he missed. I was just a little ticked off at this foolhardy act. I just jumped on my good horse, Nig, and took off for a saddle where I thought these bulls might cross into the main fork of Lost Creek. I hadn't said a word to Jack so he just stood there dumbfounded with his mouth hanging open. The bulls were smarter than I was and they just circled back into the East Fork where they had come from. All I got was my horse all sweated up trying to cut them off.

When I got back to Jack we decided that we had probably spooked everything out of this drainage so we would go on up into the upper Lost Creek basin. We built another fire to toast our sandwiches while we watched for animals from this new lookout spot. By 2:30 p.m. we hadn't spotted any game so we went back down to where the East Fork Ridge trail intersects the main Lost Creek trail.

We had just passed this junction and rode out onto the brushy East Fork Ridge, and were looking across to a flat ridge that breaks off into rock cliffs down into the East Fork Lost Creek. Over there on the edge of the trees were our two bulls, bedded down. The bulls were only about 400 yards away, so I told Jack to get a rest this time and maybe we would get an elk. Now this wouldn't be that far of a shot for the .308 Norma Magnums that Jack and I were both shooting. Jack picked the bigger of the two bulls and commenced shooting at it. I snuggled in behind a big alder bush, and then put my glove into a crotch in the bush for a good steady rest. I very carefully aligned the dot reticule in my four power scope on the smaller bull's back-line, and tight behind the shoulder. There was no indication from the bull that my shot had connected, but I was confident that it had. I aimed again with the same point of aim as the first time and touched off another round. This time the bull just walked off over the ridge-top out of view. Jack had shot three times, and reloaded and shot again. I was watching his bull and saw him stumble, and then go over the ridge following my bull.

We hurried and tied our horses in a clump of trees, and then took off across the steep rocky draw to see about the elk. When we panted up onto the ridge-top where the bulls had crossed, I looked directly into the bottom of the next draw and there, fifty feet up the opposite slope, lay my bull, dead. We went down to the elk and field-dressed, skinned, quartered, and hung the quarters from a tree, making it ready to pack on our return. Then we hurried back to where Jack's elk had turned off around the sidehill. We had about four inches of snow in which to follow the track and a faint blood trail. However, it would still require patience, and persistence, to follow this bull because he was following the trail of another herd of elk.

I told Jack to watch ahead for the bull, and I would try to keep us on the right track. We had jumped this bull several times from his bed but hadn't been able to see him. We had been on the trail for about an hour, and now only had about that long until sunset. We had continued on for another half hour when I just happened to look up and spot the bull standing behind a tree, watching us come along his back-trail. I hurried to get my scope on the bull before he jumped into the dark timber. Most of the heart-lung area was behind the tree so I aimed as close to the tree as possible and shot. Nothing, Jack stepped up beside me and shot; nothing again. I shot yet again and this time the bull elk collapsed in a heap. On inspection of the elk after we had opened him up for field-dressing, we found that my bullet had dissected a rib, torn the lungs to shreds, and then passed all the way through his body. The only other wound we could find was a slight wound through the muscle high on the left front leg. We assumed our first shots had been deflected by the dry branches on the lower tree trunks because the elk's side was splattered with copper jacket from our bullets that had been deflected by the brittle, dry tree branches before impacting the elk.

I was amazed that we were able to catch up to this bull with such a slight wound. I guess that he was just so insecure that he didn't want to leave his buddy. I don't believe we would have harvested this bull if I hadn't been there with my tracking skills to recover him. Jack, tagged this bull, but I was the one that found him and then was lucky enough to kill him.

Darkness was coming on fast so we had to build a fire for the warmth, and the light it would provide. A nice fire always takes away the gloom of the coming night. Jack didn't want to skin and quarter this bull, but knowing what a miserable job it would be if we let it freeze overnight, I prevailed and started the job. With both of us working on the elk it only took about one hour and we had another elk ready to pack on our return.

Before it had gotten black dark I had noticed that we were just south of the main trail so it was no problem finding the trail. We had to hike about two miles before we found our horses, and then it was another five miles to the truck. However, our horses were anxious to get back to the ranch so in about twenty minutes we were back at the truck.

Our midnight arrival at the ranch was welcomed by two very worried wives. After filling us up with one of their delicious suppers, they listened to the tales of our hunt. We were all content as a kitten on a warm blanket.

Jack and I returned early the next day with my horse, Nig, and three other horses that we had borrowed from a friend. It was an uneventful pack trip, no horse troubles or anything of that nature. We were mighty grateful to have the hunt over, with two nice elk hanging in the meat locker to fill our bellies through the cold, dreary winter. I believe that Jack and I both gained some very knowledgeable experience from this hunt. That is the reward of hunting, anyway.

A nice mule deer buck shot by a kid, Chris Neville, in 1985.

Chapter Thirty-two

NEW COUNTRY

Fall 1975. We had decided to hunt some new country up on the Idaho-Montana state line in the head of Lost Creek, in Shoshone County, Idaho. This hunt would be over the Labor Day weekend.

We were just a small party of two families. My sister, Linda, and her husband, Randy, and their two children, Vickie and Gene. My wife and son were along as well as the dogs, Ben and Missy. Randy had a new dog along that was a Black Labrador named "Big D".

I had asks Randy where he had come up with the name "Big D". His answer was I named the dog after you, and when I got this puzzled look on my face wondering what "Big D" had to do with me. Randy got that big old Indian smile on his face and said, "The dog is a big 'D—k Head', just like you."

We set up our two Road Runner camp trailers on the heliport by the spring in the head of the West Fork of Eagle Creek. We were not alone here, either, as there were several camps of Washington hunters, bow and arrow hunting for deer and elk.

The first morning we just walked along the road out across the forks of Lost Creek, watching for bears. We had seen everything but bear and got enough blue grouse to feed the whole group. That evening Randy and I sat out by a nice campfire while I cooked our birds to a nice golden brown on the campfire. We had plenty of time to swap lies and have a few toddies while our birds steamed until they were mouth-watering tender. After supper I walked over to the spring to fetch a pail of water for washing the dishes.

When I got to the spring a Washington hunter was there putting some fresh tomatoes in the spring to cool. When I asked him if he had had any luck hunting, his reply was a snotty remark about all the goddamn dogs running around scaring the game away. This was just sour grapes because we never got off the road, and the dogs were at heel all of the time. So I just ignored the comment, and filled my water bucket, and then called my dog, Ben. When I looked to make sure the dog was coming, it was just in time to see him dip his head into the barrel that the spring ran into

101

and snatch one of the other hunter's tomatoes out of the water and eat it. I just ignored that too, because the Washington guy hadn't seen Ben steal his tomato.

The next morning Randy and I got up real early and went down and drove up the West Eagle Creek road. We went all the way to the top and didn't see any game at all, so we headed back down the mountain. When we got down into the bottom where we usually saw ruffled grouse, I let my dog Ben out to run ahead of the pickup and see if he could scare up a grouse. We were just above the first bridge when Ben started getting gamey so I stopped to see what was up.

Once out of the pickup it was easy to see some big old wet bear tracks crossing the road. The bear was headed up the mountain. There was an outcropping of rock about 100 yards above the road so we climbed up there to be able to see better. We hadn't been there two minutes when Randy saw a bear walk out onto an open rockslide about 150 yards around the hillside. I told Randy to go ahead and shoot the bear because he had spotted it. He came around behind the rock bluff and got a rest over the edge of the bluff. I had gotten into position right beside Randy in case he missed. Randy missed his shot, so I just touched the trigger on my .308 Norma Magnum. The bear was only 150 yards away so it was no big deal to hit him right in the neck where I was aiming.

That afternoon we took both families and drove up the East Eagle Creek road towards the old Jack Waite Mine. We looked into several of our old favorite spots but didn't see any bears. Coming back down the creek that evening, my sister, Linda, spotted a bear crossing a rock slide below the cliffs at Sellers Pitch. We weren't fast enough to get a shot at that bear and he never did expose himself again. So we went on back to camp empty-handed.

That night the Washington hunters decided we were having too much fun sitting around the fire, so they came over and joined us for a few drinks. The hunting tales got pretty tall before the fire died down, but the one bear was the only big game harvested on the whole trip. It is surprising to me how much fun people can have if they just lighten up and not worry about getting their game, and enjoy the outing for what it is. Memories are made of good times had by all, not on the number of animals harvested.

Chapter Thirty-three

OLD PETE THE PACK HORSE

Fall 1976. Friends Jack and Jerry wanted me to make an elk hunt into Kelly Creek with them. Kelly Creek is a tributary of Loop Creek, which is a tributary of the North Fork of the St. Joe River, which flows into the main St. Joe River at Avery, Idaho, in Shoshone County, Idaho.

Kelly Creek heads up against the Idaho-Montana state line divide.

The State-Line Ridge is a high alpine ridge running east and west with the finger ridges down the south facing slope bracketing the Kelly Creek drainage. Kelly–Manhattan Creeks main divide ridge breaks off the main divide in a gentle slope, and a third of the way down the slope benches out flat for about one mile, and then gets steeper the closer you get to Loop Creek. The flat area is covered with jackpines and huckleberry brush, and the steeper portion has red fir and tamarack trees with openings of alder brush. The whole Loop Creek drainage is good elk habitat on both sides.

I had already gotten my elk on an earlier hunt, so I would let the guys off on top of the divide and then drive around into the bottom of Loop Creek and pick them up at the mouth of Kelly Creek. Jack and Jerry would hunt down the divide ridge between Kelly Creek and Manhattan Creek.

When I arrived at the bottom I parked my truck where I could glass the slopes on the Kelly Creek-Manhattan Creek face. It wasn't long and I spotted a bull elk moving across the face above the first bench. I still had a deer tag and this is good deer country, so I decided to climb up there and have a look around. Maybe, just maybe, I could drive some elk up the hill into Jack and Jerry. I circled around to the east side of the bench, so I would have the wind in my face, and be upwind of any animals. It was a blustery, grey sort of day with the wind gusting and swirling out of the southwest, so I would have to watch the wind constantly. It would still be a good day to hunt because the forest birds and squirrels were all scurrying around like they wanted to get fed up in case a storm came in on that southwest wind.

When I got up onto the jackpine-covered bench I encountered some fresh elk sign. The huckleberry brush had already shed their leaves, so visibility was a good seventy-five to one hundred yards, making for good stalking conditions. I thought to myself, I will just sneak along real slow through this timber and see what happens. I hadn't gone very far when I could hear something ahead of me but couldn't spot anything. I was pretty well across this bench and hadn't seen what was up ahead, so I sat down at the base of a tree and lit a cigarette, thinking maybe whatever was ahead of me would settle down if I wasn't following it. I was about through with my smoke when something made me look off to my downwind side, and there, looking around a tree at me, was a real nice 5X5 whitetail buck. I could only see the buck's head, but he was only fifty yards away so I slowly raised my .308 Norma Magnum to my shoulder and when the dot in my scope centered on the white patch on the buck's neck, I touched the trigger. Boom, I had my deer. It didn't take me long to hog-dress the deer and drag it down to the road below. This big hog-fat whitetail buck weighed in at the locker plant at 150 pounds, big for a whitetail in this area.

This deer kill brought to mind some whitetail hunting strategies that a little old man from Maine had told me. He said that you get into an area that you know is inhabited by whitetail deer, and then just sneak along upwind until you jump a deer. When the deer jumps and takes off, you turn around and run back downwind about fifty yards and hide, and the deer will come back looking for you. I believe that when I stopped and sat down, my buck came back looking to see where I had gone, just like that old man said they would. I can believe it, but you don't have to.

When I arrived back at the truck about noon, Jack and Jerry were already there. Jerry had killed a calf elk. Jack had missed a cow elk trying to shoot through brush. They had jumped a herd of elk crossing the main ridge between Manhattan Creek and Kelly Creek. Jack had spotted the cow elk and pointed it out to Jerry, so Jerry assumed that Jack would shoot the cow elk, and Jerry went ahead and got his scope on the calf as it moved off. When Jerry saw the calf in his scope he shot it through the ribs. They said that they had just hog-dressed the calf and left it draped over a log, and then tried to catch up to the elk herd again. Of course they were unsuccessful, because if elk know that you are following them it is a good bet your not going to catch up to them. We decided we would come back the next day with horses and pack the calf elk the mile back up to the road on top.

The next morning Jerry and I were up on top a-waiting daybreak so we could pack out his elk. The expected storm had passed through during the night, leaving a six-inch white mantle of snow covering everything. Up along this high alpine ridge the wind had plastered the southwest side of everything with snow. It was kind of eerie on this foggy morning with the trees all bent over looking like ghost in the fog.

For pack stock we had my horse, Nig, an old veteran, and Jack's horse, Pete. Pete was a gelding about ten years old, of some kind of an Appaloosa crossbreed. Pete weighed about 1,100 pounds, a nice size for a pack horse. Pete was a strawberry roan with bigger roan spots blanketing his rump. I didn't think that old Pete looked just right; his ears were too close together, as were his front legs. They both came out of the same spot giving him a pinched, narrow appearance. Pete wasn't hard to handle; he was just stupid. Anyway, as we proceeded down the ridge, Pete was falling over everything in his path. Finally, Pete ran head-on into a tree and fell back on his haunches. Jerry dismounted, and told me that he wasn't going to ride that stupid bastard one more step. Jerry got the halter rope off the saddle and started down the ridge leading Pete. As we worked through the jackpines, a pine marten ran up a tree alongside the trail. Jerry hadn't seen the pine marten and when he walked by the tree the marten stuck his head around the tree and almost touched noses with Jerry. Jerry jumped back against Pete, almost knocking Pete down. The marten just came on around the tree curious, as a cat. That is what he reminded me of, only he had and orange bib on his chest.

When we arrived at the elk the carcass was frozen solid in a U-shape. We hadn't any more than gotten started with the skinning job, and our hands were frozen also. This caused a delay while we gathered some dry wood to build a fire to warm our cold, stiff hands. The hide had a layer of ice between the hide and meat, so we had to more or less pry it off. By the time we got the elk skinned and quartered, Jerry was about tired of my continual bitching and griping.

Old Pete stood with his head hanging down, moaning and groaning the whole time we were preparing the elk carcass to pack. I told Jerry that I didn't think Pete could pack half of the elk, and that he would probably be lucky to pack himself out. I would just pack the whole elk on Nig, and then ride out on top of the packs too. I inserted the hindquarter into the rib cage of the front quarter with the hind leg coming out the neck channel, and then wrapped it all up tight in a canvas mantle.

Here is a way to pack a riding saddle with elk quarters that you don't see used very often. I took a thirty foot rope and tied the middle to my saddle horn, and then doubled the rope back through the cinch ring on the saddle. This gives you a loop for a basket hitch, and then you just sling your packs on each side like you would using a basket hitch on a pack saddle. When the meat was secured to my saddle, I climbed up behind the packs and pointed Nig up the mountain towards the truck. I was at the truck unloading the meat in about thirty minutes. Jerry came in thirty minutes later with old Pete still complaining at every step. I think poor old Pete hurt his neck when he collided with that tree earlier that day

The sun came out and burnt the fog off, and now the temperature was quite comfortable and the snow was melting. This made that road down off Dominion Peak both slick and dangerous. We didn't realize how slick it was until we started down for Dominion Saddle. With two horses in my 4X4 pickup the front wheels had little traction, and if I let off the throttle at all, all four wheels would lock up and slide.

This is an old CCC road built in the 1930's by the Civilian Conservation Corp, so it is steep, and slopes to the outside edge for drainage. The only thing I could do was to keep shifting into a higher gear to keep the wheels turning and at least give us enough traction to steer. When we went through Dominion Saddle we were doing about fifty miles per hour. We finally got stopped about one half mile out towards Rainy Creek Pass. The first thing we did was put tire chains on all four wheels before we continued down the mountain. That was one spooky ride coming off that peak. All of this excitement caused us to have to make a beer stop at Saltese, Montana, to settle our nerves. With everything that had happened, poor Jerry was about at the end of his rope.

When we got home and got the meat in the locker plant, and the horses back in the pasture, we stopped to tell Jack about Pete's mishap. Jack never took Pete to a vet because we knew he would put him through the sale ring the next week for horse meat. It still makes the chills run down my back when I think of what would have happened if we had rolled my truck, and the horses, down the side of Dominion Peak. I guess someone was looking out for us, because we sure were not thinking for ourselves. Keep alert for the unexpected to happen when you least expect it. Good luck and good hunting.

Chapter Thirty-four

MONTANA BEAR

Fall of 1978. I had purchased a nonresident Montana big game license for the sum of $475, if my memory serves me right. We had missed the annual Labor Day bear hunt in Idaho, and went to the Plains, Montana, rodeo instead.

I guess just because I had a Montana hunting license my wife, Karen, and I decided to go bear and forest grouse hunting in Montana. We left our home in Wallace, Idaho, and went over to Trout Creek, Montana, via Bloom Peak. We had driven through some of the best big game country in Montana right after daybreak and had only gotten one little ruffled grouse.

We left Trout Creek, Montana, and went on up the highway to Whitepine, Montana, and then turned off onto the Beaver Creek road that went up towards the pass on the Idaho-Montana border, and back into Idaho above the old Jack Waite Mine. When we came to the Little Beaver Creek road we turned off and went out below Daisy Peak and Beaver Lake to the end of the road on the ridge in Twenty-Four Mile Creek. On our drive out this road we managed to get three blue grouse, but had seen no big game at all. We were on our way back out to the main road, and then right below Daisy Peak a bear ran across the road.

Karen was all excited and was telling me to get that bear. I didn't think there was a chance of ever seeing the bear again, but being an obedient husband I took one cartridge and my .308 Norma Magnum and walked over to the road bank and looked over. To my complete amazement there was the bear standing there looking up at me not fifty feet away.

By the time I put the cartridge into the chamber and shouldered my rifle the bear was seventy yards away, bounding over logs, and was just a black blur as he vacated the scene as fast as possible. I took off down the hillside hot on his trail, and was able to catch the bear crossing a draw only 100 yards away. As bears often do, the bear stopped with his front feet up on a log, and looked back to see if I was following him. It didn't take me long to sit down and get into a solid rest, with my elbows locked into the inside of my knees. When my .308 Norma Magnum

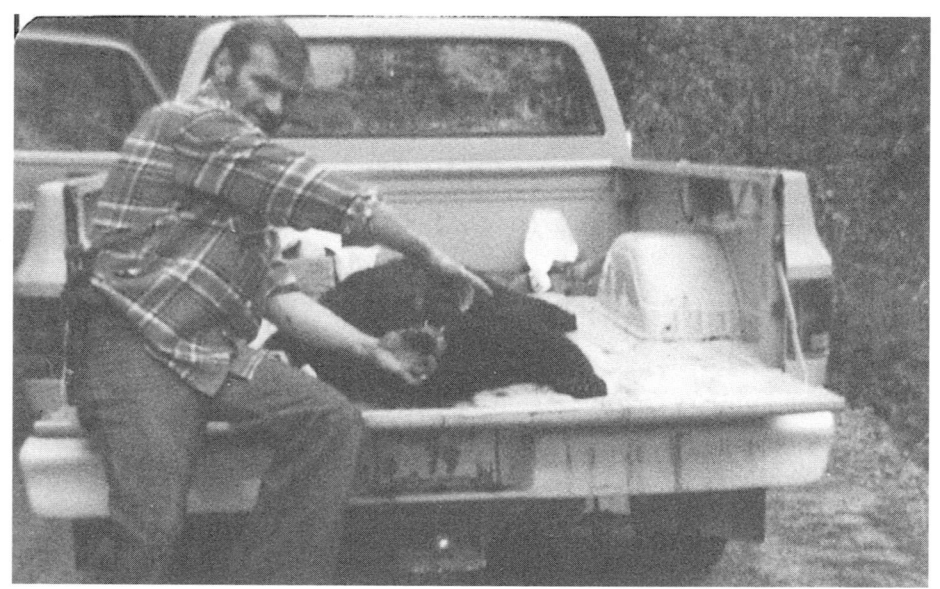

Fred's Montana bear in the pickup, at last.

went off that bear dropped into the underbrush. I had hit him right below the head in the neck so he wouldn't be hard to find. Not over ten minutes before the bear ran across the road in front of the pickup, Karen had been bitching about the lack of game in Montana. But now she was complaining because she had to help me get the bear up to the road, which mostly consisted of lifting it over about ten thousand downed trees. Sometimes a hunter's good luck turns out to make him think that maybe his luck hadn't changed for the better after all.

When we got our bear taken care of, had taken a photo and eaten our lunch, we started back out to the main Beaver Creek road when we came across an old pickup parked along the road. We thought whoever had the pickup must be cutting firewood, but now it had a flashing blue light sitting on top of the cab. A Montana game warden stepped out and flagged me down and wanted to check my hunting license. I think he was disappointed when I had the proper license and tags for big game and birds. We then went back up over the pass into Idaho and then returned to our home in Wallace, Idaho

I guess we had as good an outing as you could have on your first hunt into strange country. That is, of course, if you consider driving along back roads hunting. I think it was more of a scouting trip than a hunting trip, so just do whatever you have to do and enjoy the outing for what it is.

Chapter Thirty-five

LADY LUCK

Fall 1978. This elk hunt would take place in early October in an un-named drainage on the St. Joe side of Moon Pass, which is in Shoshone County, Idaho.

My wife, Karen, and I had wakened up at 4:00 a.m. so we went up to Sweet's Café in Wallace, Idaho, for an early breakfast. There were several local elk hunters in attendance that morning to "JOSH" me about having to take my wife elk hunting. I didn't want to tell them that they were the losers, not me. After a good hearty breakfast we were off up Placer Creek to Moon Pass, and then down the south side of the pass to a small unnamed drainage below where Roughen Creek flows under the road.

We parked my 1977 Chevy 4X4 pickup on the point of a ridge just to the south of Roughen Creek. The sky was just getting that pink blush that announces the coming of a new day as we started our climb up the steep, brushy ridge. This area is covered about seventy percent by brush-fields that are the results of the famous 1910 forest fire, and additional fires in the teens and twenties. The brush fields are wonderful cover and habitat for the elk, but a nightmare for the elk hunters that have to fight their way through the heavy alders. It is both noisy and hard to see any distance. As we moved up through this frost mantled landscape, our noses wanted to run and drip and felt like they were being pinched off from the cold air we were inhaling.

Finally, we intersected the next dividing ridge and then an elk bugle came rushing on the wind out of the next drainage. The bull elk doing the bugling was directly below us, but out of our view over the bulge in the hillside below us. The bull continued to bugle every few minutes, his excitement exciting us as we listened to him bugle right in our face. What luck, Karen's first elk hunt and we were into elk in the first hour of the hunt.

It appeared that this bull elk was right in the canyon bottom. If we tried to move higher up the ridge the bull would smell us on the descending air thermals. We determined that our best strategy would be to move down the back side of the ridge we were on until we got below the bull, and then we could cross the ridge and try to see into the canyon bottom from a spur ridge jutting out into the other drainage. We had just started down the ridge and I was doing my best bull elk imitations, bugling, raking the brush with a stick – just making a heck of a racket hoping to keep the bull elk all excited. We hadn't gone thirty yards when all hell broke loose. We had walked right into the middle of the main elk herd. There were elk crashing off in all four directions like a covey of quail flushing. Our bull in the bottom was still bugling like crazy so we still followed our first plan and ignored this new herd of elk.

We finally found a spot where we could see into the canyon bottom, and there in an elk wallow was a nice 5X5 bull elk. The bull was putting on quite a show for the five cow elk that he had stolen from the herd bull up on the ridge. He would run his antlers into the ground, and fling mud and sticks every direction, and then urinate all over his neck mane and front legs. Then he would bugle a challenge to anything that might dare enter his domain.

Upon seeing the elk, Karen was all excited and wanted me to hurry and shoot before the bull moved off into the brush. However, we were in a bad place to shoot from because I would have to stand on my tiptoes to see over the brush, and there was no place to get a rest for my rifle. The range was a good 350 yards and shooting offhand is not my best position. I had to try something, so as my scope reticule wove across the bull's chest I touched off a round. I hit right under the bull's brisket. Boom, my next shot hit in the same spot, and then the bull stepped ahead two steps, and boom, I missed him again. My .308 Norma Magnum was capable of making this shot. I was the one not performing up to par. Now my rifle was empty of cartridges; these magnums only hold three cartridges. Karen is all excited. hollering at me to shoot that bull before he gets away. I put one more cartridge into the chamber of my rifle, aim, fire, and the bull goes down on his head. Karen is really excited now that the bull is down, she is whooping, and hollering. She says, "Let's get back to town and tell those smart bastards that were in the café this morning that we have a big bull on the ground."

However, first things come first so I directed Karen through the heavy brush to where the bull had fallen, and then I joined her. On my arrival at the bull I was able to see why he hadn't gone anyplace. My last bullet had passed through both front shoulders, and the lungs, for an instant kill. I dug into my pack and got a "Coke" for Karen before starting the chore of caring for the elk carcass.

It was only a little past 8:00 a.m. when we made the kill, but it would be 3:00 p.m. before we got back to our truck. Boy, talk about a rough place to make a kill. I would have to swamp out a place to work on my elk out of the mud and water of the elk wallow. With this chore accomplished I just pulled the bull up onto the brush I had cut to keep it out of the blood and gore as I field-dressed it. I just took my time and did a good job so I would have good, tasty elk meat to eat during the coming winter. I let Karen pack the trophy antlers down that brushy canyon to the road below. Upon our arrival on the road she informed me that she had just been on her first, and last, elk hunt all in the same day. Heck, it was just too much work for her.

The next morning I got my good horse, Nig, and another good horse named Smokey loaded onto my pickup and then stopped in Wallace to get my brothers, Lawrence and Don, to help pack out my elk. The elk was about three miles up a brushy canyon, but after doing some exploring we found a game trail that led right to the elk wallow the bull was by.

Lawrence was a little apprehensive as he had heard some pretty bad packing stories that involved my horse Nig. Lawrence asked Don and me what he should do when we got ready to load the elk quarters onto Nig's packsaddle. We told Lawrence to get back, way back. Hell, Lawrence must have gone up the hill 200 yards; we thought he had gone home for a while. Of course the horses never gave us any problems. They both performed like good horses are supposed to perform. We were back at the truck in less than two hours.

I have said it before and I will say it again, if you use well trained horses you will not have any trouble with them. Do your horse training at home in a corral where you can control things, not on some brushy, rocky, steep mountainside. Take care, and good luck.

Chapter Thirty-six

MONTANA BUCK

Fall 1978. I had purchased a nonresident hunting license for Montana. The opening weekend of bear season I was successful in filling my bear tag and then on opening day of elk season I also harvested my elk. Now it was the last weekend of the deer season and I hadn't been deer hunting yet.

Upon returning to my job in an underground mine after the elk hunt, I had been caught in a "rockburst", which is like an explosion in the rock from the great pressure that builds up in the rock of deep mines. When openings are created by the extraction of the ore material, this gives the tremendous pressure in the rock some place to implode to, and that is where the term "rockburst" comes from. Anyway, my brother, Don, and I were timbering the raise-up hole in our stope when the roof burst out on top of us. Big slabs of rock came down on top of us and broke through the floor underneath us, sending us, timber, and everything else into a big pile on the floor of the stope below.

Miraculously, Don was just skinned up badly, but a big slab of rock had fallen right down my left leg, almost cutting the end of my foot off. The only thing that had saved my foot was that all underground miners are required to wear steel toed boots. I spent a week in the hospital while they repaired my broken foot and grafted skin onto the wound. I also was bothered with a trick knee injury, for the rest of my life, that the doctors just couldn't seem to find. My knee just buckles without any warning, and I usually end up flat on my face.

Thanksgiving weekend had arrived and with it the Montana deer season would close on Sunday. Even though I couldn't walk yet, I talked Don into taking me deer hunting. We had decided to go over into Tamarack Creek, a tributary of the Clark Fork River. There was no particular reason for going there other than we had fished that stream, and had seen lots of deer on those trips.

We had spent the whole day driving from one lookout spot to the another, seeing lots of deer sign along the roads but no wildlife. About 3:00 p.m. we had started for home and were just about out to the main road when it happened. A buck deer jumped across the road and ran up an old logging spur road. Even though my foot was still in a cast I bailed out and went hobbling down the road through the snow to where I could see up the spur road. And there was my buck getting further away by the second, I shouldered my rifle and aimed low on the buck's neck out of habit. Boom! My big .308 Norma Magnum went off and almost knocked me down because my balance wasn't that good trying to keep the cast out of the snow. However, the buck went down with a broken neck, and then I turned towards Don with a smirk on my face, "Like, am I good or not?" I turned the field-dressing chore over to Don, while I expounded on what a great rifle shot I was, even crippled! The deer was a nice little 3X3 mule deer buck.

Another week went by and then I was back in the hospital with an infected foot. Apparently, earlier when the doctor had cleaned out the wound he hadn't gotten all of the crushed tissue out, so it wouldn't heal. I spent the next ten days in that room all by my lonesome; you wouldn't have believed the stench when they cut my foot open again. I wasn't very popular with the nurses, but I guess you couldn't blame them. It was hard on me because I like to tell stories, and there was no one wanted to listen, because of that bad smell that permeated that small room.

Now you probably don't think I have very good hunting ethics, road hunting and shooting from the road. But I had a good excuse because my wife was about to go crazy from having to baby sit me, and was about to throw me out. Whatever, just do your own thing and have a good time doing it.

Chapter Thirty-seven

DOZEN DAY BULL

The year of 1982 was to bring many changes for Fred S. Scott, some good, and some not so good. One of the bad things was that I was laid off my job as a hard rock miner at the Star Mine at Burke, Idaho, in June. I spent the whole summer fishing and the early fall bear hunting. I had great luck fishing, and had several chances to harvest a bear, but it wasn't a very high priority so I didn't kill one.

Fall 1982. The 1982 elk hunt would cover both sides of the St. Joe Divide, from Bullion Pass on the east end to Striped Peak on the west end. The St. Joe Divide is south of Wallace, Idaho, and separates the Coeur d'Alene River and the St. Joe River drainages.

September 29th. Brother Don and I went into Slate Creek to set up our elk hunting camp and to scout for elk. Brother-in-law Randy would join us on September 30th, the evening before elk season opened. We set up Don's pickup camper on the east bank of Red Top Creek in the same place we had our elk camp last year. In the evening we took a drive up to the power-line road off of Moon Pass, and drove out this road to where we could watch down into Horseshoe Creek. We watched until black dark without spotting any animals. However, we did get a grouse with the .22 rifle on our way out from Slate Creek Saddle.

September 30th, we were back up on Horseshoe Peak at dawn. That morning we spotted a 5X5 bull elk with six cow elk in the Horseshoe Creek burn. We also spotted a mule deer doe with a fawn down in the bottom of Slate Creek. We watched until about 10:30 a.m. without spotting any other game, so we decided to take a drive down Slate Creek road when we came off the hill. We drove down to Fritz Creek and back up to camp. This trip produced two more grouse and one dove. So now we had enough for dinner. Shooting the heads off of birds with a .22 caliber rifle is good practice and will make a marksman out of you. The food on a hunting trip is a big part of the trip for me.

So, grab yourself a beer and sit back and relax while I tell you how to prepare a grouse dinner that you will never forget. We brown our birds in bacon drippings over high heat, and then turn the heat down real low, and add a little water from time to time as our birds just simmer in the steam for about four hours. While were waiting for our birds to cook we prepare some boiled potatoes, and a vegetable, and then we make milk gravy from the drippings in the pan the birds were cooked in. While we're waiting on our birds to cook we like to sip some good whiskey and creek water, tell stories about past hunts, and plan future hunts. You just try this, because I know you will like it.

After dinner and a nap to settle our dinner we decided to make a scouting trip up the bottom of Red Top Creek. We were only up the creek about one-fourth of a mile at 6:30 p.m. when we spotted two cow elk, each accompanied by their calves. We watched these elk climb up the west side of the creek and cross over Red Top Ridge. Only minutes after the elk disappeared over the ridge-top a big cougar followed their trail up the hillside, but about two-thirds of the way to the ridge-top the cougar evidently found a better scent to follow because he turned off to the right and went out of sight in the trees.

When we returned to camp, Randy was there along with Doc from Lewiston, Idaho, and the five guys we had met from Sandpoint, Idaho, the previous fall. Doc and the Sandpoint crew had set their camp on the west bank of Red Top Creek. We sat around the fire until midnight discussing where the elk were hanging out and what had gone on in everyone's lives since last fall.

October 1st, opening day of elk season. Don, Randy, and me would just hunt together that day. We went up to Slate Creek Saddle, and then traversed around through the head of Summit Creek and crossed a saddle into the (dog-leg) in Red Top Creek. We went on stand by an old snag overlooking all of Red Top Creek. About 8:00 a.m., as the sun started to warm things up to where it was almost comfortable, we spotted a 5X5 bull elk with three cow elk and one calf elk moving through the brush over across the dog-leg on the north side of Red Top Creek. The elk were only about 400 yards away, but moving through heavy brush, so we didn't attempt a shot. We never did get an opportunity, so we just continued to glass the hillsides for other game. We were able to spot two really nice mule deer bucks too, but we weren't hunting deer so we just watched until they bedded down for the day. The weather was nice and sunny, so it was easy to just spend the whole morning enjoying the peaceful surroundings, and the silence. There was no shooting in the Red Top drainage on opening day of elk season, unbelievable.

After returning to camp for a lunch of leftover grouse, we decided

115

to make our afternoon hunt up into the hidden pocket where Don and Randy had gotten their bulls in 1981. The guys in camp the fall of 1981 had decided that this drainage should be named "Fred's Secret Spot". However, during the summer I had packed six hundred pounds of rock salt in to establish a salt lick, so we changed the name to "Lick Creek".

Fred coming in with empty horses after packing salt into Lick Creek.

Randy had decided to spend a lazy afternoon around camp. Don and I left camp about 2:00 p.m. and just took our time hiking up Red Top Ridge trail. At 4:00 p.m. we had traversed around into Lick Creek, and had settled in to watch for game. In just minutes, right across the canyon and above the spring, I spotted a 5X5 bull elk, with two cow elk and their calves. I had been giving Don and Randy a hard time since the previous fall that it had just been an accident that they had hit their bull elk in the neck at 200 yards. This would be my chance to show Don what a-heck-of-a-shot his brother was on big game. I told Don to keep his binoculars focused on that bull elk, because I was going to shoot him in the neck. I lay back against a stump and drew my knees up so I could use them for a rifle rest, and then settled into a good solid position before aligning the crosshair in my scope on the center of the bull elk's neck and squeezed off a shot. When my .30-06 Winchester recoiled, that bull elk went down like he had been struck by lightning. The bull went flopping down the hillside into some heavy brush. Finally, the brush quit waving around, so I told Don to watch the area where the bull had stopped rolling down the hillside and I would cross the draw and find the bull. When I got to where the bull had stopped rolling, it looked like someone had been placer mining. The ground was all churned up where the bull had struggled trying to get up. But get up he had because he was gone! I called Don over to me, and he couldn't believe that the bull had gotten up and left either. He said he had been so sure that the bull elk was dead, that he had been watching the cows leave. There was no blood visible, so we decided to let the bull go and try for him again the next morning. We were early to bed that evening, because of the long day of hunting, and we wanted to be fresh for the next morning. It isn't hard to fall asleep after a hard day of elk hunting in these steep brushy mountains of north Idaho.

October 2nd. It was raining cats and dogs that morning. We decided that Don and Randy would go on stand in Lick Creek, and I would hunt up the west side of Lick Creek and try to drive the bull elk that got away yesterday out where Don and Randy could get a shot at him. There are several game trails going across through this drainage, so we had Doc go on stand on one of them above where Don and Randy were. After it got good and light, I started my drive. I had climbed up and crossed the first bench and band of trees and just got into the heavy brush on the hillside above when I heard the "thump, thump" of and elk taking off above me. I didn't even get a peek at the bull, but I could hear him going up the hill above me. I hollered for Don and Randy to be watching because the bull was moving up the hillside across from them.

The fog and rain wouldn't let up; first the fog would blow into the canyon bottom, and then rise up for just a moment. It would be difficult to get a shot with conditions like they were. Thirty minutes had passed by when I heard a shot on the upper end where Doc was on stand. After the shot I moved across the creek, and made contact with Don and Randy. We waited and watched for another hour without spotting anything. The rain was coming down in a heavy northwest downpour, so we decided to go back to camp and get dried out, we were soaked through to our skin and were getting chilled.

Doc came into camp about 1:00 p.m. with a story that he had gotten a shot at the 5X5 bull elk about 150 yards away and thought that it was a good shot, but he wasn't sure because he had lost sight of the elk when his rifle recoiled. The fog had settled back down into the bottoms, so he couldn't see the area where the bull had been standing when he shot.

Doc looked for two hours, but in the heavy fog he couldn't pinpoint the spot where the bull had been standing, so he came to camp to get dried out too.

The rain and fog continued the rest of the day so we all stayed in camp and didn't make an afternoon hunt. We all got together for our supper and it turned into a potluck affair. Everyone brought something, and we all shared each other's food, and of course everybody was trying to out-do the other fellow in preparing the most, and provide the gourmet dish of the evening. The after dinner drinks and stories would last until midnight again.

October 3rd. We woke up to a black, blurry, blustery day, and it had snowed just a skiff on the ridge-tops. After enjoying a good camp breakfast and several cups of that hot black coffee, we would finally get nerve enough to try another hunt in the wet brush. Don and Randy wanted to hunt Lick Creek again, so I would hunt up the bottom of Red Top Creek to the dog-leg, and then I would hunt the south side of Red Top Creek up under Red Top Knob in what we called the "Spring Draw". After and uneventful morning Randy decided to call it a day and return to camp. Don decided he would climb up the brushy hillside and hunt the area where Doc had gotten the shot yesterday. As Don approached the area, he was watching for any signs of the bull Doc had shot at the day before.

Sure enough there was the snag that Doc had described in his story. What the heck was that in the heavy brush right below the snag, it looked like an elk lying there? Why I'll be go to hell there was an elk lying there. It was Doc's 5X5 bull, deader than Wallace, Idaho, on a Sunday night. Don rolled the elk over onto his belly, and then split the skin down the back to check and see if the elk had spoiled. An elk carcass will sour in the shoulders first, because of the heavy muscle and thick hide there. The meat had soured and the stench was almost unbearable. As Don examined the elk he saw where Doc had hit the bull through the lungs, just like he thought he had. Don also saw where my bullet had creased the bull across the back of the neck. That old bull sure had a bunch of bad luck, but then so did Doc and me for not harvesting him. It just makes everyone sick to see an animal go to waste like this bull had. The only thing Don could salvage was the, "Ivories", or bugle teeth as some folks describe them. Don returned to camp to tell Doc about what he had found.

I had managed to spend the whole day on the mountain with out having any luck, just getting soaking wet again from the wet brush. Doc had sneaked back to camp that morning, and laid around camp all day sick from too much booze the night before. He was a heck of a lot sicker when Don told him what he had found. It was only 3:00 p.m. so Doc hiked up to the elk to see if he could salvage anything. About dark Doc came into camp with the hide and the trophy rack. Early the next morning, Doc attached his elk tag to the rack of antlers and went back to his home in Lewiston, Idaho.

October 4th. It had rained all night, and didn't show any sign of letting up. We had all had enough of the continual downpour of rain, so we pulled our camp and went home to wait out the storm.

October 5-6-7th. I stayed with my dad, because he has been sick for days now.

October 8th. Another friend, Joe, and I returned to Slate Creek Saddle, to resume elk hunting. Our expectations were high because the storm had finally passed on, leaving a little snow to read sign in. I sent Joe out to the snag in the dog-leg of Red Top Creek. I would take the Bad Tom Mountain. trail out to the saddle between Experimental Draw and Red Top Creek. Once there I went down onto the brushy north side of Red Top Creek, and started an elk drive back towards where Joe was on stand. Most of the sign I encountered looked like it was about one day old. We were a day late. When I got back to where Joe was on stand, he informed me that I had driven out two 5X5 mule deer bucks, but no elk. We stayed on this stand until about noon without seeing any elk; however, we did see three more mule deer bucks, two 5X5's, and one 4X4. We didn't want to pack a deer up out of this hole so we didn't shoot any; and we went on back to the truck empty-handed.

Avery, Idaho, and lunch with a cold beer appealed to us so off down Slate Creek we went. Joe shot the heads off of two grouse with his .270 Winchester, all the game we saw going to Avery. After lunch we went up the North Fork of the St. Joe River road towards Moon Pass. Right at the bottom of the pass there were two fellows loading a big 6X6 bull elk into their pickup truck. I had seen this bull back on the 26th of September during a scouting trip, but I hadn't hunted him. When we got up on Moon Pass we turned off onto the power-line road, and drove out to Ramsy, and Railroad Creeks. We jumped four more deer on the road in the head of Railroad Creek. There were three mule deer does, and a little forked horn buck. About one hour before dark we parked in the head of Horseshoe Creek to watch for game. At 6:15 p.m. we spotted a lone 5X5 bull elk on the northwest side of Horseshoe Creek.

October 9th. Joe and I were back in the head of Horseshoe Creek before the break of dawn. We had decided to watch until we spotted the bull elk from last evening, and then we could plan a stalk on him. At 7:10 a.m. we spotted a big 6X6 bull elk with five cows, but they were away and away across the drainage on Summit-Red Top Ridge divide. By 9:30 a.m. we hadn't spotted the bull in Horseshoe Creek again, so we decided to hunt down through the heavy brush in hopes of flushing him out. Joe would hunt the north side and I would hunt down the south side. I saw two mule deer does on the Fisher Creek side, but nothing on the Horseshoe Creek side. Joe's luck was even worse than mine because he never saw an animal. It was dark when we came out on Slate Creek road at the mouth of Horseshoe Creek. We had left Joe's car there that morning so we had a ride back up to my truck.

October10th. Joe and I arrived at the turn-around in the mouth of Red Top Creek about one hour before daylight. We wanted to try and get into the herd of elk we seen the day before from Horseshoe Creek. We had high hopes, and great expectations as this was also the first day cow elk would be legal game. We took off into the ink-black night to get into position before first light. Joe would go up the main Summit-Red Top divide ridge and I would go up Red Top Creek about one half mile and then get up onto the Summit-Red Top divide ridge also. We wanted to be up on top where we might catch the elk coming up onto a flat area in the ridge to bed down for the day. I was only up the creek 300 yards when I jumped a herd of elk in the dark creek bottom. Damn it, what rotten luck. I found out later that Joe also jumped elk in the heavy brush without seeing them. Come nightfall, all we had seen were other hunters, and each other.

October 11th. This would be Joe's last day to hunt. We were back at our favorite lookout spot in the dog-leg of Red Top Creek by the snag. We settled in to glass for game. About 8:30 a.m. Joe finally spotted a cow and calf elk down on the west side of Red Top Creek below the dog-leg. We watched until the elk bedded down and then made plans to be in position to murder them when they got up that afternoon. We didn't want to stalk them that morning because we didn't have a rig at the mouth of Red Top Creek and it would be a terrible climb back up that steep canyon to the truck. We went back home and spent the whole day telling ourselves how smart and clever we were. We thought we sure had these elk dead to rights. That afternoon we came up from the mouth of Red Top Creek and stealthily crept into position across from where the elk were bedded. We thought the elk should be getting up any time now, and we were ready. However, the elk hadn't read the script; they evidently had left during the day while we were home bragging about how smart we were. At black dark we went stumbling down the creek bottom to the truck, and we were very humbled elk hunters.

October 12. I hunted the Red Top-Summit divide ridge again. I parked at Slate Creek Saddle and hunted across the head of Summit Creek, and onto the ridge. My wife would pick me up at the old Slate Creek Ranger Station at dark that evening. I spent the whole day on that ridge. My only success would be three grouse that I shot the heads off of with my .30-06 Winchester at the bottom of the ridge. Walking down the road to the Slate Creek Ranger Station, I saw a gut pile in the middle of the road where some lucky sucker had killed an elk. I was probably the sucker that had chased it off the ridge. Karen was waiting for me like all good obedient wives are supposed to.

October 13-14-15-16-17th. Karen and I went to Dillon, Montana, to visit our son, Jeff, who was attending college there. When we came home I had to take my dad to the doctor in Spokane, Washington, because he has been feeling poorly all fall.

October 18th. I was back at Slate Creek Saddle that morning accompanied by another friend, Herb. There had been another storm pass through, leaving a fresh layer of snow six inches deep to read sign in. It was a beautiful morning, cold, but the sun would warm things up later. We thought it should be a good day for hunting after the storm. First we went into the dog-leg of Red Top Creek, and watched until 9:30 a.m. without seeing any animals or sign that any were around. Then we traversed up onto the Bad Tom Mountain trail and walked out to the head of Dry Creek, where we watched for about one hour without any luck. We still hadn't encountered any sign, so we moved on out to the saddle between Red Top Creek and Experimental Draw where we could look into both drainages. We never had any luck there either, so we took the Dry Creek-Experimental Draw divide ridge down to the Experimental Draw trail and then went up the trail to its end in the head of Experimental Draw right under the saddle we were in earlier.

By then it was way past lunch time so we chopped some wood off an old snag and built us a nice cheery fire to toast our sandwiches and warm our hands. We still hadn't seen any sign so we would just climb up to the saddle and walk out the Bad Tom Mountain trail back to the saddle where this hunt had started. We had just started up the hillside when we jumped some elk in the thick trees above us. The elk went crashing off to the west towards the divide ridge between the forks of Experimental Draw. I told Herb to stay put and I would cut them off and drive them back towards him. Maybe that way one of us could get a shot at the elk. I cut them off all right, but they didn't drive very well; they just circled up-wind and climbed around and above Herb, and went back over into Dry Creek. We got back to the truck at black dark, two very tired elk hunters.

October 19th. Herb and I decided to just try to spot something from the truck this morning; we were too tired to walk from the hard day of hunting the day before. Just as the eastern horizon started to get the blush of a new day we parked my truck about half-way down on the Idaho side of Bullion Pass. We just sat in the truck cab watching the brushy hillside on the south side of Bullion Creek. It wasn't any time at all before I spotted a big 5X5 mule deer buck up on the divide ridge between the Bullion and Frazier Creeks. We argued about how far away the deer was, how high we would have to hold over to hit it at that long range, and all the other malarkey that hunters argue about. We didn't even attempt a shot. I know that I could have killed that buck, even if it was 400 yards away. I had my .308 Norma Magnum along that day, and I have killed many a head of game at that range before. We would spend the rest of the day just driving from one lookout point to the next, without seeing another animal. Our luck wasn't the best.

October 21st. After a day of rest I decided I had better get with it and get an elk. The season would close on the 24th. I hiked up the Cranky Creek trail from Placer Creek to the St Joe Divide ridge, and then turned to the east towards the head of Experimental Draw. As I walked along the old jeep road I came upon a fresh elk track going down the road. The track turned off the road into the head of Cranky Creek, so I just followed it. I thought when I get to where I can see down into Cranky Creek I will just watch for awhile and see what happens. I wasn't 100 yards off the road when a cow elk exploded up off the ground from behind a little bushy fir tree. I about messed my pants I was caught so unaware. Boy, talk about an idiot, I'm really on the ball that morning I should have had that cow. When following elk it helps to be alert. I hunted on out the divide ridge, and then hunted down the divide ridge between the forks of Experimental Draw. There were lots of elk signs, and I hunted hard, but I didn't have any luck. The only game I saw was eight grouse but I didn't shoot any for fear of scaring the elk off.

October 22nd. I was up early to find it raining again, I figured there was no sense in fighting the wet brush again, so I called my brother-in-law, Randy, to see if he wanted to go road hunting. He did, so I picked him up in Mullan and we drove over to Bullion Pass again. We watched for that mule deer buck again until 8:30 a.m. and then we started down off the pass towards the bottom of Bullion Creek. We were just creeping along watching the slopes on both sides of the road for elk when, right across the creek, I spotted a 3X3 bull elk standing on the hillside about 175 yards away. I told Randy to go ahead and take the bull. Randy kept moving around looking for a rest for his rifle, but he wasn't getting ready to shoot. The bull had spotted us and was getting nervous, so I slipped out of the truck cab and over the road bank with my .30-06 and got into a solid sitting position. The crosshair in my scope settled on the bull's neck, so I touched off a shot. The elk just stood there! I quickly worked the bolt on my rifle and inserted a live round into the chamber and then dropped my aim down to his shoulder and shot again. This time the bull elk dropped like road apples from a tall horse, and then he rolled down the hill into heavy brush out of our view. The brush quit waving so we figured he was down for keeps.

Randy never did get a shot off, and never did say why he hadn't. It was raining hard so we got into our rain gear and hurried across the draw to the elk. Holy Judas! The bull was still alive, and we had left our rifles in the truck. The bull was a-straddle of a log with both legs on the upper side of the log pinned under his body, and pointing to the rear, and the other two were waving around in the air. We needed to do something fast because if that bull ever got off that log we were going to be two sorry suckers. I came up behind the bull on the upper side, and put my foot on his right antler, and then grabbed the other antler in my left hand to hold the bull's head still while I beat him in the forehead with the back of my hand axe. Finally, I knocked the bull unconscious and was able to cut his throat with my knife.

I had to sit down and get myself together after this wrestling match. Randy hadn't offered any help; he was smart enough to stay away from that bull elk and I can't say as I blame him. When we skinned the bull out we discovered that the bullets had hit side-to instead of point-to. The heavy brush had deflected the bullets before they impacted the elk. It was really strange. The first bullet hit the neck right in the center, but just went in under the hide, and then went up over the neck and was on the opposite side of the neck under the hide directly across from the entry hole. The shot that hit the shoulder was right on also, but went up at an angle to come to rest against the backbone, that was what put the bull down. I believe if that bull could have gotten off that log he would have escaped, and recovered, because his wounds weren't that bad.

Fred's Dozen-Day Bull Elk.

After slipping and sliding all over the hillside, and falling down about one hundred times, we finally got the elk quarters up that steep hillside and into the truck box. We didn't have any pack-boards with us so we had to just pack the meat in our arms. The wet brush hadn't gotten us wet, but we about drown in our own sweat, so we were soaked from the inside out.

I had been getting a little worried that I wasn't going to get an elk after twelve days of hard hunting, before I was able to score. There was only two days remaining before the elk season closed. Persistence and patience, that is what it takes to harvest an elk. Some folks call it luck, but I think there is something else involved that is bigger than luck – it is called God's grace. You can figure it anyway you want to, but you know how I feel about it. So pray my good man, and good luck.

Chapter Thirty-eight

NO BUCKS – No. ONE

1982 was the year I lost my job at the Star Mine on June 2; which was also my 20th wedding anniversary. I decided that I should just take some time off and enjoy life. My family and friends and I spent the whole summer fishing and camping, and what a blast it was!

Come September we changed to hunting black bear and forest grouse. We had lots of opportunities to harvest bears but didn't feel we needed to! The grouse were a different story. We took everyone we could, and most of them were shot through the head with a .22 long rifle. October 2nd brought the opening of elk season and we hunted almost every day until October 22nd. That was the day I finally got my elk but that story is in my earlier book. (*"Memories of Hunting Idaho's Golden Era"*).

November 3rd came and it was time to start hunting deer on the late season in Units Six and Seven. We had made an agreement that we would only take big mature bucks as the deer populations were not what they once had been. After several hunts on which we saw bucks, we still hadn't seen the one we wanted.

On a cold clear day when the thermometer was way down on the minus side of zero, I called my Indian brother-in-law, Randy, and asked him if he wanted to go deer hunting over into the North Fork of the St. Joe River in Shoshone County. From here on I will quote from my 1982 scouting journals:

November 24th. I picked Randy up at his home in Mullan and we headed over Moon Pass to the St. Joe country. When we got down past the mouth of Hammond Creek we took the access road up onto the railroad right-a-way by the trestle spanning the North Fork of St. Joe River. Right away I spotted a 5X5 bull elk bedded out on the point of the ridge on the north side of Hammond Creek. It was only 7:30 a.m. and the light was still real flat when I put my binoculars on the little bull elk again. Only now his head was in profile against a snow background and I could see that I was looking at the biggest whitetail buck I had ever seen in thirty years of hunting.

I judged this big 6X6 whitetail buck to be about 300 yards away, which would be no problem for my .30-06 Winchester Model 70. I slipped out of the truck and over to the railing on the trestle for a dead rest and put the crosshair in my scope right on top of the buck's back-line. When I shot, the deer jumped to his feet and just stood there trying to figure out where the shot had came from. Randy called my shot low, but I held the same and shot again. This time when I shot Randy called the shot low again, but I argued that I thought I had shot high. On this last shot a little whitetail doe jumped out from behind a bushy evergreen tree and went bounding around the hillside out of our view. The buck followed her. After arguing with Randy for twenty minutes, I decided to climb up the hillside and see where I had hit. I found the deer's bed and saw where I had hit right under his chest, and there were a few drops of blood sprinkled on top of the snow.

The bullet had kicked up so much dirt where it plowed into the ground that I didn't know if the deer was gut shot or not. I didn't have a gun with me but decided I would follow the buck's track for a little ways and see if I could determine where the deer had been hit. I had only gone around the hill 200 yards when I looked up and there was the buck only fifty feet away licking his hind leg right above the foot. I could have cried! Here was the biggest whitetail buck I had ever seen, which I was sure would have made the Boone & Crockett record book, and me with no gun. And to top that off for being stupid, my Ruger .44 Magnum pistol was lying on the dashboard of my pickup.

When I looked right in front of me not ten feet away was the little doe bedded behind a bushy tree. I said to her, "Get the hell out of here." It was so funny because she was on her side looking back at me and her feet were flailing the ground so fast that she was throwing a rooster tail of snow into the air. She actually went twenty feet on her side before she came up on her feet. I never even saw the buck's reaction, but I bet they didn't stop for miles.

When I got back to the truck and told Randy about the deer, he laughed until he cried. That was when I suggested that we go into Avery, Idaho, and get some beer and lunch, and maybe I could cry in my beer.

We had our lunch and headed back up the river, and Randy spotted a whitetail doe standing on the hillside in 49 Gulch. The deer was about the same distance away as the buck had been this morning but, like I said, we didn't want any does. That was when my Indian friend said,

"You couldn't hit it anyway!" I said, "We'll just see about that," and I got a good rest alongside a tree just over the road bank and shot. Down went the doe like she had been dynamited. I gave Randy my smart aleck smirk and then took off up the hill to retrieve my deer.

It was afternoon when I got back to the truck and we started upriver. We saw three elk in Stetson Creek, and another herd of thirteen in Hammond Creek. We were just up around the corner from Mozer Creek when I spotted a 3X3 whitetail buck out in the creek bottom. I told Randy to take him! He shot at the deer three times at fifty yards as it ran straight away across the creek bottom. Even though the deer hadn't reacted to Randy's shots, I couldn't imagine that it wasn't wounded. So as Randy fumbled around trying to get his gun reloaded, I stepped out and missed the deer once, and then busted him in the neck, and down he went.

I put my gun away and pulled my truck off the road, and when I looked at the deer he was just going out of sight into the trees. Why Randy hadn't shot when the deer got up I'll never know; he just stood there with a big grin splitting his round Indian face. I grabbed my gun and took off after the deer without even putting my jacket on. There was a good blood trail so I just stayed on the high lope thinking I would find the deer dead at any time. I never did catch up to it. In retrospect I should have let him bed down before I started pushing him so hard. I'm sure he died somewhere on that mountain. And this had been the very thing I was trying to avoid when I got involved in this calamity.

One of the things I have learned about deer in extreme cold is that they will stay bedded in good thermal cover until the sun starts to warm things up. This usually doesn't happen until about 11:00 a.m. Oh well, just do the best you can.

Chapter Thirty-nine

SOME FUNNY HAPPENINGS

In the mid-1950's some friends and I were up Lost Creek, a tributary of the Coeur d'Alene River in Shoshone County. We were just driving around in the spring looking at the abundant wildlife out browsing the new grass on open areas. We had spotted a sow black bear and her twin cubs on an open hillside just below the mouth of Hat Creek. The sow bear had heard the car and had walked out onto the end of a rock bluff sticking out of the hillside for a better view of her surroundings, and the two cubs were sitting right behind her awaiting orders. I'm sure the mother bear had given them the alarm that all was not right. Anyway, we got out of the car and were yelling as loud as we could to make the bears run off. I don't know what kind of insult that the mother bear perceived, but she turned and came off that rock bluff and was galloping down that hillside towards us like she meant business, and was going to straighten out some loud-mouthed humans. We bailed into the car and sped off up the road, as we didn't want to find out what that sow bear had in mind to do to us.

Another time I think in the mid-1960's we were fishing on the North Fork of the St. Joe River in Shoshone County. When we came in sight of the bridge spanning Rye Creek, a small black bear ran across the road and up into a big white fir tree next to the road. We pulled up and got out of the car and started throwing rocks at the bear's paws where he held onto the tree trunk. We're not very accurate rock throwers but did manage to hit the bear's paws occasionally. It wasn't long and the bear started to moan and whimper when ever we hit one of his paws with a rock. Finally the bear had had enough of our shenanigans and started squalling and slapping the side of the tree with his paws. Then the hair came up along his back and he let a blood-curdling roar out of him as he started backing down the tree. The tires spinning in the gravel peppered his face as he lunged up into the road as we got the heck out of there.

It was a cool September morning as a friend Herb and I walked out along the alpine ridge from Sunset Peak to Pony Peak. We were going into the head of Pony Gulch to try and bugle up a bull elk to shoot with our bow and arrows. We had just come down the steep part of the ridge where you pass the intersection of Vendetta Ridge and Pony Ridge. That was when we saw some deer down on the Pioneer gulch side of the ridge we were following. So we devised a plan: Herb would circle out ahead of the deer and then get down on the hillside out in front of them. The deer heard Herb running out along the ridge-top and went down into a corpse of trees, out of sight. When I saw that Herb was in position, I dropped down the hill and started pussy-footing along towards the trees the deer had gone into.

Sow and cub black bear. (Photo courtesy Jay Van Kuiken)

I had just entered the trees when I spotted a big mule deer doe standing in the shadows watching Herb. I didn't want to shoot her so thought I will just see how close I could get to her before she discovered that I was there. I wasn't five feet from her when she finally noticed me standing beside her, and I think she wouldn't have noticed me then if I hadn't reached out to touch her with my bow and she saw the movement. She spun around with her eyes bulged out and blew snot all over me as she made a big leap down the mountain. It must have been close to twenty feet before she hit the ground the first time, and then the woods just erupted with deer getting out of there.

I picked Herb up and we went out and dropped off into the head of Pony Gulch. We were past the wallows and on the next hogback ridge to the west when we finally heard an elk bugle. It was no time at all and bulls were bugling on all sides of us. We just stayed put and would give a little squeaky bugle occasionally to keep the bulls excited. We had been sitting there for a good forty-five minutes and nothing had developed. The bulls had gone silent. I whispered to Herb that we would wait for a few minutes in case the bulls were trying to sneak in on us. It has always amazed me how those elk can pinpoint your position on a mountainside whenever you make the slightest noise. We had gotten up to start on up a game trail leading to a bedding area when, not twenty feet away, a 5X5 bull elk whirled and ran up the mountain. It didn't surprise me that I hadn't heard the elk, but I don't think there was anything wrong with Herb's hearing.

It was September of 1980 and brother Don and I decided to go out into the dog-leg of Red Top Creek to scout for elk. We were out past the old snag where we usually sat to watch on the edge of the big brush field where we usually spotted elk. We were able to spot a 5X5 bull elk directly across from us, bugling and raking the brush with his antlers. We couldn't hear him bugle as both of us are extremely hard of hearing, but we could watch. We would bugle at the bull and he would answer but wouldn't come towards us. He must have had some cows hidden in that brush hole across from, us even though we never did spot anything besides the bull.

We probably spent most of and hour watching that bull before deciding to leave and go back out to Slate Creek Saddle. When we stood up and turned to leave, there was another 5X5 bull elk standing in the edge of our brush pile trying to peer over it. This other bull must have snuck in on us and couldn't spot us lying there on the ground. It startled us to see the bull standing there not fifteen feet away when we hadn't heard a thing. I'm sure that my hearing impairment has cost me more than one elk, but on the other hand I have been blessed with good eyesight and the ability to spot game when others fail to see anything.

It was and October afternoon in the 1990's that I had decided to make and afternoon hunt out into the dog-leg of Red Top Creek from Slate Creek Saddle. It was about 2:00 p.m. on a bright sunny day when I crossed the ridge into Red Top Creek. Sitting there on the hillside were five fellows from Post Falls, Idaho. I told them that I was sorry about disturbing them and would go some place else. They replied that it was alright as they were leaving anyway, as they had been there for over one hour. As this conversation was going on I noticed a herd of elk grazing in the brush on the side of a draw just across from where they had sat watching. They left and I was having a hard time containing myself from sliding down the hillside to get within good range of the elk herd. It wasn't long and I was only 300 yards from the elk across the draw. I picked out a nice big cow elk and got my scope onto her shoulder before dropping her with my .308 Norma Magnum with one shot. When I got back into camp late that afternoon after taking care of my elk, these same guys came over for a visit. One of them said they heard me shoot once, and then asked if I had shot a grouse. I showed them the ivories out of my big cow elk as I told them about the easy kill. They were kind of disgusted that they hadn't seen the elk, and also disappointed that I had been lucky enough to get one of the elk with one shot.

Fred fishing in the St. Joe River.

Chapter Forty

NEW HUNTING PARTNER

Fall of 1983. I hooked up with a new hunting partner named George, who was also a fellow worker at the Lucky Friday silver mine where we worked underground.

George and I tried some bow hunts for elk and deer which didn't produce any results. I never did have enough confidence in my bow shooting ability to even try a shot on an animal. As it turned out, George wasn't any better than I was. However, he was lucky enough to miss everything completely, so no animals were wounded. The highlight of our bow hunting happened one day when we were just driving around looking for game. I had stopped my truck in a turnout where there was a low saddle in the ridge the road followed; I walked over to the edge of the road to take a pee, and while I was performing this chore I was scanning the opposite slope with my binoculars. Of course I spotted a herd of elk and when I turned to tell George about them he was frantically pointing at me. When I turned to look at what he was pointing at, there, not five feet in front of me, stood a bowhunter in full camouflage. He wasn't very happy because I had peed right behind him. I profusely apologized while trying to keep from smiling. I also wanted to tell him that his cover scent smelled like fresh horse manure, but I thought better of it at the time.

Later George and I went bear hunting and I showed George how I could miss a black bear's head at 100 yards with my favorite rifle, a .308 Norma Magnum. Later in the day we saw two blue grouse sitting along the road, and I missed them at fifty feet with my .44 Magnum pistol. Now I was the one that had to take the ribbing about my marksmanship.

Come late November, George and I hooked up for a late deer season on the North Fork of the St. Joe River in Shoshone County, Idaho.

November 25th. During the early morning we saw three whitetail does but no bucks. This was and either-sex hunt but we were after big trophy bucks that were right in the heat of the rut. We saw twelve elk in Miller Creek, and one of them was a spike bull.

Noon. found us in the old railroad town of Avery, Idaho, where we stopped to have lunch and a beer. The local loggers kept us entertained through lunch with their ribald stories of their love conquests and fighting ability. Now if you should ever get the hankering to find out how tough you are in a barroom brawl, the loggers in Avery, Idaho, will surely accommodate you. For them it is just part of a fun weekend!

Coming back up the river we decided to drive up on the railroad bed at the mouth of Hammond Creek and watch over onto the ridge where I missed a huge six-point whitetail buck the previous year. This time we had driven across the railroad trestle that spans the North Fork of the St. Joe River, so we were directly across from the point where we had seen the deer the year before. It was 2:00 p.m., a very good time to see game on most days, and that is when a whitetail doe and fawn came out of the trees with a real nice five-point whitetail buck trailing them .This beautiful buck was only about 150 yards away and wasn't even aware that anyone was around. I slipped out of the truck onto the road bank, got into a good solid sitting position, and when my scope reticule centered the big buck's neck I touched off my shot. When my .308 Norma Magnum shattered the tranquility of a beautiful sunny fall day, the buck's troubles were over, and mine were about to begin. I had harvested my buck with one well-placed shot. George couldn't believe that I had shot the deer in the neck, but with that gun and my good luck shooting it, I could have shot the buck in the eye at that distance.

Going back up river we stopped in the mouth of Rye Creek, and right away I spotted a nice four-point whitetail buck standing in an opening about 400 yards away. George got out and got a good rest with his .270 Winchester Model 70 and missed the buck clean. He didn't get a second chance.

December 3rd. George and I were back on the St. Joe looking for a big buck for George. Going down the river we saw the same four-point whitetail buck that we had seen a week earlier, only this time he had two does and their fawns with him. He was in the same clearing in Rye Creek that we seen him in the first time. George very carefully missed him again! We went on downriver to Big Creek and back, seeing six elk and three more deer, all does.

High noon found us back in Avery, Idaho, having lunch again. Going back upriver at 2:30 p.m. we stopped in the mouth of Rye Creek again. And this time I spotted the same four-point whitetail buck, without his lady friends, standing in a clearing only 250 yards away surveying his territory. George eased out of the truck, got into a good rest, and

133

missed that buck for the third time.

I started giving George back some of the same joshing he had given me about my shooting ability earlier in the fall. It made him mad and he told me, "The next deer we see, you can shoot it." I informed George that I didn't shoot other people's game, and especially with their gun. I didn't even have a gun along as I had already harvested my deer.

This is where knowing your rifle and where it shoots makes a difference of harvest or no harvest. One of the best practices that I know of is to learn to shoot a pistol. It will teach you to concentrate on the sight picture, not the game, and also to control the trigger so that the gun goes off at the instant the sight picture is just right.

You do what ever it takes, but don't forget to enjoy every outing. Now I wish you good luck in all your hunting endeavors.

Fred's big buck.

Chapter Forty-one

THREE FOR THREE

Fall 1984. The elk hunt for 1984 was in Slate Creek, a tributary of the St. Joe River in Shoshone County, Idaho. This hunt could be used as an example of a perfectly executed elk hunt.

Brother Don and I, and a friend, Herb, had set up our camp on the east bank of Red Top Creek where we had camped for the past several years. Across Red Top Creek from us, Doc and his brother-in-law had their tent trailer. Five guys from Sandpoint, Idaho, had a wall tent set up there also. George's group was camped in the campground at the mouth of Summit Creek.

Our group had spent the past two days scouting out the different drainages that we knew held elk. It appeared our best chance to score on elk would be in Lick Creek-Murray Creek area, especially the open face to the west of Murray Creek where we had seen elk in the past two days of scouting for elk. On the afternoon prior to opening day we ate up a big dinner, and then Herb and I mounted our motorcycles to go up the creek and spend the night in the woods. Don would stay in camp and watch, with the spotting scope, the ridge on the west side of Flume Creek. However, his plan was to hunt Lick Creek.

Herb would ride up to the mouth of Dam Creek and then climb the ridge on the north side of Slate Creek about half-way to the top, and then camp for the night. Herb told us later that he saw a real big 5X5 mule deer buck on his climb up the ridge. He also had heard a bull elk bugling over on the south side of Slate Creek.

I rode my motorcycle up to the mouth of Murray Creek and then climbed the steep brushy ridge on the east side of Murray Creek. When I got up to the flat, timbered bench I traversed around into the forks of Murray Creek. When the middle ridge in Murray Creek came into view there was a big 6X6 bull elk headed across to the west. I got my sleeping bag laid out in an old deer bed on the upper side of a big red fir tree. I was right where I wanted to be, I was just below the forks of Murray Creek where I didn't have to worry about my scent carrying up to the elk higher up the mountain. There were several bulls tending cows across

135

Top photo: Don's big bull elk.

Below: Fred with Buck and Blaze. Notice that brushy elk habitat behind me.

this area that we had staked out. We hoped to catch them in a pincher move between us on opening morning of elk season. No matter who got the first shot, everybody had a chance to score as the elk moved east or west.

At 5:30 p.m. I had just started watching for game when I spotted two big 5X5 mule deer bucks right across the draw from me, and then at 6:15 p.m. I spotted two cow elk up high on the west fork of Murray Creek. About this same time away and away across on the south side of Slate Creek where the ridge comes down into the mouth of Flume Creek, I spotted a big old straw-colored elk. It just about had to be an old bull judging by the cream color on his sides.

The cloak of darkness finally wrapped around me like a blanket, and then a big harvest moon came climbing up over the horizon bathing everything in an un-real brightness. The stars came out by the millions, winking, and blinking their way across the heavens. The days had been almost balmy, but now the cool bright night would make it easy for me to sleep.

October 6th. Opening morning! I had hardly gotten the sleep rubbed out of my eyes when a new day burst upon me. It looked like we were in for another beautiful sunny October day, my favorite kind this time of year. At 6:40 a.m. I spotted five cow elk and two calf elk up on the west fork of Murray Creek where I seen the two cows the previous evening. Just minutes later I saw George walk out onto the middle ridge, and then he moved to the west towards the elk. Suddenly, two shots went off on the timbered ridge across from George and right below the elk. The elk I had in my view stampeded back into the trees, and then a whole herd of elk burst out the upper edge of the trees headed up the bald ridge towards Bad Tom Mountain. Now I saw another guy come out of the trees right in the path of the escaping elk. The elk just veered off and went around the hunter and into the trees above him. Evidently there were no bulls in that herd.

The minutes were ticking away, and then I saw a big 6X6 bull elk step out into an opening right across from George. George shot six times, but the bull didn't appear to know that he was being shot at. He just turned back into the timber and headed for the trail coming down the west fork of Murray Creek, right to where I was sitting. Now, maybe I would get my chance. Then there was another barrage of shots right across from George. I patiently waited for an elk to appear on the trail in front of me. The minutes kept ticking away but I still waited for my chance. Like a mirage, an elk appeared, going across the face of the middle ridge. Through my rifle scope it appeared to be a small cow elk. I laid my rifle down and picked up my nine power binoculars to watch the elk as it crossed. Holy Judas! It is a small spike bull elk, just what I wanted to harvest.

Up came my old trusty .308 Norma Magnum, I found the bull in my scope just before he passed from view. I aimed for a high shoulder hit, and then touched off a round. The elk disappeared just like he had fallen down a well, and then I saw him rolling down the hillside into some heavy brush. The bull was only about 250 yards away when I shot.

Fred's little "trophy" bull elk.

The shot I had just made I call an "Elmer Keith lung shot" because this was a hold that Elmer had recommended in many of his magazine articles. This is a good aiming point because you have several chances of a killing hit. If your shot is high you will break the spine, or just a bit lower break the shoulder, or lower yet you hit the lungs or heart. My bullet had hit the bull dead center through the shoulder joints, almost severing the off shoulder from the body. When I unloaded my rifle I found I still had my 165 grain hollow point bear loads in the magazine, instead of the 180 grain loads I normally use for elk.

Now that the elk was down the work was about to commence. With the balmy Indian summer weather we were having it is just about mandatory that the elk be dressed, skinned, quartered, and hung in a tree to keep the meat from souring. On second thought I always do it that way no matter what the weather is, and enjoy doing it, besides knowing it was done right. I had killed my bull at 8:30 a.m. and was on the Slate Creek trail at noon. Herb was waiting by my motorcycle. I gave him a ride up to the mouth of Dam Creek to retrieve his motorcycle and then headed back to camp.

This is the story Herb related to me over a cold beer as we rested in camp. When he wakened up that morning the hills were echoing with the bugles of the rutting bull elk. Herb never even broke camp. He just grabbed his rifle and ammo and then took off after the elk. He never did go back for his tent and sleeping bag. Upon entering the trees on the ridge where he had heard the elk bugling he came face to face with a spike bull elk. Bang, bang! He missed the spike bull twice at fifty feet! He could hear elk running around him in the timber, so he took off in the direction of the sounds. When he came out of the trees, George hollered that there was a wounded bull elk right below where Herb was standing. Herb started down the hillside, and a 5X5 bull elk jumped out of a tangle of bushy fir trees and ran around the hillside only twenty five yards away. Herb let loose with another barrage of shots, seven altogether, he

Herb's big bull elk.

139

said. Five of the shots were marginal hits or misses; whatever, they did put the bull down.

The two hunters met at the elk and after surveying the damage, George just cut out the ivories, or bugle teeth as some hunters refer to them, as his reward for having wounded this bull prior to Herb shooting it all to hell. Herb tagged the bull, proud as a fourteen-year-old father. When Herb told me that he had just hog-dressed the bull elk and left it lying on the ground, that was when the shit hit the fan. The last thing that I had told him before we left camp the afternoon before the opener was, "You kill one elk only, and you don't leave that meat until it is hanging in a tree skinned out. One thing we are not is 'Party Hunters'." Herb's father-in- law, John, hit the nail right on the head later when he said, "Herb is a, 'a killer' not a 'hunter'. It really gets in my craw when someone can't show an animal more respect than that after they have taken its life. After I had chewed him out, Herb's feeling were hurt so he took off for town.

I was stomping around camp with my feathers all ruffled up when Don came into camp about 1:00 p.m. Don had been successful, too. I broke out a bottle of good whiskey to sip on with a cold beer while Don told me about his hunt. Now things were perking right up!

Don had gone on stand by the fir tree in Lick Creek. He watched from there until about 9:30 a.m. and there hadn't been any shooting for awhile and he hadn't spotted any animals, so he decided to climb up and hunt the bedding area in the head of Lick creek. About half-way up that brushy hillside he was surprised to see a 5X5 bull elk trotting along the hillside across from him. The elk was only about 150-200 yards away. Don shot once and missed, and then on the next shot the bull went down and slid and flopped back into the bottom of the draw. Don found his bull wedged under a windfall in the bottom of the draw. He had to completely dismember the elk, on the spot, to get it out of that jackpot, and up into a tree to cool out. Don was pretty well tuckered out when he toddled into camp that afternoon.

We continued drinking beer and booze all afternoon while we puzzled over how we were going to get our elk packed out. Our first plan had been to hire a friend and his horses for the job. However, that plan was nixed when we discovered his truck parked in a wide spot just below our camp, and horse tracks leading off up the trail via Fool Hen Mountain, towards Mastodon Lookout.

About 4:00 p.m., Doc came into camp and joined us for supper. Doc had been successful too, so he told us his story. Doc was just above Don on the next game trail up the canyon, on stand watching for elk. Doc first spotted a cow and calf elk that Don had flushed out. Don had seen those elk, too, but they were not legal game for the first ten days of the season. Then Doc watched Don kill the 5X5 bull and when Don moved over to claim his bull, another 3X3 bull elk ran up the hill past Doc. Doc wasn't able to get a shot that he wanted so the bull got away. That is one of Doc's better qualities he is not a slob hunter.

Anyway, there wasn't anymore game moving about, so Doc moved up onto Red Top Ridge. He hiked over to where he could see down into that draw on the west side of Red Top Creek just before it makes the dog-leg to the west. As Doc stood there watching, a spike bull elk jumped up out of his bed and went crashing down across the draw. When the spike bull came out on the opposite hillside, running straight away at about 100 yards, Doc raised his .308 Winchester to his shoulder and then put a bullet right in the back of the spike bull's head. Now you might think that this is just storytelling, but I have seen Doc shoot and I believe that he made the shot just like he told it. It was about 11:00 a.m. when Doc made his kill.

It is Doc's custom to shoot an elk and then take care of the meat and pack out the hide and trophy antlers on his return to camp. Then he will spend whatever time it takes to pack his elk out on a packboard. Doc is a guy to ride the river with, and I will vouch to that.

After supper everybody gathered up at the Sandpoint camp for the opening day bull and bugling stories. Some of the bunch got a little carried away with the drinks so a couple of us were kept busy moving chairs, or heading off the ones that wanted to walk through the campfire. It stayed pretty civil; nobody got to the fisticuff stage. Heck, everybody was friends or about to be friends, a good group of fellows.

Everybody had a story to tell. One fellow said he had seen seventy elk, but didn't get one, and then another guy missed his bull because his scope was off, or a tree got in the way, anyway something happened that caused him not to get his bull. George claimed that he had gut shot the bull that Herb got at 400 yards. From my viewpoint I would have estimated it at 150, possibly 200 yards maximum. But then estimating range can be tricky in this clear mountain air. Anyway, it is George's story so what the hell, let him tell it his way. One of the fellows made the snide remark, "So what, a gut-shot elk is just a gut-shot elk, so it's no big deal." Everyone had their say and told their story, and went to bed happy. Man, what an opening day.

October 7th, Don and I were up at 4:00 a.m., blurry eyed and bushy tailed. As the old saying goes, "You can take the boy off the farm but you can't take the farm off the boy." Now Don and I never were farm boys, or ever will be, we just wake up early in the morning. We were sitting there racking our brains for a solution to the elk packing chore, and then Herb and John came rolling into camp in their pickup with John's horses in the horse trailer. What a relief that was! I fixed up a big breakfast for the whole crew and then we planned our day's packing as we ate breakfast. Herb and I would ride our motorcycles to Bad Tom Mountain and then drop down into Murray Creek and take care of Herb's elk. I thought it was a wasted effort because the elk was soured; however, there was no way we were going to leave it there. Don and John would trailer the horses back to Slate Creek Saddle and then come out the Bad Tom Mt. trail and meet us at Herb's bull. Before Don and John arrived, I went down and put my elk quarters into game bags to keep them clean while packing. When Don and John arrived, Herb asked John if he thought the elk was soured. John's reply was if it isn't, it sure as hell missed a perfect opportunity!

John had canvas pack bags that fit over the riding saddles, so he just threw an elk quarter in each side, tied the hocks together, and headed up the ridge. We packed Herb's bull to Bad Tom Mountain and then Don and John went back to pack my little bull down to the Slate Creek trail. Herb and I made two trips on the motorcycles to get his bull out to the saddle, and then loaded our bikes into the horse trailer and went to camp.

Once in camp we had some sandwiches for lunch and then I fixed more sandwiches for Don and John. I gathered up the lunch and jumped on my motorcycle and headed for the mouth of Murray Creek. When I arrived up there, the guys were just starting down the brushy ridge off the timbered bench. They had gone back down that steep middle ridge in Murray Creek to my elk in the forks of the creek. I had forgotten to tell them to swing into the bottom of the west fork side, and then they could have come down the bottom on a good game trail right to my elk. Anyway, after that steep climb up to Bad Tom Mountain, and then back down that steep ridge to my elk, the horses were all in. So they had to give them a good rest before coming down with my elk.

John was in the same shape as the horses when they came sliding down into the Slate Creek trail. I told him to take my motorcycle and go on into camp. Don and I would lead the horses the one and one half miles down the trail to our camp. John's horses were nice big horses but hadn't been used much over the summer, so were not in shape to pack out two elk the same day. When we made it to camp they were done for the day, and so were we. These steep brushy Idaho hillsides have a way of taking the starch right out of man or beast.

We rubbed the horses down and then fed them what hay was left in the trailer and turned them out into the creek bottom to rustle what they could find to eat. Herb and John had a good start on supper, so after a couple of stiff drinks we were ready to eat. John had to work the next day so he took Herb's truck and went home right after supper. It wasn't very long after the dishes were cleaned up that all of us hit the sack. Now sleep comes easy after a hard day on the mountain.

October 8th, we were up early and Don and I caught and saddled horses while Herb fixed breakfast. Herb volunteered to do the domestic chores and start dismantling camp. So right after breakfast Don and I took off to pack in Don's elk.

Blaze and Buck, John's horses, were not all that excited about going up that steep brushy ridge to Don's elk and we felt guilty about not going to town the previous evening and getting those horses some decent feed. Hell, they had earned it, that's for sure. We had to spank those big broad butts with a switch a few times but we finally urged them up the hellish two miles to Don's elk. The elk was in a hell of a brush pile, and the pack-bags were all torn apart from the pack the day before, so I told Don let's try something different on this elk. We put the quarters in the bags, and then took a piece of rope about twenty feet long and half-hitched it to the saddle horn in the middle, and then we doubled the rope back through the cinch ring to make a sling for a basket hitch. This put the quarters up on the horses' backs, not hanging down where they'd beat them in the ribs. This deal worked real well and we were back in camp by 10:30 a.m.

The Sandpoint fellows were in camp resting so we had a few beers and took some pictures, and then loaded our camp and horses and went home. When we took John's horses home we gave him $150 dollars to buy those good horses some grain for their reward for a job well done. John put up a little fight about paying him for using the horses until I explained to him that he wasn't the one being paid, he was just holding the money.

I thought the trip was an extraordinary success. We had good weather the whole trip, good food, good booze, and a heck of a good time. The camaraderie was exceptional, not counting the good luck of getting three elk, and the elk packed out in three days total time. We had offered to finish packing Doc's elk out on the horses, but he wanted to pack it all himself. That just goes to show you what a good character old Doc really is. We all wish you the best of luck in your hunting endeavors.

Joe and Don with our pack string at Mallard Lake.

Chapter Forty-two

THE LEGEND OF THE MALLARD MOUNTIE

1985. I acquired this nickname on a horse packing trip into the Mallard Larkin Wilderness on the St. Joe-Clearwater Divide. We had camped one night at Mallard Lake and found a big mess where someone had left a camp the previous fall; bears had subsequently scattered tents and garbage all over hell's half acre. We spent one whole day cleaning up this mess, burning what we could, and ended up with two packhorse loads of garbage to pack out to the trailhead.

There were some feed sacks from Moses Lake, Washington, so that gave us a clue as to who had left the camp.

When we got back out to the trailhead and were unloading our horses, a fellow come running over and asked if we were planning on hunting in this area later in the fall. I just happened to glance over towards the camp this guy came from and noticed that his truck had Washington license plates. So I told this bird that we were Idaho residents and we hunted anyplace that we wanted too. Mr. Washington hunter says to me that his party had been hunting there for the past ten years. A light came on in my head and I got suspicious, so I asked this jerk if he was the S.O.B that had left that camp out at Mallard Lake. He got all bristled up and told me that a storm dumped fourteen inches of snow on them and they had to get out. So I came back with, "Did it scare you so bad that you couldn't have come back during the summer and cleaned up your damn mess." The guy just walked off in a big huff.

By then my companions started getting on my case for being so rude to this guy. Joe said, "One day somebody is going to call your bluff and clean your plow." I said, "They won't be getting a virgin, because it has been done before, and will probably be done again. I just have a low tolerance for incompetence."

Anyway, after that deal whenever anybody did something that wasn't just right, one of my friends would say to this person, "You had better be careful, because the 'Mallard Mountie' is watching!"

March 16th 1992. We had had a real open winter so I decided to go into Slate Creek and take care of some unfinished business from the previous summer. My wife, Karen, dropped me off at the mouth of Dry Creek, a tributary of Placer Creek in Shoshone County, Idaho. I had borrowed a "Big Bear" 4-wheeler from a friend and would ride it into Slate Creek on top of the snow where the snowmobiles had packed down a trail. My mission was to burn some brush that we had cut and piled the previous summer.

I had just started up Dry Creek when I spotted seven cow elk on the west side just below the forks. I had a hard time making it over the hill because the snow was soft from the high temperatures, and all of the creek crossing was melted down to bare ground, leaving banks four feet high on both sides. It was noon by the time I arrived at the end of the road at the mouth of Red Top Creek. I was actually surprised to find lots of elk sign on the lower third of the hill, and even some moose tracks. There was about eighteen inches of snow on the level at this point and I had a one and one-half mile hike to where we had piled the brush. And me with no snowshoes; I had thought it would be bare ground down in the bottom.

I hiked the one and one half miles up to my tree stand where I would burn the brush. This was on a south facing slope so once I got out of the timber, the snow had melted off around the brush piles. I set all of the piles on fire and then tossed the ends into the fire until everything was burnt up.

I hadn't gone to bed the previous night after working the graveyard shift in the shaft at the Galena Mine, so now I was getting tired pretty fast, and my legs were starting to cramp up from fighting the deep snow.

I started down the hill anyway, and in just a short time I was back to the 4-wheeler. I didn't think that the elk wintered up this high in Slate Creek, but apparently there hadn't been enough snow to move them down. It was 3:30 p.m. when I started up the hill for home, and now, to make things even worse than they had been that morning, a light rain had started falling. By 5:30 p.m. I had decided that I wasn't going to make it out because I kept getting high centered in the soft snow. The 4-wheeler was getting hot, and old Fred was getting mighty tired.

I decided maybe I could get out through the bottom of Slate Creek, and up to Avery, Idaho, and then up over Moon Pass as it was plowed. At 6:00 p.m. I saw five elk in the brush-fields in Horseshoe Creek, I think they were all bulls but I didn't have time to check with my binoculars. By 7:30 p.m. I was down to the mouth of Cedar Creek, and what a

146

hellish trip it had been. I had deep snow, landslides, windfalls, washouts, and then I was up against a twenty-four inch thick windfall right in the creek because the road had washed out on the hillside. I got my little chainsaw out with its measly twelve-inch bar and started cutting. And what did I end up doing? I got the bar pinched in the tree and I didn't have an axe to chop it out. I took the saw off the bar and just left the bar in the tree. I would come back for it later.

A friend, Rick, retrieving my chainsaw bar.

Now I only had one way to go and that was back the way I had just come. As I fought my way back up the stream bed in the high water, I got bucked off the 4-wheeler into the water. Now I was soaked to the skin, boots full of water, and my options started going to hell in a hurry. I needed to get a fire going and get dried out or I was going to be in a world of deep poop. Thank God I had on all wool clothes, and lots of them. I decided that with no saw or axe to cut some firewood, I had better get back to Summit Creek campground and pray that someone had left some wood.

It was one happy camper who arrived at the campground and found a pile of fire wood piled between two trees. By the time I got my fire going good it was 9:00 p.m. so I got up on the picnic table and got out of my wet clothes. It wasn't very long and I had dried my clothes over the fire and gotten dressed. I figured there wasn't any sense in trying to get over the hill until it got colder and firmed up the snow. There was an old split-log bench handy so I skidded it over next to the fire and lay down as I was getting exhausted.

Unbeknown to me, my wife, Karen, had started the big rescue of the infamous "Mallard Mountie" (that's me, the dummy). The famous righteous Mallard Mountie caught out with no axe, no knife, no extra food or a flashlight (That's the kind of things legends are made of).

About 10:30 p.m., brother Don and Vinnie Self walked up to the fire. I ask Don how in hell they had found me, and how had they gotten in to the campground? They had come in on a snowmobile, but had run out of snow about one mile up the road, so had walked in the rest of the way. I asked how they had figured out where I was? Don said Vinnie had seen the fire and looked down to the site with binoculars, and then exclaimed to Don that, "There is some crazy S.O.B. down there dancing around on the table naked!" Don said, "That's Fred, all right!"

We all got aboard the 4-wheeler and got back up to the snowmobile, but from there on my machine still couldn't go on the snow because it was still raining. Finally, we got the 4-wheeler tied to the snowmobile and up that hill we went about fifty miles an hour. Once on top I could go down Dry Creek so Vinnie went back to get Don.

We got to my house at about 12:30 a.m. to find my wife very upset, and pissed off. Just what I needed to top off my day, a good butt chewing from my wife. I felt like I had been stomped on, romped on, and run over by a Brahma Bull. But anyway, that ends the saga of the Mallard Mountie.

Chapter Forty-three

TWILIGHT BULL

Fall 1985. This elk hunt took place in Horseshoe Creek, a small tributary of Slate Creek, which is a tributary of the St. Joe River in Shoshone County, Idaho.

I had parked my pickup camper on the east bank of Red Top Creek, three days prior to the opening of the Idaho elk season. Brother Don and brother-in-law Randy would join me on Friday evening. Don arrived on schedule but Randy's dad had passed away so he couldn't make it. Doc, from Lewiston, Idaho, and his brother-in-law showed up along with four of the guys from Sandpoint, Idaho. It was quite a reunion again this year.

I had been scouting for elk for three days and I had determined that our best chance to score on opening day would be in the Horseshoe Creek drainage. There was a herd of elk in Horseshoe Creek with four bulls in attendance, a big 6X6 bull, a nice 5X5 bull, a 4X4 bull and a spike bull. All of the other fellows chose to hunt in Lick Creek, where all the action had occurred the previous year. One of the fellows from Sandpoint that we all call "Hog" decided to hunt up under Corvus Creek ridge on the south side of Slate Creek. I had taken him aside and pointed out the ridge where I had seen a 5X5 bull elk that morning.

October 5th. Opening day of elk season! Don and I were up by 4:00 a.m. but we were late. The rest of the hunters were already out of camp. I guess they wanted to make sure that they beat us up into Lick Creek. We hadn't bothered to tell them we were going to hunt Horseshoe Creek. We took our time fixing breakfast, cleaned up the dishes, and then took a Thermos of coffee to drink while we drove the jeep up to the power-line road off the top of Moon Pass to access the head of Horseshoe Creek. As we came out along the ridge between Slate Creek and the Little North Fork of the St. Joe River, we saw hunters there waiting to go down both sides of the ridge. There were at least a dozen hunters standing along the road in the head of Horseshoe Creek, all humped up in that cold cruel wind that always blows at dawn and dusk. Evidently, this herd of elk was no big secret.

Don and I parked the jeep and then slipped over the road bank into the head of a dry draw that went down the brushy hillside to an open knob where we would have both forks of the creek under observation. I had discovered this route the year before.

It was still dark when we arrived on that open knob above the forks of the creek, so we settled in to await the coming dawn. It was only 6:10 a.m. and it wouldn't get light until 6:30. At 6:20 a.m. Don heard a bull elk squeal just to the north of us, right across the draw. I got my 15X60 Ziess binoculars out of my pack and started trying to spot the elk that had squealed. It was so quiet you could hear your heart beating in your chest, and we were just bursting with anticipation of getting on these elk before someone else fouled up our hunt. Any time now something should happen. Suddenly, an elk came into view in my binoculars; the elk were only 150 yards away across the draw. Eleven head of elk filled the view through my binoculars. Wow, there was the big 6X6 bull standing broad-side in a little opening below the rest of the herd. Don couldn't see the elk so I told him I was going to shoot that big bull before someone spooked the herd. I laid the binoculars to the side and picked up my .308 Norma Magnum. Using my pack for a rifle rest I looked through my scope and I was having trouble seeing the dot reticule in my scope in the low light. Finally, I could see the dot reticule against the light color on the elk's side, so really concentrating on the sight picture, I touched off a shot. The elk went down, and then went lurching down the hillside trying to get back on its feet.

The elk herd was milling around now, unsure of where to run to. They were confused by the sound of the shot ricocheting around the basin. I snatched up my binoculars just as they took off down across the hillside right in front of us. Then I spotted a 3X3 bull elk going down the draw right below us. Don finally got focused on the elk and started shooting. After three shots we couldn't really tell if he was hitting or not. The bull was about to get into the heavy brush so I started shooting before we lost a wounded elk in the brush like I had the year prior to this year. I got the elk in my scope as he leaped across the hillside, just as the dot reticule passed his nose I touched off a round. I shot his lower jaw off. Then he stopped on the edge of the brush, so I shot him again through the shoulders. The bull just collapsed in a heap, and he never even shivered.

There were elk going every direction. A 5X5 bull elk pushed two cows down the draw right below us. As the elk disappeared around the brow of the hill, out of our view, a barrage of shots crashed and rolled echoes across the mountain. There was shooting from all points of the compass. However, later we heard of only one kill being made, and that was by George, who got the 5X5 bull right above the Slate Creek road.

I showed Don the brush pile my bull was in, and now he would guide me to it. When I walked up to the brush pile, I got the biggest surprise of my life. Lying there on the ground was the biggest cow elk you ever laid eyes on, and it was a bull only season for the first ten days. How in hell could this have happened? I had Don guide me to his bull, and then called him over to me.

Don showing off his 3X3 trophy bull elk.

My only explanation was that the bull moved off while I was getting my rifle, and then the big cow elk walked into the same opening. A weak excuse, yes, but that was the best I could come up with. I was concentrating so hard on the sight picture that I never even noticed that it was a cow. The bottom line is that we should have waited and not been in such a hurry. Patience that is the virtue missing here, we were just too greedy to get our elk and be the big heroes in camp on opening day.

Don had joined me at the 3X3 bull elk, and then I explained what I had found down the hill where my bull was supposed to be. We were both just sick about it but there was no way of changing it now, and we would just have to take the cow out and if we got caught so be it. Don had hit the 3X3 bull twice also, and either hit would have eventually killed the elk. Where the elk died would have been the question. When both elk were taken care of, we slid the big cow out the bottom to the road and took her to my home. That was minus her head, of course. We then arranged to have the little bull packed out the next day by a friend, Joe, with horses.

Joe and Fred pack out Don's 3X3 bull on Joe's horses.

We were in camp that evening sitting by the campfire drinking a beer when our friend "Hog" came limping up the road, dragging his rifle alongside his leg. Old "Hog" asked, "Did you guys get your elk." "Yes," was our reply. "Son-of-a bitch," Hog screamed. "I walk my butt off and only get tired, and you lucky bastards kill two elk before daylight and on opening morning, too." I gave old Hog a beer to settle him down and then he started telling lies faster than three normal people could think them up. I guess you would have to say old "Hog" was an uncouth character, but a likeable son-of-a-bitch. He wasn't even a normal son-of-a-bitch but a self-made one, if you get my meaning.

Doc came in with a success story also. He had killed a spike bull elk on Red Top Ridge that morning. His brother-in-law had never left camp, the same as the year before. I think he has an alcohol problem. That evening everyone gathered for the opening day bull session, shooting match, and bugling contest. Doc would win the shooting match by shooting a knot through a tree offhand at 100 yards. The rifle wasn't even his but belonged to one of the guys from Sandpoint, and it was a big shoulder-busting .375 H&H Magnum. Hog even sawed the snag down and brought back the chunk with the knot shot out to verify Doc's hit. The bugling contest ended in a standoff, but I think Hog should have won on volume alone. One of the Sandpoint boys got a little war-like with Doc until I took him to the side and explained to him that Doc had boxed in the military. This old boy mellowed right out then, by golly. Anybody that has ever seen Doc's nose would know that he didn't get it by falling on his face.

Our friend met us on top the next morning just like we had planned. Everything went smoothly and we were home by noon. The afternoon turned into another bull session as we discussed what great elk hunters we were.

This hunt sobered us up a bunch in the end. I didn't write this story to try and justify our actions, but rather to show what the results are when in haste to accomplish something we face unacceptable consequences. On future hunts, patience will be practiced and we will damned sure make sure of our target before we fire a shot. That is a promise I intend to keep.

Chapter Forty-four

RHEUMATOID, NO BULL

The year of 1987 was a bad year for Fred S. Scott. In the early spring of 1987 I was stricken with severe Rheumatoid Arthritis.

Fall 1987. Don had set his pickup camper up in our usual spot on the east bank of Red Top Creek. Doc, from Lewiston, Idaho, had his tent camper set up on the west bank of Red Top Creek. However, the Sandpoint, Idaho, crew didn't show up. I think maybe they had wife troubles after the trip last year when they showed up late with some young female companions.

On the opening morning of the 1987 elk season I come off work at the Galena Mine and tried to make a hunt up into Lick Creek. I spent two hours hobbling up the hill to the fir tree on the east side of Lick Creek. I was so sick by that time that I had to take a two hour nap to recoup enough to hobble back down to the camper, and then I went most of the way on my butt, hunching along like a snail. I felt about that low also.

Don and Doc didn't have any luck either. However, Doc had located a herd of elk in Murray Creek He asked Don to accompany him to Murray Creek the next morning to put a hunt on this elk herd. Don declined the offer because he didn't want to leave me alone in the condition I was in.

The next morning I wasn't any better so we went home; it made no sense for Don to have to listen to me moan and groan any longer. Doc made his hunt into Murray Creek and got a small 5X5 bull elk. When Doc went through Wallace on his return trip home he called to let me know that this would be his last year hunting in Slate Creek. He told me that he was going to start hunting in the Clearwater River country in hopes of getting one of those record class bull elk.

However, if you research the Idaho State Record Book, there has been more trophy bull elk come out of Shoshone County, then any other county in Idaho. However, to each his own thoughts on where, when, and how to conduct their personal hunts.

I was unable to return to work until December. Whenever I would feel up to it, my wife, Karen, would drive me around in the pickup. We were able to spot two big 6X6 bull elk, and one 5X5 bull elk, and two spike bull elk. However, not being able to get out and walk I was unable to hunt any of those bulls.

The cow elk season was open and Karen and I were parked on the road above Horseshoe Creek. We had been watching for hours when two cow elk and a calf walked into a clearing fifty yards below the road. I fumbled the gun around and got it pointed out the truck window, but not in time. The elk moved off before I could get my scope on them, but that was a blessing because I couldn't have done anything with an animal if I had shot one. It was totally frustrating for me to be so crippled up that I couldn't even walk.

I did manage to murder a nice 5X5 whitetail buck from the pickup in late November, but that is another story. (To read the story about this buck you will have to get my first book, *"Memories of Hunting Idaho's Golden Era"*).

I quote from my memos for 1987. October 28th. The elk season closed, and I hadn't been out hunting since October 17th, that is if you call driving around in the pickup hunting. It would be a year with no elk meat in the Scott larder, but cheer up old lad, maybe your luck will change next year. Well so long until next year and hopefully we will meet on the mountain someday; until then good luck, and good bye.

Roger Trumbull packing out a deer on his motorcycle for Don.

155

Chapter Forty-five

MONTANA BEARS

Fall 1990. We had a very wet month during August so it was with great anticipation that we started our 1990 black bear season. My wife's niece's husband, Dan, wanted me to guide him in Montana for bear. So on August 26th when I came off the graveyard shift at the Galena Mine we made our first scouting trip up onto the state line above the old Silver Cable Mine in the head waters of the South Fork of Coeur d'Alene River.

We hadn't hunted this area before, so we weren't sure how best to approach it for the best view. Dan and I hiked up onto the ridge from the road going out above the Silver Cable mine and were looking down into the West Fork of Crow Creek on the Montana side. It was a beautiful, clear, sunny morning as we hiked along the ridge top looking for a good spot to glass the basin with our binoculars and spotting scope. It was still on the cold side for August but all the better for the bears to be out feeding later. As we hiked along I spotted a small black colored bear down on the side hill below us.

Finally we found a spot where we had a good view of the whole basin, so settled in to watch. I thought I had spotted an elk over across the basin in some heavy brush so I got my spotting scope and focused on it. Instead of and elk it was a very large bear, which I thought was a grizzly until it came out into an opening; then I could see it was a black bear. The only dark area on the bear was on its ankles and feet. Even the head was a light blonde except for the nose and eyes. I estimated the bear's weight to be somewhere between 350-400 pounds. As we watched she was joined by a solid black cub.

We watched until about 11:00 a.m. before the bears went into the trees to bed down for the day. I would have to work that night, so we went home well satisfied with our morning of spotting for bears.

On September 1st, opening day of Montana bear season, we were back on the same ridge ready to start the bear season. Right after full light we spotted the big blonde bear up towards the top of the basin. It was another bright clear morning so we just continued to watch. And then the blonde sow and cub came out further down the basin so we assumed the other blond bear was a boar.

The bears just about had to be related because they both had the very same markings. After viewing the new bear with the spotting scope we decided that he was quite a bit larger, so was probably a boar. We spotted four mule deer bucks on the ridge above the big bear, and all were at least 4X4 typicals. However, one of them was much bigger bodied and his antlers were higher and wider, not a B&C buck but still a very respectable buck. As we continued to watch we saw a big Canada lynx cat cross the hillside below the bear and deer.

About 8:30 a.m. we started our stalk on the bigger blond bear in the head of the basin. We would have to climb down the steep canyon wall and get into the bottom of the basin to keep downwind of the bear and get within shooting range. As we crossed the bottom through scattered timber and brush I kept a sharp lookout for the bear. Suddenly I could see him about 150 yards away on the hillside through a opening in the trees. Dan couldn't seem to spot him and the bear finally heard us talking and left. We had done our best but didn't score. It was now after 10:30 a.m. so I told Dan we would leave and come back the next day as I needed to get some sleep.

September 2nd. We were back by a shorter route that we found when we'd left the day before. If the bear was on the same hillside as he had been the day before, we should be within 250 yards of him. When I finally got to where I could see the area the bear had been in the day before, it was just in time to see his big broad rump disappear into the heavy brush. I think the bear had gotten our scent because the ridge was real open and I don't think he heard us approach. We watched until noon without seeing any other animals. We decided to let this place rest the rest of this day and go to the Jack Waite Mine for the afternoon hunt.

Dan and I got up onto the ridge in the middle basin on the Montana side and settled in to watch by the old claim discovery hole we had always sat by when we were kids. I had shot the heads off of three blue grouse coming up the sidehill with my .22 long rifle. It was 6:00 p.m. when I saw a medium-sized black bear come out into an old snow slide scar. I wanted to get within about 250 yards so Dan could make a good shot and we wouldn't be looking for a wounded bear half the night. When we got where I wanted to be, I sidled out enough to see down the slide and our bear was still there.

I whispered to Dan to crab crawl out into the slide and the bear would be about 150 yards directly below him. When Dan got into position he couldn't spot the bear so I slid out beside him and tried to point the bear out. Dan couldn't seem to spot the bear and pretty soon he heard my frantic whispering and looked up and spotted us and took off down onto the bench.

I had watched hundreds of bears cross that bench in the past so knew exactly where the bear would go. I hurried to point out an opening that had a log lying across it and told Dan to get his rifle on that log because when the bear got into the opening he would put his front feet up on the log and stop. The bear ran out into the opening and stopped just like I had predicted. However, Dan was watching the wrong opening so never got a shot off. It was way after black dark when we arrived back at my truck.

September 3rd. We were back on our first lookout on the ridge above the West fork of Crow Creek again. Right at 7:30 a.m. we spotted a black sow with twin black cubs but didn't see the big blond boar we had seen on the previous two mornings. We watched until about 9:30 a.m. without spotting any other animals so started hiking back along the ridge towards the main Crow Creek basin. Dan could hear a bull elk bugling down in the basin but we never did spot him. When we hit the road and started hiking back to the truck a friend, Chris, came along. He had been lucky and harvested a small chocolate-colored black bear in the main Crow Creek basin. However, he hadn't seen any other bears, and I had to return to work on the graveyard shift that night so we gave it up.

We had seen lots of animals, including the lynx cat that you don't often see, so it was a very successful hunt even if we didn't harvest a bear. Just being out in the beautiful mountains is reward enough for me, and I am sure Dan would agree.

Chapter Forty-six

REPLAY BULL

Fall 1990. The 1990 elk hunt would take place in Murray Creek, a small tributary of Slate Creek, which is a tributary of the great St. Joe River in Shoshone County, Idaho.

For a full month prior to this hunt I had been scouting every chance I got, which was often. I worked on the graveyard shift at the Galena Mine in Lake Gulch across from Silverton, Idaho. So I was scouting every morning and evening.

I had found several different herds of elk ranging the drainages that radiate out from Bad Tom Mountain like the spokes in a wagon wheel to all points of the compass. I hadn't been able to arrange any vacation leave for the hunt, so it would just be a matter of choosing a herd of elk that I could hunt after I got off my work shift. I decided that the elk herd ranging the Murray Creek drainage would be my best chance to harvest an elk, because I could ride my motorcycle right to the mouth of the creek and I would only have a steep half-mile climb up the east side to be in a good area. That would be the forks of Murray Creek. Brother Don and a friend, Joe, would hunt in the Lick Creek area just east of Murray Creek.

September 30th. Opening day of the elk season, which would be, "bulls only" for the first ten days. I didn't take my lunch break that night at work, and then fudged a little on quitting time so I managed to be at the Slate Creek trailhead at 6:00 a.m. In minutes I had unloaded my motorcycle, and was roaring up the trail to the mouth of Murray Creek. I arrived up there at 6:20 a.m. and it was just breaking day. It appeared that we would have another balmy fall day with frost in the morning, and eighty degrees in the afternoon.

I was dressed light for the fast climb up that steep brushy ridge. I had on blue jeans with shorts and a light tee shirt for underclothes, and a light felt shirt over the top. I was also wearing light-weight hunting boots. Have no doubt about it; I pushed my old out-of-shape body up that mountain in record time. By 7:20 a.m. I was in the forks of Murray Creek, which wasn't bad time for a recovering arthritic.

The bull Don gave to the Kellogg hunters.

I arrived at my destination sweating like a teenager at a strip show! I was mopping my face with my handkerchief as the sweat gushed out of me like a spring torrent. Unconscious-like, I caught a glimmer of movement back in the trees on the west fork side of Murray Creek. Something was coming through the trees on the game trail that crossed the middle ridge, only 150 yards from where I sat.

A cow and calf elk, followed by a spike bull elk, came trotting out onto the open face of the middle ridge, and there were more animals coming. Another cow and calf elk rushed out of the trees with a shad-gutted 6X6 bull elk in hot pursuit. Now this 6X6 bull elk was about as sorrowful looking a critter as you might ever imagine. It looked like he hadn't bothered with sleep, or food, for about two weeks. The bull's eyes were bloodshot, and his hide hung on him like a hound dog. He was pure decadence!

That fat spike bull elk just radiated good health as he trotted along with his head up in that alert stance elk have when they are on the move. In another forty feet the spike bull would disappear into the timber again and be safe. I hurried to raise my .308 Norma Magnum to my shoulder, and then swept the reticule in my scope up through the spike bull's body to his shoulder, and touched off a shot without stopping the forward momentum of my rifle. The bull flipped head over heels off the trail like he had been shot from a catapult. End over end he tumbled down the steep hillside, and then, like a sudden act of magic, he was on his feet and headed west like a pony express rider. I managed to get off another shot just as the bull dove from sight into a sharp draw. I wasn't sure if I had hit the bull with that final shot, so I waited for several minutes to see if he would come out of the draw. He didn't come out, so evidently he was mine.

The trailing cow and calf elk and her six-point boyfriend turned back up the west fork side to the area they had just come from. After I watched for about fifteen minutes, I saw the cow and calf going to the west out of Murray Creek; however, her boyfriend stayed behind in the timber. The spike bull hadn't come out of the draw he disappeared into, so I moved over there to check on him. He was dead on arrival!

This little spike bull was a twin to the one I killed in the same drainage on the 1984 elk hunt. It was the same hillside and the same trail, and I was on the same stand that I had been on back in '84. It was like reviewing and old movie you had seen in the past.

Upon opening up the carcass of my bull I discovered that my first shot had dissected a rib on entry and just shredded the lungs. I don't know how that spike ever regained his feet. This was just an example of how tough elk really are, and only a spike bull, too. My second shot had broken the left front leg right above the knee joint.

I took care of my elk and hung the quarters around a big pine tree, and then draped the hide around the whole she-bang to keep the rain off. And just in time, too, because there were big black rain clouds building up off in the southwest. Rain was on the way! I didn't beat the rain back to my motorcycle so I had to endure a miserable ride out to the trailhead. I arrived at my 1989 4X4 Chevy pickup soaked to the skin and chilled to the bone. I left a note on Don's jeep, and then hurried home to get dry clothes and warm my poor cold body.

Don and Joe had gotten into the elk in Lick Creek. However, when a small 6X6 bull elk chased a cow elk over a hog-back ridge, and then slid to a stop only 125 yards away facing straight on, Don muffed the shot and only broke a front leg on the bull. The bull hobbled off down the hill through heavy brush with Don in hot pursuit. Some young fellows from Kellogg, Idaho, intercepted the bull and shot him in a back leg, so now he was wounded fore and aft. Don finally got another chance and head shot the bull to put him down.

The young fellows from Kellogg were all excited and they didn't realize that Don had shot the bull first. Don was disgusted with himself over his poor marksmanship, so he just took a photo of the bull and then relinquished it to the two young fellows. It was their first elk so it was a happy experience for them.

I hired Joe to pack my elk out the next morning. We left Slate Creek Saddle early with dark black clouds threatening rain again. The clouds were right down on the ridge-tops, making visibility, zero. When we rode out onto the end of the middle ridge in Murray Creek there was a rifle shot, and it sounded real close. I started counting horses and they were all still standing. Then there were two more fast shots and someone hollered that they had an elk down. We were fifty yards down the ridge when we emerged from the fog, and right away we spotted two guys walking up to that poor old run down 6X6 bull elk that I had passed on the day before. The bull was still in the same timber patch, and would have probably died there in the coming winter anyway. After a quick break for lunch we packed up my bull and headed out for the trailhead.

The sun was burning the cloud cover off, scattering the clouds until it was almost nice again. I had an experienced packer with experienced horses, so it was an uneventful pack trip back to the truck.

I had been lucky again to get my bull on opening morning of elk season, but I still missed the camaraderie of elk camp. The smell of wood smoke and wet wool clothes drying, good food cooking, the laughter of friends in a warm tent, the clean, wholesome smell of the trees and the wet earth after a rain shower, and the wind whispering through the tree tops. But I think I missed my companions having a good time the most. Oh well, maybe next year. I will try and see you then old friend, and good luck too ya' in the interim.

Fred's nice spike bull elk.

Chapter Forty-seven

MUZZLELOADER MISHAPS

Fall 1991. In the past few years I hadn't been finding the quality of bucks that I wanted during the rifle season, but have had some success at getting friends into both deer and elk with muzzleloaders. So far that fall of 1991 I had hunted seventeen days, and had hunted hard without any success. So I finally decided to borrow a muzzleloader from a friend and try hunting closer to home in Unit 4.

November 27th. It finally started clearing in the afternoon after several days of snow and rain, so I left my home in Wallace, Idaho, and drove up Placer Creek to Experimental Gulch Trailhead. I planned to just hike up the trail real slow, hoping to catch a buck out feeding after the storm. I was only about one mile up the trail, just past the forks, when I came around a bend in the trail and there was a three point whitetail buck feeding on the brush along the trail. The buck was completely unaware that anything was up. I pulled the hammer back, put my gloved finger through the trigger guard and started to mount the gun to my shoulder. I almost had the gun to my shoulder when, BOOM, the damned gun went off. Unintentionally, I had set the set trigger and when I pushed the gun forward to put it to my shoulder my gloved finger hit the trigger and fired the gun. The little buck didn't even look my way before he jumped into the brush and was gone. I guess maybe some time spent getting familiar with an unfamiliar gun might have been appropriate.

I hunted all the way to the end of the trail without seeing another deer. However, I did see the tracks where four deer had heard me, smelled me, or just plain sensed me and taken off running. I also jumped one elk without seeing it. I think the higher I went the old snow was crusted, making for lots of crunching sounds.

November 28th. Thanksgiving Day! I left home early and went to the top of Dobson Pass north of Wallace, Idaho, and drove out the Mountain Goat Lease road. I spent the whole day walking through about fourteen inches of snow and jumped several deer and elk without seeing any. Walking in the crusted snow wasn't very productive. I went home to a nice Thanksgiving Dinner and then called a friend, Jim. Jim and I would hunt the Coeur d'Alene River the next day.

November 29th. I woke up to a foot of new snow overnight. Mike, the fellow, I had borrowed the muzzleloader from, had come and gotten it the previous evening, so I was a hunter without a gun. Jim had a muzzleloader so we went anyway. It hadn't been very productive stalking through the crusted snow so on this day we would try to locate a deer we could access from the road.

A large bull elk skull and antlers found by my friend, Jim.

We spent the whole morning driving around seeing only does, so we decided to go to Prichard, Idaho, for a beer and lunch at the Prichard Tavern. We were only about one-fourth mile out of Prichard when I spotted a big whitetail doe standing on the edge of the river. I told Jim to get his gun ready and I would coast to a stop right next to the deer. Then, in the brush behind the doe, I saw a monster whitetail buck watching the doe. This buck's antlers were so wide that at first I thought it was a mule deer buck. When we came to a stop the big buck walked out onto the river bank, and stopped to check out the doe. The buck didn't even notice us sitting there forty yards away; he had eyes only for that hot doe. There was a lone red fir tree on the road bank so Jim slipped over the road bank to use that tree for a rifle rest. Jim took plenty of time aiming, but when he shot he missed the deer completely. Jim is a good shot so I was disappointed when he missed a buck of a lifetime. The buck was both tall and wide, and had six long points. I would have bet a lot of money that this buck would have made it into the Boone & Crockett book. This was the biggest buck either one of us had ever seen.

Jim said he had aimed high because he thought it was about a seventy yard shot. But I think he was looking at that big rack instead of through the sights. Whatever, we had to get across the river and make sure the deer hadn't been hit. We got some heavy duty trash bags out from behind the truck seat and taped them to our legs so we wouldn't get our feet wet crossing the river. There are very few things as useful in your survival kit as heavy duty trash bags; you can fashion a poncho out of them for wind or rain protection, make a shelter, any number of things if you use your ingenuity. We crossed the river and followed the deer for about one half of a mile without finding any sign of a hit or that the deer was wounded.

We hunted the rest of the day without seeing any other deer. We didn't really have our mind into the game because all we could see was that big buck that got away. I even borrowed Jim's gun and came back the next day and followed the deer for about two miles trying to jump them again. I didn't see an animal all day, but I still had that crunchy snow to contend with.

Prichard Creek

I want to comment here on the uniqueness of the mouth of the Prichard Creek area. As a boy here back in about 1946 I remember seeing two bighorn rams on a rock bluff right above the bridge crossing Prichard Creek. And I have my brother, Don, and my father as witnesses. In all my research I have never found any evidence that there ever were any sheep in this area before or since that time.

In the early 1950's a fellow by the name of Bert Williams caught, on a gob of salmon eggs, a thirty-seven-inch rainbow trout weighing about nine pounds out of the mouth of Prichard Creek. In the late 1950's we would start seeing lots of big black bear in the cliffs across the river from the mouth of Prichard Creek. What attracts them there I can only guess, but I think it is the green grass coming on in the early spring from the heat of the sun reflecting off the rocks. In the spring of 1988 my wife, Karen, and I were hunting spring bear in this area. I was telling my wife stories of seeing so many big bears here back in the 50's, and what do we see, but a huge chocolate colored black bear. His head was huge and I estimated he would weigh 500 pounds at least. If that bear wasn't Boone & Crockett I'll eat my hat.

The river was in flood stage so we couldn't cross without a boat, and then it would have been taking a big chance because the river was up in the brush and wall to wall water across the valley floor. I could have killed the bear easy with my .308 Norma Magnum because he wasn't one foot over 200 yards away.

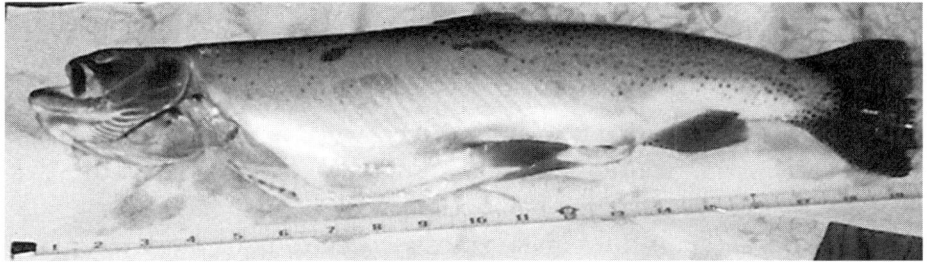

A 20-inch cutthroat trout caught by my friend, Jim.

Spring of 1991. We would see mountain goats on the cliffs across from the mouth of Prichard Creek. These were the first goats I ever saw there but other people have reported sighting them there earlier.

Fall of 1991. A friend, Jim, missed a big six-point whitetail buck on the river bank just up from the mouth of Prichard Creek. I'm pretty sure that buck would have pushed 300 pounds on the hoof, he was so huge. Back in the fall of 1964, I would harvest a 9X9 nontypical bull elk that scored 403 7/8 Boone & Crockett. Twenty-five years later, in 1989, my bull elk that was the Idaho State Record for many years was harvested up Prichard Creek, seven miles from its mouth, in the Vendetta Gulch drainage coming off the south side between Idaho Gulch and Granite Creek. On East Eagle Creek a tributary, of Prichard Creek, all during the 1950's we would see timber wolves, and I was lucky enough to kill three of them that were after Wayne Tester's milk cows in the pasture at the forks of Eagle Creek.

In 2008 we are seeing wolves moving back into the area, and the Idaho Fish & Game said we can't do anything about it. I think they need to remember who funds the department of Fish & Game, and rethink their priorities. What will happen in this area in the years to come I could not guess, but I would bet it will be something unique.

Chapter Forty-eight

BORDERLINE GUIDE

Fall 1992. October 20th, my brother Don and a friend, Dan, from Montana needed to fill their elk tags. We decided that the area along the state-line above the old Jack Waite Mine would be our best bet. Dan would be hunting Montana and Don would hunt the Idaho side. Our main objective would be the Bear and Butte Gulch drainages on the Idaho side, and the Beaver and Little Beaver creek drainages on the Montana side.

This was country that Don and I were very familiar with. We had spent our childhood only four miles from this state line ridge at the Jack Waite Mine Camp at Duthie, Idaho. This is a mile high alpine area, with big open basins tucked up under the state line in both states. Don and I had cut our hunting teeth chasing black bear in the high huckleberry patches of those high basins.

The basins abounded in big mule deer bucks so unsophisticated that you could get your buck, any hour, of any day you chose to. The forest grouse were everywhere. We had even seen grizzly bear on occasion and this was also a corridor for timber wolves moving out of Canada into the wilderness areas of central Idaho. The elk were few and far between back in the 1940's and 1950's, but at this writing they are plentiful. Yes, it was a wonderful game field for young boys with a burning desire to hunt.

This would be the last weekend for Don to hunt, though Dan's season didn't open until Sunday the 21st. We were right behind a wet fall snowstorm that had dropped about fifteen inches of snow, encasing everything with a thick layer of snow. With the mountains also encased in a pea-soup-thick northwest fog and a big old full moon shining down from above, it gave the snow-encased, stunted alpine trees a bent old-person effect. All of this combined created a graveyard like appearance, a spooky effect like in the movies.

The snow would be no problem for my 1989 Chevy 4X4 pickup, equipped with brand new Toyo traction tires that were siped – the whole deal. If that wasn't enough, I had two sets of heavy truck chains behind the seat of the pickup.

Just past the Jack Waite Mine camp the road changed to and old CCC road built by the Civilian Conservation Corp in the early thirties. One mile up this road we encountered fresh elk tracks meandering along the road through the unblemished snow. The drag marks in the snow indicated that a bull elk had fed along the road for about one mile. We were all the way across the Butte Gulch drainage before we saw where a herd of elk had come over out of Montana and gone down the divide ridge between Bear and Butte Gulch. I suppose the elk camps moving into Beaver Creek for the Montana elk opener had driven these elk up over the state line ridge.

It was still dark so we pulled over into a turnout and drank coffee until a dark, dank, dreary daybreak finally lightened the horizon to the east. After it was full light, Don and Dan took off on the trail of the elk. I would drive around on the Maple Peak road and meet them in the saddle between Butte-Bear gulch. The elk had already crossed this saddle and gone on out the divide ridge. When my hunters arrived we walked out along the Maple Peak road, hoping to catch this elk herd farther out towards Maple Peak. This wasn't real productive, either, as the fog would only occasionally blow up out of the bottoms to allow us a view. During one of these intervals we were able to spot some deer down on the Bear Gulch side. My 20-40 power Bushnell spotting scope revealed that one of the deer was a forked horn buck and Don still had a deer tag so he and Dan took off after the buck.

I decided to go out the divide ridge and see where the elk had gone. I followed the elk trail for about a half a mile, and then the elk went down onto the Butte Gulch side of the ridge. I just moved on out the divide ridge until I came to a favorite lookout spot under a huge ancient fir tree. From there I had the whole upper Butte Gulch basin under observation as the fog lifted and dissipated. I spent about two hours scanning the hillsides for game; the elks' trail through the snow indicated that they had passed through the basin. I was unsuccessful, so I returned to the truck. Don and Dan were already there. They had jumped their buck but didn't get a shot at him. Oh well, I guess that is why they call it hunting.

It was now about 10:30 a.m. so we took a drive down into Beaver Creek on the Montana side of the state-line divide. We would come back that afternoon to check on the elk herd we left in Butte Gulch. There was nothing but hunters down on Beaver Creek, so we decided to have a look into the big alpine basins up on the state-line ridge.

We all went together up into the middle Montana basin which was only one-fourth of a mile from the road crossing the head of Butte Gulch to a low saddle in the state-line ridge. After watching for about one hour with no results, we decided that Don and Dan would go to the north to look into another big alpine basin. I would do the same to the south. It was 3:40 p.m. when I spotted two cow elk, a calf elk and two spike bull elk crossing the bottom of the basin. I watched this herd cross over a hog-back ridge into the next basin to the south. I spent another hour watching for any other game that might cross with out any luck so I returned to my truck.

I turned the truck around and went back down to where I was supposed to pick up my hunters. They had not seen any game in Montana, but had spotted some elk on the south side of Butte Gulch on the Idaho side. I'm sure it was the same herd that had been in the road that morning because they were on a ridge just one-half of a mile from where I had left them that morning. I set up the spotting scope and found two rag-horn bull elk, plus fifteen cows and calves, bedded on a steep hog-back ridge.

We left this lookout and drove back out towards Maple Peak to see if we could plan a stalk from that side. We were not able to spot anything from that side, and we were about out of daylight for this day. So we decided to come back the next morning and start anew. Don could hunt this herd and Dan could hunt the herd in Montana that I had seen.

It was getting into the late evening, about 6:00 p.m. so we decided to head for home. As we crossed the creek in Bear Basin the second time we got a pleasant surprise. Standing in the road was a big 6X6 bull elk. We slid to a stop not twenty feet from him. In one big bounding leap the bull cleared the road-bank and disappeared into the trees. Don had the Idaho elk tag and was riding shotgun, so he popped out of the pickup cab almost before it stopped. Don ran over to a game trail coming down the road bank and then ran up the hillside into the trees. He had only disappeared into the trees when we heard him shoot; seconds later the big bull elk rolled down into the road. The bull had stopped fifty feet up the hill and was looking back over his shoulder at Don, and Don was able to shoot him in the neck with his .270 Winchester with 150 grain Nosler Partition bullets. The time was 6:20 p.m., almost dark.

After field-dressing the bull we were faced with loading the elk whole from the ground. We removed the tail-gate from the pickup box

170

and used it as a ramp to slide the elk into the pickup box. It was a good thing that I had a "come-along" ratchet hoist behind the truck seat. It is hard to imagine just how soft and loose a whole warm elk can be. The bull would weigh in at the locker plant at 600 pounds even, and that was minus his hide and head. The Idaho Fish & Game took a tooth and aged the bull at ten years. The antlers were evidently not the largest set the bull had ever grown because he only scored 287 5/8th Boone & Crockett points. That is small for a mature bull elk in that area.

After many stops to show off our trophy it was 1:30 a.m. when we got home. Sunday was a day of rest. Always keep in mind that the hunt isn't over until the last minute, of the last hour, of the last day of elk season. So be patient and persistent, and you will achieve success.

Don and Dan with Don's big 6X6 bull elk.

171

Chapter Forty-nine

GUIDE'S INTUITION

Fall 1992. It was the day after Thanksgiving. I had gotten my elk during the rifle season, but a couple of young friends, Jim and Shawn, had not. Now the late muzzleloader season was open for deer and elk. I decided that a hunt into the upper St. Joe River area might be productive for the boys.

Early Friday morning at 4:00 a.m., I picked the boys up at their home in Mullan, Idaho. We took off over Lookout Pass into Montana. We would drive almost to St. Regis, Montana, and then take the Two Mile Creek road to the top of Gold Creek, which is a tributary of the St. Joe River in Shoshone County, Idaho.

Just as we came out of the east end of the St. Regis River canyon there were four elk crossing the highway. One of those elk was a huge 6X6 bull elk. The boys were ready to fill their elk tags. I said, "I don't think so, not in Montana."

We went up over the hill and down into lower Gold Creek to where the Crooked Ridge road turns off. As we started up the hill on this road we started encountering lots of elk sign and some deer sign. However, we saw only one little whitetail doe coming up the hill and the boys wanted to kill her, too. But I overruled the boys on that deal, too. When we broke over the saddle onto Crooked Ridge, there were two elk just going into the trees. We never had a chance to see if they were bulls or cows, and our muzzleloader season was for bull elk only.

We had only one muzzleloader, which belonged to Jim. So Jim and I took off on a fire break trail that went up over the top of the mountain above the trees the elk had gone into. When we got up on top we were able to determine that the elk had not crossed over the ridge-top. We had about and eight-inch layer of snow in which to read sign, so we shouldn't miss anything. I told Jim that we would move around to the low side of this knob and then sneak down through this timber and see if we can jump an elk. As we eased down through the timber we were on our backsides more than on our feet. The ground was frozen iron hard and was slick under that snow cover, and it was steep as a cow's face, also. One thing in our favor was that the timber was pretty open, allowing us to see 100 to 150 yards.

As we got near the bottom of the timber patch a narrow steep draw developed, and across this draw a movement caught my eye. When I put my binoculars to my eyes I spotted two spike bull elk standing right at the limit of our visibility. One of the bulls had a tree blocking out most of his body; however, the other bull was out in the open. This bull was looking back over his shoulder at us in a quartering position. Jim got set down into a solid position and squeezed off a shot. Boom, the smoke boiled out of the end of that old smoke pole, obstructing our view. I didn't see anything to indicate a hit. Jim said, "I guess I missed him."

The elk had been only about 100 yards away across this steep, windfall-choked draw. But when I asked Jim if he thought we should go have a look-see, he replied that he was aiming at the elk's neck and the elk would have fallen if he had hit it. So we dropped on down the hill into a logging clear-cut and walked the road back to my pickup.

We got Shawn woke up so we could get into the pickup cab, and then drove out along Crooked Ridge road for about three miles. There were elk tracks all along the road but the boys didn't see any game. I turned the truck around and parked on the edge of the road overlooking a flat ridge running down into the St. Joe River country. The boys said what did you stop here for? My answer was to look for elk, and they replied that they had both been watching all the way out here and there were no animals around.

Well I said, "If you look right at the bottom of that big tamarack snag down there, I can see two cow elk standing there." After glassing the area for about twenty minutes I was able to spot six elk, all cows. Finally, the elk saw us and moved over the ridge-top out of our view.

Going back out the ridge, I kept having this thought that we should have checked on that spike bull that Jim had shot at that morning. So I pulled up where we had parked that morning and told Jim to grab his muzzleloader because we were going to go check on that elk. Jim said,"I know I missed him." I said, "I will know that too after we go check it out." Jim wasn't liking it very much, but we went to where the elk had gone into the trees that morning and then followed the trail in the snow to where we thought the elk was when Jim shot at it. We found no hair, blood, or any indication that it had been hit. Jim said, "Are you satisfied now?" I said, "No, let's follow it a ways to make sure it isn't hit." Only fifty feet along the track, Jim said, "I can't even see where the bullet hit, can you?" After turning to face Jim I replied, that he had hit the elk was the reason he couldn't see where the bullet hit. "What the hell are you talking about," Jim asked? I said, "Turn around and look behind you in that little depression." There lay the elk, dead as dead can be.

Upon inspecting the elk we found that Jim had hit the elk through the heart, and that was two feet from where he was aiming. The bullet had just poked a clean hole all the way through the chest cavity. An animal hit through the chest won't always leave a blood trail right away. I have followed elk hit in the chest with a modern rifle for 200 yards before they started leaving a blood trail. So be persistent and follow the animal for at least one-half of a mile if you can before giving up. You will be surprised at how often you will recover an animal that you thought you had missed.

I gave Jim my knife and belt saw and told him to get busy dressing his elk. I walked back to the pickup and woke Shawn up again and told him to go help his brother with the elk while I took a nap. As it turned out we didn't even have a packboard along. But it was easy enough for them to just drag the elk quarters through the snow.

We were home by early afternoon, and had the elk hanging in the cooler. Whatever you do on a hunt, if you get a shot be responsible and go check it out whether it was across a draw or across the canyon. I'm sure glad that we did. It would be unprofessional to do other wise. There are not enough elk alive to waste any because of haste or bad reasoning. Well, good luck with your hunting endeavors and make sure that gun hits where you point it.

Chapter Fifty

NO BUCK No. TWO

1993 was another year when I had been off work for about one year, and I got a job as and equipment operator on the Crouse Creek Mine construction. This mine was located on the Yankee Fork of the Salmon River in Custer County, Idaho.

Opening day of deer season in Unit 36B on the west side of the Salmon River found my wife, Karen, and I hunting up Birch Creek behind Blue Mountain southwest of Challis, Idaho. Just as the sky started to lighten up we spotted two buck deer sparring on a ridge-top, silhouetted against the brightening sky. The deer were a good 500 yards away so we drove up onto a saddle before I attempted a stalk. I climbed up the backside of the ridge the deer were on, and when I peeked over the ridge-top I was only fifty feet from the deer. They were two typical four point mule deer bucks that were almost identical in size. Even though the deer never had a clue anyone was about, I decided not to shoot one as they had pretty small and slender racks. They would have maybe gone twenty-four inches wide, but were not what I wanted to harvest.

Four days later we were down on the Salmon River about ten miles southwest of the city of Salmon, Idaho, when we saw a herd of elk in an alfalfa field. There were four branch-antlered bulls in the herd, two 5X5 bulls, a small 4X5 bull, and a really nice 6X6 bull with thirty-odd cows and calves. The season wasn't open for six more days so all we could do was write this herd in our hunting log book. Later the same day we saw a very large black bear on Lost Trail Pass north of Salmon. I had a bear tag and my .308 Norma Magnum to harvest the bear with, but we didn't want a bear so we just watched until he fed into the trees and out of sight.

We went out again on the 16th of October in the Bayhorse area, and we saw four 4X4 mule deer bucks, but for what ever reason we didn't harvest any of them.

On the 19th, of October I was hunting in the Bayhorse area again when I saw a herd of thirteen bighorn sheep, all of them rams and some of them were well over full curl.

On November 24th., we were returning from Wallace, Idaho, after the Thanksgiving holiday, and about four miles north of Salmon, Idaho, we saw a big 5X5 whitetail buck in a field along the highway. The season was closed so we were out of luck on that nice buck!

Some seasons you harvest the buck you want and some seasons nothing comes together just right so you don't harvest anything. It is all just part of why they call it hunting and not about killing animals. When you have matured enough that you don't have to harvest an animal to have a successful hunt, that is when you can call yourself a "HUNTER".

Deer trophies from previous hunts.

Chapter Fifty-one

SALMON RIVER COW ELK HUNT

The fall of 1994 found me working a new job as an equipment operator at the Grouse Creek Mine on Jordan Creek, a tributary of the Yankee Fork of the Salmon River. I was living at Challis, Idaho.

My Salmon River elk hunt actually started in August after I had called "Tag Draw" to find out that I had been successful in drawing a cow elk permit for unit 36B. This cow elk permit opened on November 10th and went through until December 8th, 1994. I had lots of time to gather information on the best areas to hunt. However, as I started my research, I suddenly became aware of the fact that I was an outsider. This was a whole different experience than I was accustomed to, and not a pleasant one.

This was the type of information that the local folks were able to supply me with. When would be the best time to start my hunt? Well, whenever the season for cow elk is open. Where should I start my hunt? Well, maybe in the mountains within unit 36B. Were there any areas that they could recommend? Yes, the area west of the Salmon River in unit 36B. With this good information I really hadn't come up with a best plan, so would just make and educated guess and start from that. The first four days of the season I was unable to get away from work so it was the 12th before I started my hunt.

The weather had turned out perfect. We had several snowstorms pass through, leaving and accumulation of about eight inches in the foothills and several feet on the mountain tops. I figured the elk would start their migration to the winter range with their habit of following the snow-line down the mountains. Usually they will move back up above the snow-line in between storms.

My first hunt was in the Pine Summit-Jeff's Flat area. This area is just a series of benches stacked one above the other from the creek bottom to the top of the mountains. It was a cold clear day developing as I followed Garden Creek road to my hunt area. There were herds of deer feeding all along the steep hillsides above the creek. I encountered lots of deer hunters with late season buck permits, but no elk hunters. Finally, I got on the Mill Creek road and turned off on the Pine Summit road and climbed up into a system of benches running northeast-southwest about one mile above Mill Creek. This road was snow covered with some deep drifts but was no problem for my 1989 4X4 Chevy pickup. I had two sets of tire chains behind the truck seat if they should be needed. This area was just crisscrossed with elk trails. However, I was unable to spot any of the animals that had made them. The sign looked to be about two days old so that explained the lack of game sighting. I spent the whole day going from one observation point to another without seeing one elk.

The next morning I stopped at the local café for an early breakfast. Again that outsider feeling surfaced as everyone just glanced over their shoulder at me like I was a stray dog that had sneaked in to steal their breakfast. I didn't enjoy the breakfast or the cold shoulder treatment so I didn't have that second cup of coffee. I have always been a magnanimous old country boy so I was beginning to develop an attitude from all this outcast treatment.

I had decided to move my hunt to the north about ten miles to the Morgan Creek drainage. A beautiful star-studded night promised another nice day as I motored up the West-Fork of Morgan Creek road. I had decided to try hunting a little higher up the mountain that morning. The higher I got the fresher the sign became so I turned off onto the Little West Fork road and kept climbing higher. When I got to the end of this road I turned around and started carefully glassing the country with my binoculars as I moved from one vantage point to another. About 8:30 a.m. I came upon a pickup parked in a turnout with a lady resting a rifle across the hood. I drove on down the road out of sight and pulled over to see if I could spot what she was looking at. Right away I spotted a cow elk coming around the hillside with two calves following her. Bang, Bang, and bang again, the lady got off three hurried shots but she didn't even get the elks' attention. Finally, there was one more shot that must have been closer because the elk trotted off around the hill, out of sight. I didn't figure that the elk were in much danger as the lady must have been shooting a good 400 to 500 yards, and with a small caliber rifle, too.

I drove all the way back out to the main West-Fork road without sighting any other animals so I proceeded on up into Blowfly Creek. Now I really encountered some fresh sign where a herd of elk had been grazing along the road in the willows along the stream. It was so fresh I could smell the elk inside the truck cab with the windows up. I parked in the first wide spot where I could get my truck off the road. Then I hurriedly grabbed my rifle, inserted two cartridges into the magazine, and put on my pack and took off up the trail of the elk herd. With the cold temperatures and the wind still as death, my scent was of no concern as I followed the elk up along a hillside game trail. I was only about 100 yards up this trail when I noticed movement about 150 yards above me. Then I spotted three cow elk and a calf standing on a little bulge in the mountainside. All that I could see of the largest cow elk was her rump, and about eight inches of her neck as she looked back at me over her rump.

She had me spotted! So, very slowly and carefully, I inched up beside a big red fir tree for a solid rest for my rifle. This would be a difficult shot. However, I felt confident that I could make it. When the crosshair in my scope came to rest at the juncture of her head and neck I touched the trigger real gentle-like. Boom, that big 308 Norma Magnum went off shattering the morning quietness. The cow elk dropped and came cascading down the mountain in a cloud of snow and other forest debris as she went past me and slid out onto the road right in front of a pickup truck coming along the road. When I arrived on the scene a cow dog was biting my elk in the butt trying to get her up. I laughed out loud as the owner called the dog off and put it in his truck.

I asked this fellow and another fellow that had driven up if they would help me load my elk into my pickup box. They didn't answer; they just stood there with disgusted looks on their faces, so I walked up and got my truck and backed up to the elk. To my surprise they helped me slide the elk up a plank into the truck box. I thanked them and then pulled off the road so they could continue their hunts. As they drove by I recognized the lady that was shooting that morning. Now I understood why they were so disgusted.

While dressing out my elk my hands about froze off. Every few minutes I was taking breaks to warm my hands. Man, it was colder than the proverbial BRASS MONKEY! The dressing job took me all of two hours but I got good results and arrived at the locker plant with a nice, clean piece of meat. After aging for two weeks the butcher cut and wrapped the meat for me. I was all set for a winter of prime eating off this cow elk. This had to be about the easiest elk I ever harvested. Maybe too easy! Whatever, just do the best you can and good luck too

179

you. Maybe we will meet on the mountain someday. Just keep your eyes open for an old Salmon River savage.

Fred fishing rattlesnake-infested Morgan Creek.

Chapter Fifty-two

BRAD'S BUCK

Fall of 1994. My brother, Don, and his grandson, Brad, were very lucky in the tag drawings. Brad received an antelope tag for a buck, as well as a buck deer tag for the late deer season in unit 36B on the west side of the Salmon River. Don was lucky enough to draw a late season tag for cow elk in unit 36B, and Brad, participating in his first ever tag drawing, also drew out for cow elk also during the late season.

About mid-September Don and Brad showed up at my home in Challis, Idaho, wanting me to help them find an antelope for Brad. The first morning we took the Goose Creek road up over the divide between Morgan Creek and Deer Creek. Don and Brad had scouted the evening before in Deer Creek and had spotted a herd of antelope that had a nice buck in it. We glassed with our binoculars for about one hour before we finally located the herd in a branch canyon off of Deer Creek. We determined that the antelope were in a canyon that had a dead-end road coming up from the river. I let Don and Brad out to make a stalk on the herd while I drove around to come up from the river on the dead end road and pick them up.

I arrived at the end of the road and could see that Don and Brad would have about a one and a half mile hike to access the road after they had gotten to where the antelope herd was located. I had come off of the night shift at the Grouse Creek Mine, so it wasn't long and I decided to take a nap in the seat of my pickup while I waited for my hunters.

Don and Brad had made their stalk but found the antelope unapproachable beyond about 400 yards. Brad had tried a shot but missed by feet. As they continued on down the canyon towards the pickup they watched a herd of elk come out of and alfalfa field and go into a canyon on the west side of Deer Creek. They also watched a herd of antelope follow the elk into the same canyon. When they arrived back at the pickup we took a drive up the canyon the antelope and elk had went into but weren't successful in finding them.

On our drive back up Deer Creek we saw a small herd of bighorn sheep consisting of several ewes and lambs. Just before we topped out on the divide a lone antelope buck squirted across the road and down into a blind canyon full of trees and mahogany brush. We continued down into Morgan Creek and went back up over the Darling Creek divide. In the bottom of Darling Creek we saw another herd of bighorn sheep. That bachelor group consisted of five rams, and several of them had full curl or better horns.

On Sunday morning we were parked at the alfalfa field that the elk and antelope had come out of the day before daybreak. However, on this morning the field was empty so we drove off up into the blind canyon the antelope had gone into the day before. When we got up to the end of the road we hiked off into a side canyon, going straight west hoping to find the antelope there. We drew a blank on the hunt, but we did find a spring high on the mountain on our way down and were lucky enough to jump a flock of chukar partridge out of the sagebrush surrounding the spring. Don and I had our shotguns so were able to get four chukars out of this flock.

We had just started down the mountain in the pickup when we approached a saddle and I saw an antelope buck look over the ridge-top and then disappear. Don and Brad exited the pickup and I drove off. When they looked over the ridge-top the antelope were in a little bowl on the back side of the ridge. The antelope saw Don and Brad when they came over the ridge-top and took off around the mountain about 150 yards away. Brad was able to get a shot off but was in an awkward position, so he missed yet again.

I had heard Brad shoot and then saw the antelope cross the road lower down the mountain, so I went back and picked them up and drove down to the saddle where I had seen the antelope cross the road. When we stopped, there was the buck antelope about 150 yards away watching us? Brad, after missing two shots already, was frustrated and didn't think he could hit the buck even though he was within good range. I told Brad I know that you can't hit the antelope if you don't try, so he fell out of the pickup and was fumbling around with his gun before he got into position to shoot. By that time the buck was vacating the scene at a fast trot and Brad missed again. In hindsight, I think Brad being new to the hunting scene wasn't familiar with all of the decisions that hunters just automatically make from past experience.

When we passed the alfalfa field on our way back to the highway, a nice mule deer buck trotted across the road and then stopped on the side of a draw to look back at us. I ask Brad to get into position for a shot

182

and look through his scope just to get familiar with his gun; because we all have to learn the steps it takes to be successful hunting by repetition. That would be the only opportunities that Brad had to hunt antelope.

However, come November they were back to try to harvest a buck deer and fill their cow elk tags. The guys arrived back in Challis the day before Thanksgiving, and I would be off work for the holiday as well as the remainder of the week. Thanksgiving morning we were out of town early and went up Garden Creek and over Big Hill. Our first game sighted was a herd of mule deer does and fawns. These deer didn't seem to excite Brad much even though Don and I were trying to impress on him to always be watching for game and to be alert and ready if and opportunity was presented. We went on up Mill Creek and then up to Pine Summit. We were driving along below Corkscrew Mountain when we spotted a herd of elk crossing the face of the mountain. Don and Brad made a stalk on the last timber patch that the elk had entered. They were unsuccessful again, only getting some good exercise for their effort, which is a big part of hunting.

As we came around the end of the mountain and before dropping down onto Jeff's Flat we spotted a real nice 6X6 bull elk bedded on the mountain. We drove up through a bowl below the bull elk and then Don and Brad made a stalk up the backside of the ridge, but the lone bull was the only elk on the mountain.

When we got down to Challis Creek we drove up to Pats Creek and started up to glass the Eddy Basin country. We weren't far up Pats Creek when a forked-horn mule deer buck stepped across the old two track trail we were following. I stopped and Brad stepped out and walked up the road and stopped, then threw his gun up and fired a shot. He ran back to the pickup and asked Don and me if he had hit the buck. After explaining to him that we couldn't see the deer when he shot, Don went back up the road with him and found the deer laying in a gully just off the road. Don dressed the deer out and we returned to Challis.

The church ladies were putting on a big Thanksgiving Dinner just across from the house so we let Don buy us dinner. Those ladies had really done this dinner up big, and all of the homemade pies, cakes, and cookies were just a bonus.

Early Friday morning we drove up Morgan Creek to the end of the road on the Little West Fork of Morgan Creek. We hiked out the trail towards the wilderness boundary, looking down into the Eddy Creek Basin and the headwaters of the Little West Fork of Morgan Creek. Late in the year like this the elk and deer migrate down out of the wilderness to winter along Morgan Creek. We spent most of the day hiking from one lookout point to another without seeing an animal. We arrived back at my pickup about one hour before dark and started down off the hill. The first time we stopped to glass we spotted a lone cow elk across the canyon from us. I estimated the range at 350 yards and Don got prone, lying in the road and shot with his .270 Winchester with 150 grain Nosler bullets going about 3,000 feet per second. I would later shoot this distance with a laser rangefinder at 420 yards. At the shot the cow elk stumbled sideways and started flopping down the mountainside. Don took off down the sidehill and Brad and I drove down to where the road crossed the creek. When we found Don he was gutting out the big cow that he had to shoot again to put her down.

There was a big bloody spot on her hip, so I started teasing Don about his bad marksmanship. However later when we skinned the elk we found that the bullet had glanced off of the big flat bone in the front shoulder and traveled down her side and came out at the hip. The elk had been standing at a quartering angle towards us so that must have caused the bullet to ricochet off the shoulder. It was black dark before we got back to the truck.

Early Saturday morning just before we approached the Little West Fork road we spotted a herd of elk in a bowl back towards the main Morgan Creek drainage. We got Brad into a good steady position next to a big sagebrush and had him pick out an animal that was away from the others so we could watch with our binoculars to see if he scored any hits.

Brad was able to shoot three shots before the elk moved up over the ridge-top. Neither Don nor I could determine where he was hitting with our binoculars so couldn't give him any advice. We drove on up into Blow Fly Creek and spotted yet another herd of elk and Brad shot twice without hitting any animals. Finally we were back to the spot where Don had shot his elk and there were two cow elk and one calf in the same opening. Brad wanted to shoot at these elk but they were about 150 yards further away than the ones he had missed so we wouldn't let him shoot.

When we got down on the creek where we would access Don's elk from I happened to look up the mountain and see a small cow elk walk out of the trees and look down at us and then go back into the trees. I told Don to go ahead up to his elk and start getting it ready to pack, and

184

I would take Brad up around the mountain on a closed road that came in behind the tree patch we had seen the cow elk go into. Brad and I weren't far up the road when I asked him to take the lead incase we jumped an elk. I could see that he wasn't very much into this deal so I asked him if he wanted to continue or not. His answer was that he didn't think he wanted to work that hard for an elk, so I said let's go back and help Don then.

Brad was about 100 yards ahead of me when we came out on the main road and when I looked up at the timber patch on the ridge-top there was that same cow elk looking down at us again. Brad got into the pickup to take a nap so I went on up to Don's elk. When I told Don about the elk still on the ridge above us he said go get my rifle out of the truck and go kill one of them, and Brad can tag it. I said I don't think that is necessary as we would have all we wanted getting his elk out to the truck.

We would wrap the quarters in plastic tarps and drag them along the cattle trails down the creek to the truck. Don said when he arrived at his elk there had been a large buck mule deer on the hillside watching him all morning.

Sunday morning early Don and Brad loaded up their deer and elk and went back to Pinehurst, Idaho, where Don lives.

Chapter Fifty-three

PERSEVERANCE PAYS

By Brook Stansil, Author

It was the 12th day of elk hunting season here in North Idaho and still no sightings. Actually, it is my 12th day of my 12th elk hunting season. Some days I've even been out both in the morning and again in the afternoon. Since I'm the youngest in an avid hunting family everyone is trying to help me locate an elk. I didn't even care if it was a cow. Horns don't seem so important considering all the time we've invested in finding my first elk. But cow season was only five days long and now it's back to bulls only, and boy can those big guys hide!

Today I'm hunting with my husband of seven months and my dad, who not only taught me to hunt but also instilled in me a love of the outdoors. We have beat the brush and come back to the pickup, probably to call it a day – Dad has some work to do and we have a birthday party to attend this afternoon. Dad said he'd like to drive out this road and see what the area looks like. So now we're sitting in the pickup on this ridge looking across the valley to a clearing. Nothing to see but since we're up high I decided to call Mom on the cell phone and tell her we'll be heading home soon. And then it happened. The elk started walking out of the woods on the other side, one by one. They're so far away that they look like ants walking on a log. Dad is looking through his binoculars and is counting, four, five, six – no horns but a bull's got to be around somewhere. What do you want to do Brook? I said, "Go for it!" About that time a bull came out. Horns!!

We jumped out of dad's Chevy pickup and grabbed our guns. Down the hill we went, running, slipping and trying not to make too much noise. Across the creek, now we head up a finger ridge parallel to the side the elk are on. As we head up the ridge we are careful to stay on the opposite side of it so the elk won't be able to see or hear us coming. We take our time so that we won't be winded by the time we round the top of the ridge. Finally, we crest the top and we are still low on the finger ridge so we look up higher on the other side where we thought the elk would be. But, to our surprise the elk were not in sight. Just as we thought the elk had outsmarted us, my husband says, "A bull" and pointed straight across from us about 250 yards away. I hurried and sat down to get a good shot but the angle was wrong so I stood up, moved over a bit, and sat back down.

I must hurry now before the elk gets away. I put the crosshairs on the front shoulder and squeezed the trigger of my Winchester Model 70 Featherweight .280cal. The bull jumps and spins all in one motion and is heading the opposite way but he doesn't run. That gives me enough time to chamber another round. Boom, I shoot again. This time the bull lunges forward and goes out of my sight. My husband yells, "He went down but he's still moving down towards the creek." I hurried, went over to my husband and he points to where the bull is. I had a full-length target at his spine, but he is in a lot of brush and is moving all around. In an instant I shot and the bull went out of sight again, but we could hear him thrashing around. My dad decided to go track him down, while my husband and I continue to watch the hillside in case he tries to make his way up it. Finally, my dad finds the animal and the elk has managed to pin himself under a windfall. My dad is approximately twenty feet away from him and he lets out two full bugles. My dad yells for me to come over and finish him off. I hate to see any animal suffer and normally I would have told my dad to kill him, but this is my first elk and I have put in many long days and miles for this moment. I hurried over and fired the killing shot. We sit and admire the beautiful rack on this enormous animal.

It's around 10:30a.m. and we have a lot of work ahead of us. My husband starts to dress out and quarter the elk while my dad goes back for the pickup. Approximately, three hours later my dad finally arrives. I'm so cold that I'm shivering from being in the cold draw with my damp clothes on. We hang the quarters in the trees; they couldn't be in a better place to cool out. It's about one mile back to the pickup so we leave the quarters in the trees and decide to come back for them the next day. When we got home, my dad called a friend who has some pack mules and ask him if he would be willing to help us pack out the meat next day.

Once we arrive back in town the following morning with the meat and antlers we stopped at the Blue Goose Sporting Goods Store, one of our local sports shops. While we were there we realized just how big the set of antlers actually were. Our local newspaper later interviewed me.

Perseverance is an important quality of all hunters. After twelve years, a successful hunt. Next year will be harder, though. Now that I've tasted the thrill of a kill, enjoyed the fruits of a successful hunt, rewarded with record antlers, recorded for posterity and basked in the limelight. How can I possibly top this??!!

Besides, Dad says, "Next time we won't be waiting for Brook to get the perfect shot."

Brook and her husband with her big bull. I really liked her story of taking this bull, so asked to include it in my book.

Chapter Fifty-four

BIG WINDY

Fall 1998. Every elk hunt has a beginning and an end. However, on this elk hunt they would prove to be a long ways apart. In December of 1997 I purchased a nonresident Idaho hunting license for deer and elk at a cost of $651 U.S. dollars. I also filed applications for a muzzleloader deer tag and a rifle controlled hunt for bull elk, in Unit 51 on the Little Lost River. I was successful drawing a tag for both hunts. The bull elk hunt opened on November 3rd and ran through December 8th and the deer muzzleloader hunt opened on November 26th and closed on December 9th.

On November 12th, I took my wife, Karen, to Reno, Nevada, to catch a plane for Missoula, Montana, where she would visit her niece, Julie. On November 13th, I left solo for Arco, Idaho, where I had a motel room reserved for my elk hunting headquarters. Several of my friends had shown an interest in this elk hunt, but they never did anything about it so I was solo. I drove hard and steady and arrived in Arco by lunch time.

Now you must remember that I had never hunted this part of Idaho. However, the best local information that I could gather said I should conduct my hunt in the Sawmill Canyon drainage on the north end of the Little Lost River valley. So after I had eaten my lunch I took off for Sawmill Canyon to scout for elk. I drove eighty-one miles from Arco to Timber Creek, a tributary of Sawmill Canyon.

By black dark I had seen one covey of "Hungarian partridge" and one small mule deer doe. There had been lots of elk and deer tracks showing in about six inches of old snow along the road in Sawmill Canyon. However, this area was quite heavily cut up with roads, so I decided I would try something different the next day.

On November 14th, I left Arco at 3:30 a.m. and drove thirty-three and seven-tenths miles to Pass Creek Summit, arriving up there at 4:40 a.m. I would only have to wait until 6:00 a.m. for daybreak. After a bright morning sun under azure blue skies lit up the valley, I started glassing all of the country that I could see from this open pass area. I moved to the north along the Wet Creek valley glassing from different observation spots as they came along. I never spotted any animals, but there were fresh elk tracks everywhere. This area is on the southeast end of the Lost River Range of mountains, which is home to Idaho's highest peak, Mount Borah, elevation 12,662 feet. To compare, Arco is at only 5,318 feet elevation. On the other side of the Wet Creek valley is the Hawley Mountain Range, both south and north ranges. Hawley Mountain, in the north Hawley Mountain Range, is 9,752 feet elevation.

This country is big open sagebrush canyons with timber from about 7,000 feet elevation up to timberline at 8,500 feet elevation, and then bare rocky ridges along the mountain tops. The south facing slopes have mahogany trees, instead of the evergreen trees found on the north and east facing slopes.

As I proceeded down Wet Creek I jumped a covey of, "Hungarian partridge" and that was the only game sighted. When I intersected the Dry Creek road I drove along Dry Creek to the top of Taylor Mountain, elevation 7,525 feet. This drive produced lots of tracks, but the only animal I saw was a coyote on Dry Creek at 10:00 a.m. I drove back out to Wet Creek, and then drove up Wet Creek to the turn-off for Deer Creek Pass. At 10:40 a.m. I spotted five cow elk bedded in an opening in the timber on the northwest end of the South Hawley Mountain Range. All of the country that I had under observation is just spider-webbed with elk trails, from timber patch to wind-blown ridges where the elk were feeding. Although I had seen no deer, there were lots of cattle still on the BLM grazing allotments, which was unusual for this time of year. By 1:00 p.m., I had driven around into the North Fork of Deer Creek, and was watching a cow and calf elk bedded in the mahogany trees. As I drove out of Deer Creek to the Little Lost River road I jumped a flock of seven sage grouse and another coyote.

I drove back around the north end of the North Hawley Mountain Range into Wet Creek again. As I drove up the creek I jumped the "Huns" again that I had seen earlier that morning. When I got up to where I could watch both sides of the Deer Creek Pass area, I pulled off the road to watch the open slopes for my bull elk to come out to feed. At 3:40 p.m., I spotted a herd of elk coming out of the trees on Hawley Mountain. The elk were coming down an east-west ridge that was just open grass and sagebrush. Through my 20-40 power Bushnell spotting scope I counted twenty-nine cow elk and one spike bull elk in this herd. I watched the elk until black dark without spotting any other animals.

On November 15th, I left Arco under a star-studded sky promising another one of those cold, crisp, sunny days so prevalent in mid-November. At 4:30 a.m., I turned off onto the Wet Creek cutoff road and at 6:10 a.m., just as I started up Wet Creek, I saw a herd of twenty antelope run across the road ahead of my 1989 Chevy 4X4 pickup. I turned off onto the jeep trail going into Hawley Canyon, which would take me up to the northeast side of the ridge where I had seen the elk the previous evening. It was 7:00 a.m., when I spotted the same herd of elk that I had seen the day before. As I glassed the elk I discovered that now there were two spike bull elk in the herd. At 7:10 a.m., I spotted a coyote up by the elk herd, and then at 7:21 a.m. I spotted five deer off to my left on the north ridge. All of the deer were mule deer does. By 8:30 a.m., the sun started shining on the ridge where the elk herd was, so I put my spotting scope on the window clamp and then turned the forty power eyepiece up so I could look over this bunch of elk. Now I could determine that there were two forked-horn bull elk and one spike bull elk in the herd. I was not interested in any of these bull elk, so I drove back out and up Wet Creek to my lookout from last evening. It was 9:10 a.m., and, when I started glassing, right away I spotted two branch-antlered bull elk coming out of a side canyon below the other herd of elk. My spotting scope revealed that there was a small 5X5 bull and another bull that was a 290-300 B&C 6X6 bull elk. At 9:30 a.m. I spotted a lone cow elk over on the north end of the South Hawley Mountain range. The elk herd on the west ridge coming down off of Hawley Mountain had bedded down right out on an open saddle, and the two branch antlered bulls had joined this herd. These elk were in a pretty safe place; they could see for miles in all directions. This herd of elk now consisted of thirty-one cows, one spike bull, and two forked-horn bulls, plus the two branch-antlered bulls.

By 11:00 a.m., I haven't spotted anything closer than the herd bedded on the open ridge, so I have decided that the 6X6 was the elk I was going to try and harvest. I knew that I would have to be smarter than an elk, so I planned out my stalk on the herd. A finger ridge about one mile west of the elk would give me access to the ridge that they were bedded on, and I would be out of their view so the sharp-eyed buggers shouldn't be able to spot me. Once on the main ridge I would still be one and a half miles from the elk herd, but with the wind out of the southwest I should be able to approach within rifle range before I would have to expose myself to the elk. At 3:00 p.m., I was just intersecting the

191

main ridge when big black storm clouds began to stack up against the mountains, and the wind started blowing at gale force, about fifty miles per hour. With that strong a wind, it wouldn't be long before the storm was upon me. The two inches of snow that I started out in had increased to two-foot-deep drifts along the main ridge and for the past one-half hour I had spent more time chasing my hat than I had stalking elk, so I was just a whisker away from aborting the stalk.

But I knew that if you are going to hunt elk you just have to get tough, and get after them. I finally rustled some flagging ribbon from my pack to tie my felt cruiser hat on my head and then I put on my heavy Carhart jacket, so that, maybe, I could get back to the business of stalking elk. The snow was both deep and crusted, so I had to lift my knees up under my chin to take a step forward, and then that damned wind would gust and about blow me over. By 4:30 p.m. I had the elk in sight but they were still out of good rifle range. I was just exhausted; it seemed at the time like over the years I had just worked my butt off only to encounter difficult situations. And now my blue jeans were soaked to my crotch, and my pants wanted to fall off. My long underwear was bunched up in my crotch, so that wasn't helping either. You would think I would have had sense enough to wear my wool pants and suspenders, but that is what happens when you get all excited about getting your elk.

Then the elk herd spotted me but they didn't seem to be alarmed, so now I was crawling around like a critter hoping that my brown coat would fool the elk. At the time I sure hoped there were no other hunters around. I needed to get closer yet, so I just pushed my pack along in front of me so I would have it handy for use as a rifle rest when I got into range. Finally, I was only 200 yards from the elk herd, but I still hadn't spotted the 6X6 bull elk.

I started crawling around again, counting elk to make sure that I was seeing all of them and then a big cow elk got to her feet and started coming towards me. I laid my face down on my pack and prayed that she wouldn't come up to me and spook the herd. After several suspense-filled minutes, I looked up to find that the cow elk had bedded back down. I had accounted for all of the elk except the 6X6 bull, so I decided that he must have left while I was laboring up the mountain. So now I decided to take the 5X5 bull instead. He was lying behind a big cow, looking right at me, so I would have to shoot him in the head. Impossible you say. No, now you just watch how an old marksman does it. I steadied

192

my rifle over my pack from the prone position, and BOOM, I missed. All of the elk jumped up and ran down off the saddle. I rolled up into a sitting position, and then spotted the 5X5 bull right below me about the same distance as before. The bull was still behind a cow (probably his mother) but this time his neck was exposed. When my .308 Norma Magnum went off, I had killed my bull elk. I don't know how to explain how I determine where to aim on an animal I want to harvest. I guess you could say that I shoot instinctively; by that I mean I don't consciously think about where to aim. I just let that computer in my head figure it out and it is seldom wrong. How else would you make that decision, in the split millisecond that you have to make it in sometimes?

Now that the elk was down, and dead, the fun began. Upon my arrival at my bull I experienced some terrible cramps up the front of my thighs. I had to sit down on the elk and massage the cramps away. I had only experienced cramps like this before from hiking on snowshoes in deep fluffy snow where you have to raise your legs high to clear the surface of the snow. Anyway, I went to work on my elk until the cramps once again tied my thigh muscles into knots and I fell over onto the elk and, again, massaged my legs until the cramps went away. I finally managed to get the insides out of the elk, and decided that would have to do for that day as I still had to get back to my truck, two long miles straight down the mountain. It is 5:30 p.m. when I stumbled off down a hogback ridge that I hoped will take me to my truck. Every time that I encountered a swale full of snow, or sagebrush, I was back to massaging the cramps out of my legs. I was beginning to wonder if I would have the endurance to make it to my truck. Every time I had to get up off the ground it took all the strength I could muster. And then I'd catch my foot on something under the snow and down I'd go, face first onto the frozen ground. Man oh man, did that ever feel good. My rifle hit the ground with the scope down, but nothing broke.

At 6:30 p.m., it was pitch black dark, and I was exhausted when I finally stumbled up to my truck. I groped around in the dark trying to find my truck keys that I had stashed under the fender. I found them and unlocked the truck door, got into the truck and got the motor running and the heater turned on. However, every time I tried to let in the clutch I would get leg cramps again, but I finally got going down the road. It was 9:00 p.m. when I arrived at my motel I was completely exhausted, but relieved to be done for the day. I never even had any supper, just a couple of stiff shots of whiskey and then I started calling looking for a packer to pack my elk out. I hit pay dirt on the first call to a friend in Challis, Idaho. My friend Will would help me get the elk out in the morning.

As I reflected back on that day, I had a revelation that right after I killed my elk the wind calmed down and the clouds dissipated, and then the temperature kept rising until it was almost comfortable. I just wonder if that old boy up yonder figured that I had had just about had all I could handle for one day. I sure like to think so.

On November 16th, after a fitful night of little sleep and lots of leg cramps, I made it out of bed and up to Pickle's Café where Will was waiting for me. We had breakfast and then took off up the Little Lost River at 5:30 a.m. and saw a herd of antelope standing along the road, Will counted fifteen head total. As we continued up the river, it seemed like every field we passed had one to five yodel dogs (coyotes) hunting mice in them. We must have seen twenty-five or thirty total. At 7:30 a.m. we arrived at the end of an old jeep trail on the side of Hawley Mountain. I set my spotting scope on the window clamp to show Will my elk, which was just a speck on the ridge-top two miles away as the crow flies. Just before dismantling the scope, I looked off to the east and spotted a herd of elk coming around the mountain. This herd of elk consisted of twenty-eight cows and calves, but no bulls.

By 8:00 a.m. we were started up the mountain to retrieve my elk. On my arrival at the elk, Will had already cut off the bull's legs at the knee joints and tied the rear hocks together so that I could come along behind keeping the elk straight by holding it back so it wouldn't run over Will on the steep slope. At 3:30 p.m. we had the elk down into a steep notch in the mouth of the canyon. This brought everything to an abrupt halt because we couldn't get around a steep bluff dropping off into the canyon bottom. After studying this situation, we decided that if we could get the pickup down the steep sagebrush slope above the canyon, we could pull the elk up to the ridge top where the pickup was parked. We hiked up to the truck and chained all four wheels before we attempted to maneuver the truck down that snow-covered slope. We finally got down within 400 feet of the elk and then we spliced together all the rope we had and, miraculously, it was enough to reach the elk. Will tied the rope to the bull's antlers and then he guided it around obstacles as I cautiously backed the truck up the hillside. We finally arrived at the jeep trail and gave a big sigh of relief.

Poor Will was all in, just like I had been the day before, but it was understandable because he had done ninety-nine percent of the work. I was so stove up from the hard day the previous day that about all I could do was stumble around and get in the way.

As Will and I drove back to Arco, we discussed the bull elk that I had harvested. We decided that the bull elk was probably only eighteen months old because the ivory teeth were pure white, with no eye at all, and his coat had those long reddish brown guard hairs like those on a calf elk. I estimated the weight at 400 pounds or less. The carcass later yielded 253 pounds of cut and wrapped meat. This little bull elk was probably a Boone & Crockett candidate had he lived to maturity.

Finally, at 6:30 p.m. we arrived back at my motel room. We were both soaked to the skin and exhausted to where we didn't even want any supper. I tried to pay Will for his services, but he wouldn't accept any money. I will get even some how, some day in the future, and you can bet a buck or two on that. After Will left I just fell into bed, too pooped to party.

After a restful night's sleep, I was up early and headed for my home in Winnemucca, Nevada. On my arrival at home I had a phone message on the answering machine from my son, Jeff. He informed me that there was an airline ticket waiting in Reno, Nevada, and I was to come to Phoenix, Arizona. I hurried my elk up to the locker plant for processing, and then packed my bag for Phoenix. My wife, Karen, was already there, so we would spend the next two weeks spoiling our grandson. I hadn't seen enough deer sign that I wanted to go back for the deer hunt, and besides, I was still tired from my elk hunt. In fact I told my grandson Tyler that I was going to let him be the family elk hunter. "No grandpa," he said, "Give the gun to grandma!"

Well there you have it. I chalk it up mostly to luck. Getting so tired and lonesome kind of bummed me on the whole trip. If I go again, I hope to have some companions along. Well, so long and good luck.

Chapter Fifty-five

BIG FREEZE

Fall 2000. On November 30, 2000, I left Winnemucca, Nevada, to take my wife, Karen, to Elko, Nevada, to catch an airline flight to Arizona. She would spend the next ten days spoiling our grandchildren, our son, and his wife. After dropping Karen off I headed on up the highway to Arco, Idaho, where I will meet my brother-in-law, Randy, and his son, Gene, for an elk hunt. Randy and Gene would be the hunters as they had cow elk tags for Unit 51 on the Little Lost River in Butte County, Idaho. I would just try to help them as I didn't draw a tag.

I arrived in Arco after dark, so I stopped and had supper. Then I was off up the Little Lost River road to Wet Creek. I found a pull-out at Squaw Springs, parked my Chevy Suburban and rolled out my sleeping bag and went to sleep.

11-04-00. After a cold night and a cold breakfast I was off to do some scouting for elk. At first light I was parked in the jeep trail in the mouth of Hawley Canyon. Between 7:00-7:30 a.m. I spotted some animals skylighted against a bright morning sky. My 20-40 power Bushnell spotting scope revealed a small herd of antelope. Further glassing reveled a coyote hunting up a hog-back ridge. As I scanned the head of the basin on the northwest side of Hawley Mountain, I spotted three bull elk feeding across the basin. Two of the bull elk were 5X5's and the other one was about a 310 B&C 6X6 bull elk. I watched these bulls until they went into the trees on a ridge running straight north. That was all the game I could find at this location, so I went back out to Wet Creek and started upstream towards Pass Creek Pass. There were lots of elk camps up along Wet Creek; most of the camps had horses, 4-wheelers, or both.

The cow elk season had opened the previous Wednesday and now it was Saturday, so we had missed opening day. There was a big round harvest moon lighting up the nights, so with the bright nights and snow above 7,000 feet elevation, and lots of hunters out, it appeared all the elk were on top of the mountains. Now let me tell you it is a long hike to the top of the mountains in the Lost River Range. There are lots of peaks over 10,000 feet elevation; the highest peak is Mt. Borah at 12,662 feet in elevation. I glassed the whole Wet Creek drainage top to bottom and both sides of the valley without spotting another animal.

I was supposed to meet Randy and Gene in Arco at Pickle's Café at 12:00 noon. When I arrived in town I still had time to have a couple of cold beers at the tavern before I had to meet the guys. We met at noon and had a hearty lunch, and then headed up the Little Lost River to Wet Creek where we would camp. We got Gene's camp trailer set up at the confluence of Chicken Creek, and Squaw Springs. After camp was established we were off for an afternoon hunt.

We drove up Wet Creek to the Deer Creek Pass road turnoff, and then off up to Deer Creek Pass. In our travels we jumped a herd of antelope right in the road on Wet Creek. By 3:30 p.m. we were parked high up under the southeast side of Hawley Mountain glassing the surrounding hills for elk. After an hour of careful glassing I was able to spot three mule deer does bedded in the mahogany brush, away and away across the canyon to the east. Finally, the descending darkness ended our glassing for this day, so we went back to camp.

Our wives had prepared our food and frozen it in bags, so we had a good supper of homemade stew, homemade bread with real butter, and of course, strong black camp coffee to wash it all down. Soon after the dishes were cleaned up, we planned our next day's hunting over drinks before hitting the sack.

11-05-00. We were up bright-eyed and bushy-tailed, ready for another full day of hunting by 4:00 a.m. We cooked up a good breakfast, cleaned up the dishes, and then drank coffee until we could only make it about three minutes between pee calls. We had decided to check out Hawley Canyon again in hopes that there were some cow elk hanging around with the bulls I had seen the day before. We pulled up to the same observation spot I had used on Saturday, set up the spotting scope and my Ziess 15X60 binoculars on window mounts and started picking the landscape apart. Two long hours later we had spotted a total of one doe antelope, and one coyote. We left there and went around to the east side of Hawley Mountain, and then up Deer Creek to where all the little drainages head up behind the Wet Creek Basin. We saw a fresh cougar track along the bottom of one of these small drainages. However, there was very few deer or elk sign. We spent the whole day glassing this area from different observation points without ever seeing another animal.

At black dark we arrived back at our camp site to a very cold, dismal evening. The high for the day had been about eighteen degrees, with a fifty-mile-an-hour wind blowing snow squalls up and around the mountains all day. Those dark, dirty gray clouds hanging down along the ridge-tops made for a very dark dreary day. We sure missed the sun, I can tell you. The camp trailer was always cold even with the propane heater with an electric fan going full blast and four burners on the cook stove burning wide open. Our beer sitting on the floor inside the trailer was freezing!

Had we not been camped at Squaw Springs, we would not have had open water to dip our water. The creeks were frozen over solid. Every minute we were in camp Gene would have to hook the pickup to the trailer to run the lights and heater fan. That relentless cold just zapped all the power out of the storage batteries. What we wouldn't have given for a couple of Coleman lanterns, and a wood stove to keep us warm!

We had another good supper of homemade chili, homemade rolls, and a cold crispy salad. After the domestic chores were done we didn't linger over our after-dinner drinks very long. In minutes we were snuggled into our warm sleeping bags dreaming about beautiful South Sea islands, which were covered with pretty girls with those twitchy hips rotating around and around.

It was a long cold night; the thermometer showed a frosty two degrees above zero when we got up that morning. We had a hearty and filling breakfast, and then we were off up the southwest side of Hawley Mountain to the timberline. We left Gene off to hunt down through the timber in the head of Hawley Canyon. Randy and I would drive around into the mouth of the canyon to go on stand to watch for any animals that Gene might flush out of the timber. However, it was a short hike, and Gene was already at the end of the jeep trail when Randy and I got around there. Gene reported a few old deer tracks, and no elk sign at all. At 7:00 a.m. I decided that Gene and I would go up onto the ridge and hunt down into the area where the bull elk entered the timber two days ago. We had just started out when we spotted four mule deer does on the south ridge. By 8:00 a.m. Gene and I had topped out on the north ridge right where the three bull elk had two days previously. As we descended down the ridge-top we encountered lots of elk sign, both old and fresh. We just continued down the ridge-top being as quiet as possible in the crusty old snow. We had the wind in our face so we had that in our favor. One step at a time isn't a very fast pace, but in a short time we were into some real fresh elk sign where the elk had been feeding that morning. Just as we were about to break over a rocky point, I climbed up onto a rock pile so that I could see down the slope below me better. We were about a third of the way down the mountain at about 7,500 feet elevation, so we were in a perfect place to find game.

It was only 8:30 a.m. and I was scanning the slope that had come into my view from my observation spot on the rock pile. Instantly, I spotted a huge bull elk lying at the base of a large fir tree almost to the bottom of the slope. I motioned for Gene to climb up beside me on the rock pile. He didn't know that I had seen an elk, so I had to speak to him quite sternly to get his attention and make him understand what was going on. The bull elk, being only 125 yards away, heard me talking to Gene. Gene finally got the message and jumped up beside me on the rock pile, and he was able to spot the bull elk just as the bull lunged to his feet and jumped off the mountain. As the bull trotted off we saw another smaller bull elk join him. When the bulls appeared in a small open sagebrush meadow across the small drainage, I squealed like a bull elk and Gene blew on his cow call. Both bulls stopped and looked back over their shoulders at us; they were only 200 yards away. The big 6X6 bull elk was a good 330-340 B&C score bull elk, the best bull I had seen in this area. He had good long main beams, long antler tines, and was real massive all the way to the tip of his antlers. The smaller bull was a 5X1 raghorn bull, which had broken his left antler off right above the brow tine. Just judging from all the sign we had seen, I guessed that the bulls I'd seen on Saturday were still there, also. What a time to have a cow elk tag. We also saw some pretty big deer tracks along this ridge. I'm just guessing, but I think there were some big mule deer bucks hanging back in this timber during the day, and coming out on these bright moonlight nights to breed the does.

When we arrived back at the pickup we decided that we needed to go to Howe, Idaho, for some gas for the pickup. Gas was $2.25 per gallon!! We filled up with gas, and got a twelve-pack of beer that didn't have ice in it, and then we headed off up the river to Sawmill Canyon. The only game we saw on this jaunt was a small cow elk dead in the back of a pickup. Those hunters' luck was surely better than ours.

By 4:00 p.m. we were back on Deer Creek Pass parked in our observation spot from yesterday evening. We had seen lots of tracks in this area, and no hunters, so that was encouraging. Gene had my 15X60 Ziess binoculars and was able to spot six cow elk high up in a pocket on the north end of the South Hawley Mountain Range. We realized that on

199

those dark, overcast days those big binoculars make a real difference. We watched the elk feed until darkness blotted them out. Then it was back to a cold, damp trailer. I don't even recall what we had for supper. I do know that this continuous cold and miserable weather was starting to get to everyone. That day was the worst day of all because it never got above eight degrees, and when you add that blasted wind to the other factors it just about made it unbearable. I think it was only about zero inside the trailer; I know it was too cold to enjoy any drinks or conversation, so we gave up and went to bed.

11-07-00. Gene and Randy woke me up about 12:30 a.m. They were up starting the pickup to charge the storage batteries enough to be able to use the heater fan and so that the lights would give light. Gene had all the burners on the cook stove plus the oven burner going trying to warm things up. It had even been too cold that night to conjure up that dream about those twitchy-hipped girls down on the tropical islands.

Over an early breakfast we planned our strategy for the day, which hopefully would produce a chance to harvest one of the elk we had seen the previous evening? Gene and I would put on our warmest clothes, plus face masks, and try to get into this last herd of elk. Randy, not being able to walk with his bad knee, would cover the escape routes. When we got to the foot of the mountain we glassed from the pickup for about one hour without any results. I like to have the elk that I'm stalking in sight before leaving the pickup, but we had to start somewhere so off up that steep mountain we went.

We had only gone about 300 yards when we found a spike bull elk that had been killed by a cougar. Judging by the tracks I would guess that it was the same cat that had been on Deer Creek two days earlier. Even though we had seen the elk first the evening before, the cougar had been successful before we were. I cut out the "ivories" out of the elk and dropped them into my pocket. From there all the way up onto the ridge it was just crisscrossed with elk tracks, beds and rubs – any kind of elk sign you could expect to find. Of course all of this sign was hours old. When that cougar killed that spike bull he had chased every elk on the mountain off. Judging by the sign the elk had been on this mountainside for a while. Evidently, they had been feeding at night and bedding in the trees out of that wind during the day. As much as we had glassed this area in the past three days, it was unbelievable that we had seen only six elk the evening before.

We returned to the trailer for lunch. After a cold lunch we drove up Chicken Creek to look at some new country. There was scattered elk sign all along Chicken Creek. When we got up into the headwaters of Chicken Creek we encountered drifting snow along the divide ridge. A badger was the only thing to challenge us for the road. As the front tire was about to smash him he backed down his hole in the road bank. When we drove by he showed me his teeth through a vicious snarl; he would give up the road, but not his dignity.

On our return down Chicken Creek we stopped to inspect an old log cabin in the creek bottom willows. The door was ajar and the back wall of the cabin looked like it was home to some beavers. There were sticks piled five feet high against the back wall. However, when I looked onto a shelf built into the wall about half-way to the ceiling I saw a huge wood rat grooming himself and giving us the evil eye like only a beady-eyed rat could. This cabin must have been the biggest rat hotel in Idaho. Anyway, we named it "Rat Cabin on Chicken Creek". We arrived back at the trailer in the early afternoon. Everyone was getting discouraged from the cold, windy weather, and the scarcity of elk. We decided to call it a trip and go home empty-handed.

Gene and Randy at the Rat Cabin on Chicken Creek.

In retrospect, I wish we would have gone into Arco and rented a motel room, taken a good hot shower, and then treated ourselves to a big steak dinner and drinks. I'm sure a good night's sleep in a warm room would have rejuvenated us. We could have replenished our supplies and then gone back hunting. I'm sure with the moon waning, the temperatures would have come back up to where it would be bearable to hunt. If we could have gotten into position to glass that country on the east side of the Wet Creek Basin, I'm also sure we would have found elk again. That big herd that the cougar had run off were headed that direction when we gave up the chase. When it is windy and cold the, elk like to get on those south and east facing slopes where they have feed and the cover of thick trees for thermal cover.

Anyway, maybe next time we will be better prepared for the cold, windy weather, and have a better game plan in place. I hope that your hunts may be successful, and that you are luckier than we were.

Two old boys with new toys, summer of 2009. We're in our second childhood.

Chapter Fifty-six

LAST ANTELOPE

2006 would prove to be a very lucky and busy year for old Fred Scott. I was fortunate enough to draw tags in Nevada for antelope and mule deer, and both tags were for bucks. I also got a nonresident bull elk tag for Idaho. I also turned 65 years old in 2006 so I was able to retire from working in July and start getting ready for my hunts.

The price of gas at over $3.00 per gallon would dictate that we start camping on our hunts instead of driving from town every day. I had all of the equipment we would need to make this adjustment; it was just a matter of getting it rounded up and checked out before we needed it. This is a very important item when you haven't used some of this stuff in twenty years or more.

Finally, my brother, Don, came down from Idaho and we loaded up all our equipment plus two 4-wheelers, and headed for the old Clover Valley Ranch up in Elko County. The weather was hot and windy, as it had been for the past month, so we just set up a "wicki-up" with a big plastic tarp attached to the pickup. We had a folding table and a gas grill to cook on, so we were in good shape that way. We got the camp all set up and squared away and were ready to check on the antelope that I had been scouting for the past month.

8-25-06. Early that morning we found all of the antelope I had spotted in about the same places, plus we found some new bucks. I had already made up my mind that I was going to try for a fifteen-inch buck with a nice prong and massive horns that had always been by himself on a low ridge separating Summit Creek valley and Clover Creek valley. However, that day I think he decided to start chasing the ladies because we observed him watching another fifteen-inch buck that wasn't quite as massive in the horns or as big-bodied as the first buck.

The other buck was with ten does just to the north of him, up the valley. That evening we were treated to a ringside seat for an antelope fight. Those two fifteen-inch bucks got together on a flat spot and fought it out for twenty minutes. They raised such a cloud of dust that you wouldn't believe it; I mean they shoved each other all over that flat. As far as I was concerned that fight would turn out to be the highlight of my antelope hunt. When it ended the smaller buck gathered up his does and headed off into a deep canyon going to the east. The bigger buck ran down the valley about one-half of a mile and came back driving two antelope does ahead of him. This group followed the other herd up the canyon to the east.

The next day would be opening day and I still had my sights set on that heavy fifteen-inch buck that I had found on my first scouting trip over a month earlier. That buck had always been in the same area on the Summit Creek side of the ridge, so I had decided I needed to come over a saddle from Clover Valley with the sun at my back and the wind out of the west in my face.

Don spotting for Fred's antelope.

8-26-06. Opening day of antelope season in Area's 67 and 68. We were up at 2:30 a.m. and had breakfast and loaded our gear on the 4-wheelers to go around into Clover Valley to start our stalk on the fifteen-inch buck. Going into Clover Valley in the dark turned into quite an adventure. I must have seen at least 500 kangaroo rats running along in the headlight beams. These rats didn't want to get out of the open tracks of the two-track trail, so I ran over about half of them. It must not have hurt them much though because Don said he never saw any rats at all. We parked the 4-wheelers just off the road and headed out across the valley in the starlight. When it finally got light enough that we could see

204

the ridge-line we found out that we were way east of where we wanted to be, so we made the correction and hurried off towards the saddle we wanted to cross. Right at 6:00 a.m. we popped over the saddle to ambush my fifteen inch buck antelope, and just like the script that we had written for this stalk the buck was right there. It surprised us when the buck was only 125 yards away coming up the hillside right towards us.

We squatted down so we would be out of sight of the antelope, and I got my shooting sticks ready so I would have a rest when I stood up. Just as I rose up to shoot, the buck went galloping across the hillside to our left into some tall sagebrush. Evidently he had scented us as now we felt the breeze seeping down from the east. We ran back up over the saddle so we would be able to see the antelope if he ran out into Clover Valley. Sure enough, there was my buck trotting across the valley, so I threw my pack off and got down behind it for a rifle rest if the buck stopped. Finally, the buck stopped out there about 300 yards and turned broadside. I put the horizontal hair in my scope right on the antelope's back-line and the vertical hair right in line with his front leg. I was using my .270 Winchester with 130 grain Fail Safe Winchester ammo. When I touched off my shot I hit right over the buck's back, right where I was aiming! My rangefinder later read 257 yards, not the 300 yards I had estimated. My dad had always said don't ever hold over on the first shot, but stuff happens I guess.

We hiked back to the 4-wheelers, two pretty humble antelope hunters. When we got back to the 4-wheelers we went on up Clover Valley towards Squaw Valley. At 8:20 a.m., just before we crossed over the divide, I spotted a doe antelope with a twelve-inch buck with her. I ranged these antelope at 228 yards, and shot over this buck also. The antelope trotted over the hill out of sight. About one half mile on up the road we came up on the same antelope again, this time the rangefinder said 207 yards. So I tried another shot and hit to the left, in front of the buck, and he turned around and I shot again, missing to the right this time. However, this time I drew blood on the second shot and it was my own where the scope smacked me above the eye.

Don was getting pretty disgusted with my shooting and suggested maybe I needed to sight in my rifle. We came up on this same buck again at 116 yards and I thought I couldn't miss him this time, but I sure as hell did. Don wanted me to try another shot at 150 yards at the same buck, but I said. "I give up." I never did get my gun to shoot right, and haven't figured out the problem yet. We saw several more antelope that day and even saw my fifteen-inch buck that evening across the valley, right where we had seen him the evening before.

8-26-06. We tried the same stalk this morning but we never did see our fifteen-inch buck. The only thing I got to miss on this day was a coyote. And then I lied and told Don I wasn't trying to hit him. By that afternoon I was pretty disappointed in my performance, and for three days it had been hot, like over 100 degrees, so we said to heck with it and went home.

Fred using binoculars while glassing for antelope.

8-29-06 Don had went back to Idaho and I was thinking about those antelope again so my wife, Karen, and I decided to go antelope hunting. This time I had my .308 Norma Magnum along; maybe I could hit something with it. At 7:05 a.m. we were almost back to the lookout spot where we had scouted antelope from all summer. Right alongside the road were two little buck antelope, and my wife was telling me to shoot one of them. So I stepped out of the truck and got a rest over a fence post just off the road right-of-way and shot the bigger buck of the two. I was surprised when the antelope just trotted off after I had shot him through the body behind the shoulder. Even more amazing was the fact that the bullet had left an exit wound eight inches in diameter and that little buck had still ran about fifty yards before going down.

When I walked up to this antelope the memories came flooding back of why I hadn't hunted antelope for about thirty years; they stink worse than an old goat. However, I did manage to get the thing dressed out and skinned without losing my breakfast. I had a six gallon can of water to wash the blood and gore off the meat and cool it down before putting it in a game bag. That little buck's horns were only ten to eleven inches tall, but he had nice ivory tips on the horns. I gave the meat and trophy both away. I'll just save the memories. I think I will quit antelope hunting forever. You can have them; they stink too bad for me.

Chapter Fifty-seven

NEVADA BUCK

Fall 2006. Here it was the 18th day of October and I hadn't filled my deer tag. The deer season had been open since October 7th and I had already hunted on opening day, and then scouted several different areas, so now I had to make and effort to fill my tag.

I had decided to go up into Elko County for a two-day hunt in the Midas, Nevada, area. I was out of town early and out to the trailhead before daylight. This should be a good day to hunt because a storm had passed through the area the day before, dumping snow on the higher elevations. This morning was clear, promising a beautiful sunny day when old sol got up, and when I left my truck it was a refreshing twenty-one degrees.

When I got up on top there were eight inches of unblemished snow to read sign in. However, I went up over Snowstorm Mountain and out to the end of the road between Kenny Creek and First Creek without seeing any deer sign at all. It was 8:00 a.m. and a bright sunny day developing when I walked out onto a rock outcropping on the west side of First Creek. To my surprise when I looked down onto the sunlit east facing hillside, there was a big 5X5 mule deer buck looking back at me. The buck had me spotted so I backed out of there and went back to my 4-wheeler and got my rifle and pack.

I slipped into the head of a draw between me and the buck, and then started my stalk as I needed to get 500 yards closer to be within good shooting range. As I made my way down the draw I happened to look back up towards the top of the main ridge, and there in the head of the draw that held the big buck I was hunting, there was another buck. I put my binoculars on the second buck and his antlers were about one inch wider than his ears, a nice 4X4 mule deer buck. When I tried to get the range on my rangefinder I discovered that the unit's battery was low and wouldn't give me a reading. This smaller buck didn't know that I was there so I continued my stalk on the bigger buck.

I got to the outcropping of rock that I had marked as the place where I would be directly across from the big 5X5 buck. When I peeked over the ridge-top the big buck was looking right at me again, so I ducked down, got my pack off and then crawled back up to the ridge-top with my pack in front of me for a rifle rest. But the buck had had enough and was bouncing across the slope 300 yards away when I looked over the ridge-top. I hated to lose this nice buck whose rack I estimated would go about twenty inches wide, and was real tall, too. But I thought all was not lost because I would go back up the hill and kill the other buck. However, when I got into position to shoot at the smaller buck, he had heard the big buck run off and he was leaving too.

Fred's muddy 4-wheeler on the Nevada deer hunt.

By the time I had climbed back up that forty degree slope to my 4-wheeler I was thanking the good Lord for not letting me kill one of these bucks. It would have been an all day project for me to pack either one of them out of that steep, rough canyon. And at age 65 I don't think I could have done it.

I would spend the better part of the day looking into other drainages off of Snowstorm Mountain with out any success. When I arrived back at my truck the mileage meter on my 4-wheeler read 47.8 miles, and the temperature had risen to a balmy fifty degrees. Me, the 4-wheeler, and everything on it were coated with about two inches of mud. What a mess!

After some hot coffee and a cold lunch I decided to go up Willow Creek, and then ride my 4-wheeler to the top of Toe Jam Mountain. I gathered the gear I would need to stay on the mountain if I didn't get a deer that day, and, after a couple of false starts and going back for forgotten items, I was off up the creek. I arrived up on top to find three to four inches of snow; however I hadn't seen any deer sign. I decided to get my camp set up, which just consisted of a plastic tarp tied to the

4-wheeler for a wind break, and then got my sleeping bag and pad ready for a cold night before going on stand above a "quaky patch" to watch for deer.

I was unsuccessful there, too, so I went back to my camp and got behind my windbreak and then heated a can of Dinty Moore beef stew on my pack stove for supper. I thought the long day would make my simple food taste better; however, my stew wasn't near as good as I had anticipated.

It had been awhile since I had slept out under the stars like I would on that night, like maybe ten years, but I still had good memories of doing just that. I anticipated a cold night so the only thing I took off before getting into my sleeping bag was my boots, and then I put them in my bag too to keep them from freezing. I also put on extra wool socks and my wool stocking cap, plus wool gloves, and then I was ready for bed. It was a bright starlit night up there at 7,123 feet elevation, and the stars seemed to be right in my face. I felt like I could reach up and pull them out of the sky. I could see all the ranch yard lights down in Independence Valley and on the St. John's Ranch away down on Soldier Creek. I finally got tired of watching the stars dancing across the heavens, so I pulled my sleeping bag up over my head and drifted off to sleep.

I woke at 3:00 a.m. and had to pee. When I crawled out of my sleeping bag the frost crystals reflecting the bright night sky reminded me just how cold it really was. It sure didn't take long to tend to business and get back into that warm sleeping bag. When I awakened at 6:00 a.m. the temperature was down in the low teens and it was frosty cold, but I still needed to get up. I had spent a comfortable night in my "Arctic Elite" sleeping bag even in the snow. After a lukewarm breakfast of warmed up beef short ribs, I headed back over the ridge to watch the Quaky Patch again.

I had the same luck as the previous evening, so by 8:00 a.m. I had my camp packed up and was ready to get down off the mountain. The only track I had seen up high in the snow was a coyote track that circled my camp during the night.

Even though there were big black storm clouds building up over in the southwest with their bellies hanging down dripping rain, I would make it back to my truck without getting rained on. I had seen two mule deer does and their fawns coming down the valley but no bucks. It was a 34.4 mile round trip up on the mountain and back to my truck.

I was driving down Willow Creek on my way home when I started thinking of a herd of deer that I had seen back in September on a scouting trip. I can't explain why this came into my mind just then, but when I looked over at the ridge on which I had seen the deer back in September, there they were, out feeding at 11:00 a.m. I know this sounds kind of odd, but I think the good Lord sets these things up when he wants us to be successful. It has happened that way for me so many times that I can't believe anything else.

I grabbed my binoculars and stepped out of my truck to see if, perhaps, there was a buck in this herd of deer. Sure enough, one of them was a forked-horn mule deer buck. I wasn't about to look a gift horse in the mouth; this buck was intended for me. So I got my trusty old .308 Norma Magnum out to try and make the 400 yard shot to the deer

However, the deer had spotted me and gone up over a ridge, out of my view, before I could get a shot off. I grabbed my cartridge and knife belt and took off across the flat to see if I could get another look at the deer. When I peeked over the ridge the deer had disappeared behind, there they were, unaware, only 100 yards away. I aimed for a neck shot and the little buck was mine. As soon as I made sure the buck was down for good I headed back to the pickup to get my 4-wheeler. I unloaded my 4-wheeler and rode across the valley to retrieve my buck.

After field-dressing my deer, when I went to load him onto my 4-wheeler, I found out I wasn't man enough to get the job done. I cut the head and legs off and then still had to cut him in half before I was able to load it onto the 4-wheeler rack. When I got to my truck I unloaded the meat onto the tailgate and then finished skinning and quartering the deer. This little buck was about the fattest deer I ever harvested. I had to wipe the tallow off the blade of my knife more than once during the skinning process. I had a clean tarp, so laid the meat out on that to cool while I drove home.

When this trip was done and over with I was sure glad I hadn't harvested one of those big bucks down in that steep, deep canyon. Every year I tell myself that I'm getting too old to do it anymore, but then after a few weeks have passed I start planning my hunts for next year. That is just the way it is with us hunters; we only remember the good times. The work and sweat just passes from our minds and the next hunting season can't get here soon enough. I hope all of your hunting memories are as wonderful as mine seem to be. Good luck, and take care until next time.

Chapter Fifty-eight

NEVER SAY NEVER

Winter of 2008 came at us in record proportions, according to the keepers of such records, although I am sure that you could find some older individual that would argue the point with you. There is one thing that I can tell you with certainty, though, and that is that our deer and elk were devastated not only from the deep snows but also the wonderful wolves that were presented to us by our government thanks to the enviro's. The wolves not only decimated our big game herds, they also killed several hunting dogs as well as family pets.

Wolf track.

On a more positive subject I was successful in drawing a special deer permit for Unit 6 in the St. Joe River drainage. This permit would allow me to hunt buck deer of either the whitetail or mule deer species, August 30th until December 10th. This was a unit where I had always seen some very nice mule deer bucks during early September before the bow hunters made them go nocturnal.

However, early in 2008 I had started the process of getting a book of my hunting memoirs published. Finally in the last weeks of August my book *"Memories of Hunting Idaho's Golden Era"* was published by Stoneydale Press of Stevensville, Montana, so we had book signing parties and stuff of that nature to deal with; and our first book signing was a real success selling close to one hundred books in a town of only 400 inhabitants.

So on September 6, 2008, I was finally able to make my first deer hunt. There was my nephew, Aaron, and friends, Herb and Justin, who joined me for the hunt in the Dunn Peak area north of Avery, Idaho. We traveled up the Dunn Peak road until we topped out where we could look down into the Setster Creek drainage where we stopped to watch for game with our binoculars and spotting scopes. Right away we spotted elk scattered along the dividing ridge between Setster Creek and the next creek to the west, which is Storm Creek. There were five cow elk and one calf elk being chased all over the sidehill by five 6X6 bulls, plus four 5X5 bulls and a spike bull. A couple of the 6X6 bulls were not only big bodied but also would score in the 320-330-B&C class.

Aaron and Justin were hunting elk with their bows but were lured away from this herd when they heard bulls bugling in the drainage to the east of us, which would be 49 Gulch. Before they left they came back and told Herb and I that they had spotted a thirty-inch mule deer buck in 49 Gulch. We were looking right into the sun and I couldn't spot the deer so I walked down the road to a low saddle where I could get where I would be looking into 49 Gulch. I finally got out where I could see into the head of 49 Gulch, and was just in time to watch two 5X5 bull elk have a sparring match. The bulls were headed up over the ridge that would take them into Stetson Creek and when the lead bull came into a small opening he whirled around and charged the following bull. Of course he had the uphill advantage so he knocked the other bull off his feet and into the heavy alder brush. I was never able to spot the mule deer buck but as I walked through the heavy alders there was a cow elk barking at me continually. When I finally gave up and went out to the road, I spotted three whitetail does on the opposite slope watching me. After the boys came back we drove on towards Dunn Peak.

It wasn't long and there were three blue grouse sitting on the road bank and I had my .22 rifle along so I proceeded to show the boys how to miss five sitting shots at those grouse. And then Justin said, "I thought we were hunting with a professional," a phrase I would hear repeated several times throughout the day. I really didn't see the humor of it! We went all the way out to the gate below Dunn Peak Lookout and back to Avery without seeing anymore game.

After a stop at the Trading Post Bar for lunch we went downriver to Slate Creek and up the creek to Slate Creek Saddle. We did see a nice bull moose across from the mouth of Corvus Creek. The boys threw rocks at that moose for a half an hour with out touching him.

On September 7th I drove out the power-line road off Moon Pass to Binney Creek tower site, where I could glass over into Rover Creek. It wasn't long and right in the edge of the sunlight creeping down off Fool Hen Point I spotted a group of mule deer bucks. Through my 60 power spotting scope I could determine that they were all 4X4's or better and one was a 160-170 B&C class buck. This was no surprise as I have seen bucks in this same area in the past.

Fred's 4-wheeler after flopping down "Suicide Hill".

On September 10th brother Don and I loaded our camping gear on the 4-wheelers and loaded one into my pickup box and put the other one on my trailer and headed for Big Creek of the St. Joe and Cemetery Ridge. We made a stop in Avery for lunch and then missed our turn-off for Cemetery Ridge and were late getting to the trailhead for Mastodon Lookout. We went out to Mastodon and then down the ridge to where we would drop off on the ridge going out to Fool Hen Point.

Don's 4-wheeler didn't have very good compression so we hooked a tow strap from the front of my machine to the back of Don's machine. Don was down the steep part when I dropped my 4-wheeler off an eighteen-

213

inch rock ledge and did a forward flip down the mountain. There wasn't time to even think before I was trapped under my 4-wheeler, which, thank God, wasn't even touching me because I was lying in a trench where motorcycles had dug the trail down powering up the steep incline. Other than having the wind knocked out of me and a bruised shoulder, I didn't think I was hurt much. Don was able to lift the 4-wheeler high enough so that I could crawl out from under it. We spent about one hour getting the 4-wheeler right side up and winched up onto the ridge again. I had broken the cover off of my gun boot but my rifle was okay; the only other damage was my six gallon water can was smashed and broken.

I decided that maybe we had better get back out to the pickup before I stiffened up to a point where I couldn't steer my 4-wheeler. We made it home about midnight and I scared the crap out of my wife when she heard me walk up the street and start fumbling around with the door lock. Don had taken my truck home because his 4-wheeler was on the trailer.

Finally, on September 18th, I decided to go to the doctor and get checked out because I didn't seem to be getting over the accident. I was x-rayed and learned I had three broken ribs and a dislocated right shoulder, plus some internal bruising. So the doctor said no 4-wheeling or hunting for four weeks.

Elk season opened on October 10th so I took my nephew, LeRoy, elk hunting on opening day. I hadn't even been out scouting so we hunted the west side of Moon Peak from the Slate Creek Saddle road. We found no elk sign at all but LeRoy did see two little mule deer does on the ridge above Moon Creek. We split up with LeRoy taking the ridge to the west while I went down and hit Trail 16 going to Slate Creek Saddle. LeRoy would pick me up at the saddle. I didn't see a thing but LeRoy saw three cow elk in the brush-field below George's Hole.

We spent the rest of the day glassing from the pickup without seeing any animals. I was still quite sore from the wreck so didn't get out again until October 18th. LeRoy went with me again and we went on stand out in the dog-leg of Red Top Creek. It was fogged in so we left there about 11:00 a.m. and went back to the truck. We decided to drive out to Moon Pass and glass across into the old burn while we ate our lunch. It was fogged in there, also, so we started down off the pass for home. Just as we came out of the fog in the head of Placer Creek I spotted a mule deer buck on the sidehill above the road. I couldn't hunt in Unit 4 with my

214

permit so LeRoy took off up the creek after the deer. When he got up on the deer's level he started back across the hillside to flush the buck out. However the buck was very cooperative and came out into an opening about 120 yards from LeRoy. LeRoy had an old Model 54 Winchester in the world famous "Ought-Six" caliber that my Dad had given him, a rifle with open sights but LeRoy made a good lung shot and harvested his buck. I had a ringside seat from the pickup for the whole stalk and shot. The buck was a 4X4 without eye guards, as most Shoshone County mule deer are.

LeRoy with his buck.

As the season continued I was pleasantly surprised to find out that I was back amongst friends. Every time I would meet up with anyone they would tell me where they had been seeing animals, and not to worry about getting my elk packed out because they would do it for me. I made several hunts but didn't see any elk or bucks. One morning I had made a hunt into Horseshoe Creek from the power-line road but didn't see anything but two mule deer does. When I came out to Moon Pass I decided to drive down to where I could see into the fern beds in the headwaters of the North Fork of the St. Joe River drainage. There were five cow elk in the fern beds feeding so I put the rangefinder on them and it read 590 yards. As I watched the elk I decided that I could stalk down onto the hillside across from the cow elk and have an easy 300 yard shot across the canyon. But if I did that, I would still have another half mile into the creek bottom and up the opposite sidehill to the elk. So, being kind of tired from the morning hunt and realizing that it would take the whole afternoon to take care of the elk, plus another full day to get it packed out to the road, I decided to pass on these elk. It is always a good feeling to know that you have friends that would do all that work of getting your elk out at no cost to you, however I didn't want to put them out that much.

The elk season closed without Fred Scott getting his elk but I still had that buck tag. I made several hunts without seeing a buck, and then on November 11th brother Don and I decided to make a hunt off of Slate Creek Saddle. We unloaded the 4-wheeler at daybreak but the fog was right down on the ridge-tops as we started out Trail 16 towards Bad Tom Mountain. As we crossed the head of Red Top Creek on the 4-wheeler trail we saw one old lone blue grouse hunkered down on the frost-covered ground trying to keep from freezing to death. We would continue all the way out to Cemetery Ridge before we got out of the fog. It was windy and cold so we continued on until we hit the road going out into Big Creek. We were out this road about one mile when we started seeing lots of deer tracks so we parked the 4-wheeler and started walking out along the road.

We came into the top end of a rocky draw that looked promising so we stopped to glass. In no time at all we had spotted a mule deer buck and one doe about 200 yards away on a hog-back ridge above some cliffs. The deer had us spotted too but didn't take off as I looked for a place to shoot from. Finally, I was able to lean up against the road bank and get my rifle on the shooting sticks and see the buck through a small opening in the brush and trees below the road bank. I had my .30-06 Winchester Model 70 so it would be and easy shot. I decided to shoot the buck right through the front shoulders to anchor him so he couldn't go down the steep slope. When the "ought six" went off the buck was knocked sideways and took one step and then started head over heels down the steep slope. He was out of sight on the first flop so we weren't sure if he was down for good or not.

Don went on up the road to where he could access the hog-back ridge the deer had been on, and I went across the side hill above the draw the deer had disappeared into in case he wasn't dead yet. We found the blood trail where the buck had tumbled down through the brush

Fred with his buck.

into the draw. After about one-half of a mile we finally found the deer dead in the bottom of the draw. He was a little 4X5 buck but would seem like a bull elk before we got him packed out to the road above. It was about 8:30 a.m. when I shot and was 3:30 p.m. before we got to the road with all four quarters. We were two pooped old deer hunters, but glad to be on the road at last. It would be black dark before we arrived back at the pickup.

It had been a hard full day for two old hunters in their sixties. However we were just thankful that we could still participate in the hunt at our age. There are lots of people younger than us who aren't that fortunate. Hopefully, we still have a few years left to enjoy the great sport of hunting.

Chapter Fifty-nine

CLOSE ENCOUNTERS

It has been my experience that whenever you unintentionally get within a certain distance of and animal, or human, they are not going to retreat in haste. I would set this distance at fifty feet; however, it may be more or less. The following are just some of the encounters that I have had personally.

In the early 1970's everyone was interested in mining claims because metal prices were higher than in the past. I was doing some contact claim staking for several individuals, and was checking out the status of some claims in the Columbus Gulch drainage. There was and old brushed-in and overgrown road leading up this drainage, with Columbus Creek gurgling alongside. My wife, Karen, and our son, Jeff, were with me that day, and as we walked up this old road, all of a sudden a black bear walked out of the brush not five feet in front of us. We stopped and the bear stopped with his hair all standing up and his back humped up like a scared house cat. My wife was about to pinch my arm off on one side, and my son was wrapped around my leg on the other side. All of us were scared speechless.

The bear was first to get over his surprise and moved off a couple of steps and then would turn his head to see if we had moved. Not once did the bear growl or make any sound. When the bear finally entered the brush on the opposite side of the road we could hear him tearing up the hillside like the devil himself was after him. I had a geologist hammer in my hand but if the bear would have charged us I don't think that I would have had time to react even if I had wanted too. I don't recall having any thoughts at all about escape or defense, either one. When the coast was clear we retreated back to the truck and I decided I'd come back to that spot another day.

Fall of 1975. I was out elk hunting by myself on the southwest side of Sunset Peak. I was just easing along through some jackpine timber watching for bedded elk when a bull moose stood up out of his bed, not ten feet away. The bull didn't offer to charge, even though the ruff on his neck and back were standing on end. After a matter of minutes the moose started to move off, but as soon as I moved he would whirl back around with his hair all standing up the wrong way. We went through this same scenario several times, with the same results, so I thought I would brand this bull for life. I raised my .308 Norma Magnum to my shoulder and shot a hole through the bull's right ear. The bull just took a couple of quick steps toward me, flopping his head like he was fighting flies, and then stopped, stamping his front hooves into the ground. Fifteen minutes passed and the bull turned to walk off again. I took another step towards him and he spun around again with his hair all standing up, so I shot a hole through his left ear. This time he whirled and ran off through the trees, flopping his head again. I thought I had pushed the issue far enough, so I let him go and changed my hunt plan to a different area.

A bull moose.

Fall of 1982. I was out bear hunting with my brother, Lawrence, and his son, LeRoy. We were on the west side of Grizzly Mountain driving up the road when we spotted a nice black bear just below the road coming down from Grizzly Mt. Lookout Tower. We continued up the road until we intersected the road coming down from the peak and then LeRoy and I walked up the road to see if we could get a shot at the bear. I didn't even take my rifle because LeRoy had his dad's Model 71 Winchester .348 lever action. We came to the edge of the trees and knew the bear should be just another fifty yards further. When we peeked over the road bank the bear wasn't fifty feet away; however he was standing behind a big boulder that stuck out of the road bank. The bear was looking away from us and just his shoulders, neck and head were visible. I whispered to LeRoy to inject a cartridge into the chamber and aim right at the edge of the rock and the middle of the bear's back, over his shoulders. Boom, the rifle went off and smoke flew off the edge of the rock right over the bear's back. When that bullet ricocheted off the rock it couldn't have missed that bear's head by a hair, but the bear didn't even acknowledge that he had heard it. It took a couple of steps further out, away from us, and stopped again. I told LeRoy to hold the same and shoot again. I don't know where that shot went but the bear just started walking away downhill so I told LeRoy to shoot again. Same result as the last shot and when I told LeRoy to shoot again he threw the rifle at me with the action open, and told me to shoot the bear.

We got the rifle reloaded and started tracking the bear down the hill as I just knew that one or more of LeRoy's shots had to have hit the bear some place because the bear never was more than twenty-five yards away. We didn't have any trouble following the bear because it was really dry and dusty. We kept following the track down towards the lower road, hoping to see the bear before he crossed the road below. We came into a patch of jackpine trees and when I looked up there was a big mule deer buck standing not thirty feet away acting like he was invisible. He didn't as much as blink and eye. It was lucky for the deer that the deer season wasn't open yet because he was a trophy that no one would pass up. The deer never moved until we were out of his sight.

Late spring of 1989. My wife, Karen, and I had driven into the Clearwater River to try fishing. It had turned into a black, gloomy and rainy day so the fishing wasn't all that good. We had eaten our lunch and decided to drive over the hill into the Kelly Creek drainage to try fishing there in the afternoon.

We had just crossed Lake Creek when three mule deer, two does and a fawn, came trotting around the corner and then jumped over the road bank when they saw our pickup. When we rounded the next corner there was a coyote trotting up the road towards us so I stopped the pickup. The coyote just kept coming up the road like he didn't see us. He was only about 100 yards away when a big cougar jumped out of the underbrush alongside the road and grabbed the coyote in his front paws. The road was blacktopped and when the cougar grabbed the coyote he fell down and went sliding across the road on his back, and let go of the coyote in the process. The coyote was running for all he was worth right at the pickup when the cougar regained his feet and, in about four big bounds, caught the coyote again in his front paws. However, he fell again and came sliding up the road on his back, letting go of the coyote again. The coyote dove over the road bank right in front of the pickup with the cougar right behind him. We could hear them fighting just over the road bank, so I stepped out of the truck with my .22 caliber pistol. I had just walked around the front of the truck when the coyote came up over the road bank right in front of me. The cougar had him by the seat of the pants with his right paw. The coyote had his head turned, trying to bite the cougars paw, so didn't see me five feet in front of him, but the cougar saw me standing there so he let go of the coyote and pulled his paw back like he was going to swat me with it. The lion let out a big growl and his paw looked to be as big as a dinner plate. I had the gun at arm's length pointed at the cougars head not three feet off the muzzle. The cat had his hair all standing on end, his head looked to be a foot wide and his mouth was all bloody from fighting with the coyote. Finally, the cougar put his paw down and moved off a couple of steps and then stopped and roared at me again. He went through that same scenario several times before he leaped into the underbrush along the road. I was relieved that he had left because I didn't want to kill him, because he was in his summer phrase kind of a burnt red. Even though I think the lion would have went Boone & Crockett, he wouldn't have been a good trophy in that short-haired red phrase.

After the lion left and we started down the road again we saw the coyote jump up the road bank and then disappear. In a quarter of a mile another logging road intersected the main road and the coyote trotted out right in front of the pickup again. We had to swerve to miss him. I couldn't believe that the coyote didn't show any signs of being injured after all the blood the cougar had on his face. I bet that coyote is still telling his offspring about that day. All during this episode we had a 35mm camera plus a video camera lying in the truck seat and didn't even think about taking a picture. A video of that sure would have been worth a thousand words.

Fred Scott fishing on Kelly Creek in 1984.

Fall of 1989 I was out elk hunting on the south side of Moon Pass. I had climbed the ridge just down stream from Roughin Creek. It was real early in the morning when the game trail I was following intersected another cross trail, and in this trail were the fresh tracks of a herd of elk. I had only followed the tracks about fifty yards when I had to duck under the branches of a fir tree next to the trail. When I rose up there was a cow elks butt not fifteen feet in front of me. The elk was feeding on some huckleberry brush alongside of the trail and didn't seem to know I was there.

Cow elk weren't legal game so I just stayed bent over, moving only my eyes as I tried to spot a bull. The cow finally fed out of sight over the ridge-top, and then I saw three cow elk standing on the ridge-top ten yards away looking down at me. They would turn away and leave and then come right back. Finally, they started stamping their feet on the ground trying to make me move. The biggest cow must have gotten a whiff of my scent because she gave an alarm bark and the elk left. I had just straightened up when out of the corner of my eye I saw a big broad butt go behind a fir tree just below me. Later in the day I ran into a friend, Bobby, hunting the same area and he told me he had missed a real big trophy bull elk on the same ridge the day before.

Spring of 1990. My wife, Karen, and I were shooting ground squirrels over on Randolph Creek in Montana. It was late evening as we walked down the road back to our pickup. A big old black bear stepped up onto the road about ten feet in front of us. We stopped and the bear stopped, looking right at us. The bear was waving his head back and forth trying to get our scent; it knew we were there but couldn't identify us, so finally he moved away a couple of steps and then turned around to see if we were trying to follow. We let out a sigh of relief twenty minutes later when the bear finally stepped off the road and back into the forest.

September 17th, 1991. I left home early and was in the saddle between Roughin Creek and Park Creek before daybreak. The purpose of this trip was two-fold as I would watch Park Creek right after daybreak for elk, deer and bear. After watching for an hour without spotting any animals I hiked out the ridge to the west where I could watch down into the two unnamed drainages between Roughin Creek and Champion Creek. I watched these drainages until 8:00 a.m. and only saw one little 5X5 bull elk. I had my shotgun along, so I hiked back along the hillside until I intersected the ridge on the south side of Roughin Creek. I had just started up the ridge when I jumped a flock of blue grouse and was lucky enough to get two birds.

I had just climbed up over the rock bluff on the end of this ridge when two ravens started dive bombing me and squawking their heads off. Being annoyed by this assault on my privacy I shot both of them out of the sky. When I dropped off the knob the sun was just starting to shine through the trees, making it kind of hard to see as I was facing kind of northeast. I noticed what I thought was a rabbit sitting at the base of a tree in the sunlight. However, when I raised my binoculars and focused on the object I could see the head of a big cougar peering around the tree at me only twenty-five feet away. What a photo opportunity and me with no camera. After speaking to the cougar and waving my arm at him didn't get a response, I started walking towards him. Evidently I was within that circle that wild animals define as their space, because the big cat would only retreat a few steps and then stop and look over his back to see if I was following. After taking several minutes to get out of my view without appearing to be leaving, I watched the big cat go bounding downwind of me to get my scent.

That was the second cougar that I have been within twenty feet of in the past two years, and both showed a reluctance to leave. In fact, every wild animal that I have been real close to has shown a reluctance to reveal fear. You can figure it anyway you want, but I think they are just protecting their dignity. In hindsight which is always 20-20, I think those ravens may have been trying to warn me of the cat being so close.

One of the Andersons' hunting camps in the Selway-Bitteroot Wilderness.

Chapter Sixty

BUCK FEVER

What is this malady called buck fever that affects all hunters at some time or other in their hunting career? Old, or young, experienced or inexperienced, it doesn't matter because sometime, somewhere it will grab a-hold of all hunters during their lifetime.

If you want to hear about my personal experience with "Buck Fever" you will have to get my first book, *"Memories of Hunting Idaho's Golden Era".* The following are tales of friends or family who were affected by this mysterious malady.

We were hunting down on the Salmon River below North Fork in the Brushy Creek drainage. As we drove up the road three deer jumped down into the old mine assessment road (dozer trail) we were following, and started bounding up the road. My friend jumped out of the jeep and threw up his Model 99 Savage in .308 caliber Winchester, and then each time that he said "Boom" he would eject a live round out of the chamber onto the ground. After three "Booms" the deer disappeared from sight and my friend looked over at me and asked, "How did I miss those deer?" I said, "You never did fire your gun. Look on the ground, that is where all your ammo is that you ejected out of your gun." Even as he picked up his unfired bullets off the ground you could see the look of disbelief on his face, and his face was chalk white with sweat dripping from his brow.

My dad was in his late sixties or early seventies when he and my brother, Raymond, went for an elk hunt one late afternoon in October. Dad wasn't able to do much hiking so they decided to drive up over Two Mile Saddle and down into Beaver Creek. They were almost to the bottom of the hill on the Beaver Creek side of the hill when they saw where some animals had slid down the road bank and crossed the road, and then went down into the creek bottom.

Brother Raymond stopped the car and got out to examine this fresh elk sign and when he looked over the road bank there were the elk, lined up along the creek getting a drink of water. Raymond ran back to the car, excitedly told dad about the elk, grabbed his rifle, injected a live round into the chamber and sat down on the road bank and shot a cow elk. Raymond must have killed the lead cow of the herd because the elk didn't even attempt to leave; they were just milling around in the open creek bottom sixty yards away. Then Raymond looked to see what dad was doing and there was dad with his rifle pointed straight up looking down at the elk. Raymond asked. "Dad, why don't you shoot an elk?". Dad exclaimed, "Come over here and pull my gun down so I can!" Dad was just frozen stiff with "Buck Fever"!

Not to pick on good old dad, but he would experience "Buck Fever" once again before he hung up his rifle. This time dad and mom had gotten up real early and gone for a ride up Elk Creek and out to Montgomery Gulch Saddle. It was just breaking day when they pulled up onto Montgomery Gulch Saddle when, smack dab in the middle of the road, there appeared a huge mule deer buck, probably the biggest deer either one of them had seen in their lifetimes. Dad's version of the story was that he didn't shoot the deer because he didn't think mom could load it into the back of his Chevy Blazer. But mom told a totally different story right in front of dad, to his complete embarrassment. Mom said dad was shaking so bad that he couldn't even get a-hold of the door handle to open the car door, let alone get out. She said dad just kept repeating over and over, "LOOK AT THAT BUCK, MOTHER." It was a funny story that dad would tell on himself for years after this incident.

Another friend, Bob, told this story on himself when he was eighty-four years old. He said he was just a young whippersnapper about twenty-five years old when he went hunting up the Trouble Creek trail off the Coeur d'Alene River above Prichard, Idaho, where he lived at the time.

Bob said he was pretty much up into the headwaters of the creek when he spotted a huge mule deer buck standing behind and Alder Bush watching him climb up the trail. Bob said the deer was only about seventy yards away, an easy shot for his Model 99 Savage in .250/3000 caliber. Bob said he'd go to the left and the deer would go to the right keeping the alder bush between them. This dance went on for about twenty minutes, and by that time Bob said he was shaking so bad he couldn't even hold the gun up. Finally, the deer turned and went bouncing up the hill into the trees, keeping the bush between them all the time.

Bob said he was so disgusted with himself he just went home with his tail between his hind legs. Bob had a pretty colorful way of describing things. When telling about a friend that was good in a barroom brawl, Bob said, "He was awful clever with his front feet" (meaning his fists).

Along the Coeur d'Alene River above Prichard, Idaho.

Chapter Sixty-one

JUST REMINISCING

I'm sure that all of you have heard the old saying that every man is entitled to one good wife, dog or horse in his lifetime. Well I have that perfect wife, the same one for the past forty-eight years. So I'll go to the dog column where I have been blessed to know more than one good dog, and make some short comments.

The first dog I recall was a Water Spaniel-Irish Setter mix that was coal black with a white spot on his chest. This dog belonged to a family that raised Irish Setters to sell, so this dog that adopted our family was probably a throwback. This dog loved kids, anybody's kids, and would follow us around making sure nobody threatened us.

We named the dog Nig because of his black color, not to disrespect anyone. We were so far back in the hills we didn't even know what a Negro was. The only Negro we had ever seen was "Aunt Jemima" on the syrup can. Yes, syrup came in gallon cans back then.

Anyway, this dog was the favorite of everyone because they knew that he would give his life in defense of any kid. We actually weren't in much danger of getting hurt or maimed, even out in the woods with all those wild animals. I can only remember one time that Nig attacked a person. Nig always slept on the front porch right in front of the door, and our neighbor, who had lived there as long as we had had the dog, got a little too much to drink so he came over to get my dad to join him for a drink in the middle of the night. There were five steps leading up onto the porch, and when the neighbor came stumbling up the steps old Nig came sailing off the porch and grabbed him by the throat. My dad heard the commotion and went outside to investigate. As it turned out the neighbor wasn't hurt, just scared sober. We had Nig for seventeen years before he passed away, and let me tell you there wasn't a dry eye in the house when he died..

We also adopted a female German Shepherd that, before we got her, had been beaten and abused until she didn't trust anyone. If you so much as raised your voice or hand she would cower down and roll over on her back and whine. It took about one year with us before she finally

228

relaxed and started to trust people again. We had her for several years and she would follow us around wherever we went, just like Nig. Her only downfall was she hated porcupines and would grab every one she encountered. There just didn't seem to be anyway to break her of this habit, which would lead to her death. She had gotten slapped in the face by a porcupine and had quills in her eyeballs, so we had to shoot her.

Whenever someone didn't want a dog anymore they brought it to the Scott residence. My dad took in a Pekinese-Terrier cross that had started biting kids and was banned from the city of Coeur d'Alene, Idaho. Dad named him Tuffy and he never left my dad's side for years. My dad was the mine foreman at the Jack Waite Mine so he had to do watchman duty one weekend every month. The mine was having problems with packrats building nests in the electric motors that ran the air compressors, which supplied the compressed air, which in turn ran the drills in the mine. A house cat wouldn't stay in the building for one second with those rats, and traps didn't work either. However one day as dad was making his rounds on watchman duty and walked into the compressor building a rat went scurrying across the floor. Tuffy caught the rat and gave it a violent shake, snapping its neck. Dead rat! Dad left Tuffy in the building for the rest of the weekend and that took care of the rat problem. No more fires in the electric motors on Monday morning. Another unique quality Tuffy had was he knew when ever we were scheduled to work and would wake us up at 5:00 a.m. on those days. Some times we would have to work on a Saturday doing repair work in the main haulage drift, and it has always been a mystery to me how the dog determined if we were scheduled to work or not.

Babe, a Labrador-Shepherd cross was my first bird dog. And not knowing anything about bird dogs, or bird hunting, I took her to a professional trainer for training. As it turned out she became a champion bird dog and retriever. There were days when she got more birds on her own than we hunters did. I will describe one of those days: it was opening day of pheasant season and only about 10:00 a.m. when I finally limited out, so headed for the pickup at the end of the draw I was hunting. When I came in sight of the road I could see a Fish & Game truck sitting on the hilltop watching us, and Babe came back to me with a crippled pheasant she had retrieved out of the heavy brush along the stream we were hunting. I didn't take the bird from her so she loped on ahead and jumped up into the back of the truck. When I hit the road the game cop came coasting down the road and arrived at the truck at the same time as I did. He checked my birds and saw that I had my limit for the day, and then asked about the bird the dog had. He knew that I hadn't killed it, so I told him he would have to talk to the dog about that bird, but I warned him that she wasn't going to give it to him. He got back in his truck and drove off, which was a smart move on his part. Nobody, and I mean nobody, took a bird out of Babe's mouth regardless of who shot it except me. It was a bad day of hunting when Babe didn't have her own limit of crippled birds by 10:00 a.m. She loved to hunt and flush birds for the gun and would get frustrated if we missed too many birds. She had learned early on that pheasants would run on her in the heavy cover, so she would circle out in front of them and flush them right into your face.

A lot of folks would have you believe that dogs are not capable of having a thought about something, and then creating a plan of action and acting it out to their own benefit. I disagree, and I think that Babe devising that plan to stop running birds proves it. I have also observed numerous dogs that having hunted and area before, they would always check out the places where they had flushed birds out of before first, and let me assure you we hunted a great scope of country. Babe only had one sin and that was if you missed a bird sometimes she would chase it until she couldn't see it anymore. No matter how many times I reprimanded her she just wouldn't give it up. I know you're supposed to shoot the dog in the butt! Not this guy. Finally one day when she did this, I didn't blow the whistle or scream my lungs out at her, I just laid my gun on the ground and took off after her, and when I caught her I kicked her in the butt just as hard as I could. I didn't say a word but she made a bee-line for the truck because she knew she was in trouble. Never again did she take off after a bird, and when I blew the whistle to whoa, she stopped and didn't move unless I told her too. Like the professional dog trainer told me the first thing to teach any dog is to whoa, or stop when you give one blast on a dog whistle. That way you can stop the dog before they make any mistakes, and the training will advance at a faster pace, and you won't have to punish the dog for doing something you didn't want it to do.

My first shot at trying to train a bird dog was a bullheaded Labrador Retriever named Caesar. The dog had been trained by about a dozen people and had been dragging a dog house all over Mullan, Idaho, for about two years at the end of a log chain. His owner started telling me all of his problems, the biggest one being that Caesar would break any kind of choker chain collar put on him. So I got out this heavy leather collar that had spikes imbedded in the inside surface and worked on the principle of a choke collar. I put this collar on Caesar and tied him up and we went into the house to have a beer while Caesar educated himself about breaking collars. We had hardly sat down when out in the yard Caesar let a mournful howl out of him that didn't stop for minutes. He had worked that collar down over the point of his shoulder, and then hit it with all of his one hundred plus pounds of weight to break it. Never again did you have to tie him with anything stronger than a piece of store string. His owner said you can't put him in the kennel because he will bark nonstop until you let him out. I put him in the kennel and went out several times and told him to shut up. Finally, I took a chain lease and doubled it over in my hand and walked out to the kennel and when Caesar ran up to the wire thinking I was going to let him out I whacked him across the face with that chain lease and went back in the house. Another problem solved. No matter what you did you just couldn't get Caesar's attention, he was always one jump ahead of you trying to figure out how to get out of doing something instead of doing it. So I took him into my garage, which had a wood floor, put a log chain around his neck and nailed it to the garage floor about eighteen inches from his head. He could get to his food dish and water dish, and I would go in several times a day to clean up and check on him, but never made eye contact or spoke to him for about six days. The next time we went into the back yard for a training session he wouldn't take his eyes off of me. It was like he was saying, "What you want me to do boss? Please don't put me back in that garage." Caesar turned into one of the nicest bird dogs you could ever own.

My next training job was with a Labrador Retriever named Lucky. We went through the whole process from basic commands to hand signals. The only flaw Lucky had was he wasn't sure of himself when he went out to retrieve until he had the bird or training dummy in his mouth and turned towards you and started back. I didn't know what to do to put some fire in him when he was going out to the bird, and then one evening my wife was watching the training session and she suggested maybe a kick in the butt might help. I didn't have any better solution, and had tried everything I thought might help, so I ran up behind Lucky and kicked him in the butt. End of problem.

I have found that the biggest challenge when trying to train and animal to do something is to make them understand what it is you want them to do. Most of them are more than willing to do it once they know what you want them to do. I also learned to not ask an animal to do something unless you're sure they understand what you want, and you're 100% sure they will do it. I also found out early on that an ounce of praise is worth more than a ton of punishment.

Another system is to let the animal train himself. Point of fact: I had a Labrador that found out he could jump up on top of his doghouse and jump over the kennel fence to get out. He didn't go anyplace once he was out, but I still wanted to break him of doing it without baby sitting him to catch him at it. Then one day I was in the kennel feeding the dogs and noticed the snow shovel sitting against the fence so I laid it up onto the roof of the dog house with the blade turned up. It wasn't long after I had gone back into the house and I heard the shovel clatter on the cement floor of the kennel. When I looked out the dog had this bewildered look on his face like how did I hit myself in the face with that shovel handle.

My Brittany Spaniel, Britts.

I'll mention one more dog a beautiful little orange and white Brittany Spaniel. Britt was her name, a little female that was too soft and timid to be harsh with. I never could get her to retrieve so I just let her do her own thing as she could smell a bird a mile away. We would just let the Labradors do the retrieving as they loved to do it anyway. Then one day four of us hunters were hunting chukar's down in the Salmon River country. A big covey of birds got up and several birds were knocked out of the sky, the dogs retrieved and we were still one bird short. No matter how many times that we sent the dogs to the area where we thought the bird had been marked down they came up empty. We even committed the biggest sin of all by scouring the area ourselves, fouling the area with our scent. Finally, we moved on to hunt the stragglers that we had marked down on a hillside.

It had been at least twenty minutes since we had moved on when Britt came up and nudged me in the leg, and believe it or not she had that last chukar in her mouth. Her one and only retrieve! My wife gave Britt a bath one day and then sprinkled her with bath powder to kill that wet dog odor. Britt was hooked. From that day forward she loved to smell like a lady, and given the chance she would get into my wife's perfume or bath powder any chance she got. If nothing else she would ride in the seat of the pickup next to my wife with her nose up in her armpit seeking out that wonderful smell.

Don's dog,
Tumbleweed.

Tumbleweed was a registered Springer Spaniel with black and white marking, just a little runt who lived to hunt and retrieve birds. She was my brother Don's dog. Tumbleweed's only problem was trying to figure out if her name was "Tumbleweed, you son of a bitch" or "You son of a bitch, Tumbleweed." She was a hunting fool, hunting with a bunch of fools.

Midnight and Tumbleweed on a 1984 bird hunt near Lewiston.

Now I will comment on some of the horses that I was fortunate enough to be involved with, and hopefully won't get too repetitious in the process. Many horses I have known have been mentioned in stories in my first book *"Memories of Hunting Idaho's Golden Era"*.

I remember going to my Grandfather Kellogg's ranch in South Dakota one summer in the early 1950's. Grandpa was one of the old school ranchers that still kept a few workhorses even though he didn't use them much at the time. I remember he had a big work horse, Stud, that he kept in a small lot down on the creek. I remember this horse as a speckled, grayish white-colored stud horse that probably weighed close to a ton. Anyway, grandpa and I went into the lot and grandpa put a halter on the stud horse and we prepared to lead him out into a paddock that had a water trough that was built into the fence to be shared with stock in another pasture adjoining the paddock.

For whatever reason grandpa handed me the lead rope and then went to do something else before taking the stud to water. I think the horse's name was Prince but I'm not sure. Anyway, without either of us noticing some other horses in the pasture came into water and when one of them nickered, the stud threw his head up and walked right out through the fence enclosing the lot. This fence was made of three-inch thick by eight-inch wide rough-cut planking for rails four high on good solid posts, but that stud didn't even look at it as he crashed through. Grandpa was shouting at me to hold that stud which was dragging my skinny beanpole ninety pounds along without even turning his head. When he came to the paddock fence which was the same as the one in the stud pen he walked through it, also, and followed the horses in the pasture back over the hill. Grandpa was beside himself and was still scolding me for letting the horse get away when the horses went out of sight. I don't think it would have made any difference if the stud had been tied to a truck because evidently one of the mares in the horse heard was in season.

I have to tell of one other unique quality that Grandpa Kellogg had, and that was that even though he owned several hundred whiteface Hereford cattle he could tell you the history of each and every one of them. He did not keep any records on his cattle, he just stored this knowledge in his head. There were no computers back then.

It was in the middle fifties that I was back in South Dakota to work for grandpa for the summer. I had gone to my Uncle Ray's ranch to spend the night as we were going to move some cattle the next day. Uncle Ray's ranch adjoined grandpa's ranch on the creek breaks. As soon as the morning chores were attended to we saddled two horses to go move the cattle. I was riding a horse called "Bug" (for what reason I hadn't found out yet). We had crossed the creek breaks and came to a gate in the fence going into one of grandpa's pastures. I had opened the gate and shut it, and when I mounted Bug he grabbed the bridle bit in his teeth and ran away with me. I didn't have a clue what to do besides pull on the reins with all my strength, which had no effect at all. Uncle Ray was at least a quarter of a mile back, hollering for me to stop that horse. I was scared out of my wits at first that he had given me this crazy horse, and by the time old Bug had run himself down, in about two miles, I was scared mad. We were up on a little hilltop and I could see Uncle Ray coming as fast as he could, at least one-half mile behind at this point. Like I said I was scared mad so I thought you son-of-a-gun if you want to run we will just run back to the gate and start over. I met Uncle Ray and was whipping old Bug across the flanks with the end of the reins going hell for leather back the way we had come. When we got back to the gate we slid to a stop and I bailed off. Bug was dripping sweat and gasping for air when Uncle Ray rode up ten minutes later. I thought I would probably get a spanking from Uncle Ray but didn't really care because I still had a mad on myself.

After both horses got their breathing back to normal Uncle Ray took hold of the cheek piece on Bug's bridle and pulled his head up into his lap while I mounted up. When we came to the pasture with the cattle in it that we were to move I jumped off and opened the gate, led Bug through the gate and mounted back up without any problems. When we started gathering the cattle I just let Bug do whatever he wanted because I didn't have any idea what needed to be done. The rest of the day I just did my best to stay in the saddle as Bug worked the cattle. That old boy knew how to hold, and cut, cattle. He could stop and turn on a dime and give you nine cents change. At the end of the day we had both earned each others respect.

Grandpa Kellogg also had a big Hamiltonian mare he called Lady that he used to gather the horses and bring them in whenever he had some little chore he wanted to use a team for. The work horses were all a speckled grayish-white color, but I don't know what breed they were

. Lady was a big mare. I am going to say she weighed about 1,200 pounds, and was probably sixteen or seventeen hands high and black as midnight with a white star on her forehead. Whenever I rode her I was just along for the ride; she knew what she was supposed to do. All I had to do was try and still be on her when we got back to the barn lot. My aunt Arlene had tried to instruct me on how to ride a horse as I think she just cringed every time she saw me and Lady going flat out down across the creek breaks to cut off a horse that wanted to turn back, I'm also sure she could see a lot of daylight between my butt and the saddle as Lady jumped across wash-outs. Arlene said, "You need to relax and move with the horse." Hell, my only thought was just staying on the top side of her.

One day one of Grandpa's bulls had gotten out and into another pasture with the neighbor's cows, so I had instructions to go get the bull and put him back into our pasture and then fix the fence. When we found the bull he didn't want to leave the cows and Lady acted like she was half scared of him as he pawed dirt up over his back, and shook those big white horns that almost enclosed his face. Finally, I was able to pop him across the back with a hard coil lariat and got him moving down the fence line. However, when we came to where the fence was down the bull didn't want to go back into grandpa's pasture and would charge the horse when she tried to cut him back through the hole in the fence where

I had fastened the wire to the bottom of the post so the bull wouldn't get entangled in the wire. We had made about a half-dozen attempts to put him through the fence, and even whacking him across the face with the rope didn't turn him, so I gave up and let Lady do what ever she wanted. She had him going the right direction down the fence line and she swung out to the side, and when the bull came even with the hole in the fence Lady came hellbent for leather and hit him with her shoulder and the bull stumbled through the hole and into the pasture.

We chased the bull out into the middle of the pasture, and then went back and put the wire back up on the post and re-stapled it good and solid. Grandpa wanted to know what had taken so long, but I didn't even answer I just unsaddled Lady and turned her into the corral so she could have a nice roll in the dust. I went directly to the house where I was way overdue for one of Aunt Arlene's lunches, or dinner as they called it.

It was 1955 and the Jack Waite Mine was shut down for a labor strike, and two of my brothers had gone to work for the Bob Connors Logging company at Murray, Idaho. They were working on a logging sale just above the Kings Pass road. Connors had this big strawberry roan horse that weighed about 1,800 pounds that they were using to skid the logs downhill to the landing. There was a fellow working with the horse that got fired, or quit, depending on which story you wanted to believe. Anyway, they needed someone to work with this horse so even though I didn't have a clue about log skidding with a horse I was given the job. As Mr. Connors explained to me, all you have to do is drive the trail dogs into the logs. Dick, the horse, would do the rest. Before we started work Dick had to have shoes put on him and my Dad, LeRoy, was selected to do the job as he had been trained by the Army to shoe mules while in the service for Uncle Sam. I rode Dick from Murray up to the logging job the first morning and even though I had long gangly legs I could not straddle Dick's broad back. I had to sit sideways on him. Dick was well up in years and had skidded logs so long that we didn't even use lines on him to drive him. All you had to do was tell him "Go to the woods Dick" or "Go to the landing, Dick" and he knew exactly what needed to be done.

The log sawyers would swamp out a trail for the horse. The logs were not that big and old Dick could judge how many he could pull down hill to the landing and would pull them out into the skid trail, spaced just the right distance apart so that all I had to do was drive the trail dogs into the ends of the logs. Dick would position each log perfectly to go into the log deck. All I had to do is hook him to each log and tell him if it were a long log or a short log.

Dick had been skidding logs for a lot of years so he didn't exert himself too much. I remember one day we had been going right along and when I told Dick to go back to the woods he refused to move, so I walked up to his head and grabbed hold of his halter to turn him around to go up the hill. He didn't budge and finally got tied of me pulling on his head, so he planted one of those pie platter-sized front feet on top of my foot to hold me in place. He only put enough weight on his foot so as I couldn't pull my foot free, and no matter how many times I slapped him in the face he didn't move until he was ready. Dick wasn't lazy, he just knew what his limits were! One morning we hooked onto a big red fir butt log that was about thirty inches in diameter and thirty-three feet long and when we hit the road it dug into the road surface a good six or eight inches and Dick couldn't pull it.

I went up into the woods to get someone to help me roll the log off the road so we could continue skidding logs. The fellow that came to help me was determined to make Dick pull the log to the log deck so he put the bridle and lines on him. Dick tried with everything he had to move that log; his belly wasn't a foot off the ground but he still couldn't move that big log. First he tried pulling it to either side but nothing worked, so then this fellow started whacking him across the butt with the end of the lines. Old Dick just set back about six inches and lunged into the collar with all his weight and the harness came apart like you had cut it with a knife. That ended that little scenario! I spent a couple of months on that job and I don't think I was paid one red cent.

Dick was also a union horse. He went to work at 6:00 a.m. and quit at 10:00 a.m. for lunch, and then went back to work at 11:00 a.m. and worked until 3:00 p.m. when he quit for the day. You could have set your watch by that horse, and he didn't care if he was ten feet away from the deck at quitting time, he didn't move another inch until you unhooked him from the trail of logs.

Next we will talk about a couple of horses you couldn't catch. The first one was a regular renegade that was kept in a three-acre pasture. This horses name was Brownie and you had to run him down every time you wanted to use him. He wouldn't come to you for a ton of oats! We had been chasing Brownie all over the pasture and had cornered him several times, but he would just open his mouth and charge you like a stud horse. Now most folks are going to get out of the way when this happens; however we had been after him for way over and hour and I was at the end of my patience. Then we cornered him next to a big red fir tree and there were lots of limbs lying on the ground about the size of baseball bats and there was no question about whether he would charge us, it was just a matter of when. I picked up one of those large limbs and when he came charging past me I whacked him right across the forehead over the eyes. Brownie went head over heels, knocked colder than hell and when he came to he had a halter on his head. At first I thought maybe I had killed him but didn't really give a damn if I had, because at that point I would have gladly paid for that privilege. You still had to corner Brownie after this incident, but he would just stand there and quiver until you had a halter on him.

A friend, Rich, had a big old horse that weighed over 1,400 pounds named Sundown that was also hard to catch. I guess the reason they called him Sundown was because he could go all day until sundown if it was required. The only person on the ranch that could catch Sundown was Rich's three-year-old daughter, Leslie. She would take a handful of oats and call him to her, feed him the oats out of her hand and then pull on his fetlock until he picked his foot up for her. At this point anyone could walk up and put a halter on him and he wouldn't move until Leslie was out of the way, usually sitting up on that big broad back as he was led to the barn.

I remember this old horse trainer from down in the West Fork of Pine Creek being quizzed by this gal that was complaining about her horse being hard to catch. This fellow told her she had been watching too many TV westerns. He said, "I have observed you when you turn him out at the end of the day, and every time when he lunges through the gate you whack him across the back with the bridle. Would you want to be caught if you knew that someone was going to smack you with that bridle and bit when they turned you loose?"

Molly & Mike were a pair of horses that their owners thought couldn't be separated. They wanted someone to ride them but you were required to follow a certain procedure. Molly was a spirited mare and Mike was this docile gelding that didn't want to get out of Molly's shadow. We had been riding them several times a week following the strict rules that had been laid down by their owners. Both of these horses were kind of a burnt brownish-black color, and of equal size.

One morning we went into the shed where they were sleeping and slipped halters on them and led them out into the corral to be saddled. It was way before daylight when we headed up the trail for Lost Lake, and would be daylight before we realized that we were both riding the wrong horse. I always rode Molly but this day my brother, Ray, was supposed to ride Mike. However we had gotten them mixed up in the dark and I rode Mike in the lead, with Molly following. We had thought the horses were just nervous and excited about all the spooky shadows or something so just let them work off their nervous energy. From that day forward they were fine no matter which horse was leading. Like I said Molly was quite spirited and her owner was afraid of her so if she pranced around or acted skittish he would jump off of her. She was a great horse just full of energy and wanted to go and get it over with and get back to the barn where she would be over fed and spoiled.

We would jump lots of deer as we rode the trails and old skid trails above Silverton, and it delighted Molly to chase those deer until they jumped off the road or trail. It really surprised me how fast those horses could catch a deer even if the deer had several hundred yards head start. Molly liked to run up behind a deer and then nip it right on the butt above the tail. It was a shame that those horses belonged to those guys that were scared to death of them, because they really liked to get out and see lots of country. The best way I know of to educate a horse to be well mannered, is to put lots of miles on them, and pull sweaty saddle blankets off a tired horse at the end of the day.

My friend, Bill, had gone to a horse sale at Spokane and bought a seven-year-old gelding that had never been handled. The horse was kind of a blue and white color in a pinto pattern with smaller dark blue spots across his rump. I think he was maybe from an Appaloosa cross of some kind. He was a nice-sized horse, about 1,150 pounds, and very athletic. His only problem was he didn't know anything, and Bill or none of the rest of us knew anything to teach him. The local sheriff's posse ride came up and I was without a horse to ride, so Bill made me the proposition that if I would ride his blue horse, he would let my son, Jeff, ride his pet Skeeter. We all gathered at a little ranch above the Hale Fish Hatchery at Mullan, Idaho, and there were about forty people and horses going on the overnight ride.

Blue was all excited and nervous with all the strange people and horses, and, knowing that I would have no control over him, I suggested to Bill that I would wait until the others had left before attempting to mount him because I didn't know what kind of rodeo might ensue. The others had been gone about one hour and Blue was dancing around at the end of his halter rope, wanting to follow the rest of the group. So without making any moves like I was going to mount him I untied his lead rope and tied it with the saddle strings before bailing up into the saddle. We were off in a flash. Blue had his ears pinned back and was doing his best to catch the group. When we did catch them ole Blue didn't slow down at all and there was nothing I could do to stop him, or guide him either, and people were being forced off the road whether they liked it or not. Finally, when we were about five miles up the road on top of Mullan Pass, Blue figured out we were all alone and stopped. He had plenty of time to catch his breath before anyone caught up to us, but he had shot his wad so I didn't have any trouble getting back on him.

One of the gals in the group was reading me the riot act for forcing her and "Baby Doll," her horse, off the road. There was a light rain falling washing the dye out of this beauty's long black hair and staining the back of her blouse, but I didn't dare mention it to her. We just plodded along down the road amidst the rest of the group until we arrived at the big meadow in Randolph Creek. The group was going to spend the night on this meadow so everyone was staking their horses out on a good long rope so they could all get tangled together. Bill was worried about what to do with Blue because he had never been turned loose outside of a corral. I thought Bill was going to have the big one when I took Blue to the upper end of the meadow and just dropped his lead rope so he could graze without getting tangled up in his rope. I watched until I saw him standing on three legs, resting under a tree, and then went and took him to water, and then tied him high and short to a tree for the night.

The next morning I turned him loose early so he could get filled up for the day's ride. Breakfast was over and we had brought the horses into camp to saddle them and get ready to hit the trail. Blue was walking kind of stiff and tired like, so I didn't anticipate any problems when I went to mount him. However, when I swung up into the stirrup he bogged his head and went pitching right into camp, knocking over tables and people both. When I jerked myself up into the saddle I came down right on my thumb, laying it back on my wrist, and all this time I was trying to get Blue's head out from under his belly and get away from the camp area. The trail boss was reading me the riot act about mounting a crazy horse right in camp, so I told him don't worry about it because I was not getting off this horse before sundown tonight.

The day's ride was up the steep power-line right-of-way to Taft Summit, and then out the ridge past the Silver Cable Mine and back down to the ranch where we had started. Blue had not learned much other than there were other places besides a corral with a full hay manger at the end of the day. Bill didn't have time to do much with training on Blue, so in the fall he took him to a trainer down on Bear Creek on the lower Coeur d'Alene River.

We were on our first ride of the spring and Bill was going to ride his Blue horse to show how well trained he was. I don't know what the trainer done to old Blue, but I swear you could punch him right between the eyes and he wouldn't even blink. We rode up the East Fork of Lost Creek ridge trail to the junction with the main Lost Creek trail at the head of Hat Creek. Then we came down the main Lost Creek trail to the first creek crossing. There was a log lying at an angle across the creek with a hole below the log about four feet deep where the water flowed over it. All of us had come down and jumped our horses across the creek, over this hole of water. There was a little meadow there so I told the rest of the guys to wait for Bill and see what might develop. Here came old Blue plodding along with his head dragging practically in the trail itself. He stepped over the log and went head first into that hole of ice-cold water. It about drowned both Bill and the horse before they got untangled and out of the creek. We were all laughing like hell as Bill about choked to death spitting water all over as he bitched us out for not telling him about the hole in the creek. I told Bill that maybe he should wake old Blue up before he walked off a cliff and killed both of them. It wasn't very long after that ride that the horse needed new shoes, so they had him tied in a low-roofed shed and Blue reared up and hit his head on a rafter and killed himself.

I'm not sure why it is but most horses will not injure a child no matter how crazy they are. A friend, Frank, and I had made a hunt into Idaho Gulch above Murray, Idaho, and had seen some encouraging elk sign so wanted to return the following morning. Anyway, it was decided that we would leave our horses staked out on the power-line right-of-way below Murray overnight. Then we went into Murray and had some dinner at the Spragpole Bar and came back to check on the horses before leaving for town. Here was Frank's horse, a big flighty 1,200 pound Appaloosa gelding named Rocky Point, covered with kids from head to tail. We couldn't figure out how they had gotten onto his back until we watched the show. There were still several kids on the ground and whenever Rocky Point put his head down for a bite of grass, one of those kids would jump on his head with their arms around his throat right behind his ears and when he raised his head the kid would shinny down his neck until he could turn around on his back. During all this, kids were falling off over Rocky's rump, shinnying down his legs, running back and forth under his belly, and not one time did he shy away or step on a kid. And all this time we had thought he was a grown man's only horse!

I kept my horse up at the Anderson Ranch so one day when my son, Jeff, and I decided to go for a ride we went up to catch a couple of horses. Jeff was only about four years old so he usually rode old Buck, his favorite horse. Anyway, the horses were in the pasture above the house so I got a pan of oats and we went up into the pasture shaking the bucket and calling, thinking I could catch the horses we wanted and go for our ride. There were about a dozen horses in the pasture at the time and here they came in one big herd, all going all out to be the first to the oats. It was too late to run so I jerked Jeff around behind me and was trying to keep the horses from knocking us down as they crowed around trying to get at the oats. When the dust finally settled I couldn't find Jeff, and then I noticed Sundown, a big old gelding, all straddled out with his eyes white with fear. Right under Sundown's belly was Jeff so terrified he couldn't move, and all the other horse fighting to get at the oats. Finally, I just threw them the bucket and reached over and jerked Jeff out from under Sundown's belly. You could actually see Sundown relax when he saw that Jeff wasn't hurt. That was the last time I did that stunt. I don't believe you could have pushed Sundown over with a bulldozer because he had all four legs straddled out and braced with all of his 1400 pounds.

Reflections play on the water of one of my favorite places, Trail Creek at the headwaters of the North Fork of the Coeur d'Alene River.

Chapter Sixty-two

I DON'T WANT TO SHOOT A BEAR

Bear hunting has always been a family tradition in our family. I believe that I first hunted bears in the fall of 1950. If I remember right there wasn't a limit or season on bears at that time; they were considered predators. However, most folks didn't start pursuing bears until after the first frost in September had killed the huckleberries and they were at their sweetest stage because that is when the bears start gorging themselves on the ripe fruit, getting ready for their hibernation period that would start with the heavy snows of late November. That also was when the bears were the fattest, and most folks wanted the lard as much as the meat.

Since that first fall hunt in 1950 I don't believe I have ever missed a fall of bear hunting. I didn't kill a bear every fall, but I probably harvested bears more years than not. I didn't keep an exact count so couldn't even guess how many I did harvest. However, I don't remember that we had any set rules or criteria that triggered us to harvest or not harvest.

It was the fall of 2009 and my wife, Karen, and I decided to take a drive through the high country, scouting for elk and deer and maybe get some forest grouse with the .22 caliber rifle. As we loaded all of our gear into the pickup for a day of driving the back roads looking for game. My wife commented, "Where is your big rifle in case we see a bear"? I said, "We don't want to shoot a bear," my excuse being that the weather was too warm.

On the bright clear morning of September 4th we were out of town at 4:30 a.m. going over into the Coeur d'Alene River Country. Our plan was to drive up Lost Creek right at daybreak to Taylor Saddle. However it wasn't full daylight yet when we arrived there so we went on upriver and turned off into the Shoshone Creek Drainage. We followed Shoshone Creek until we intersected the Falls Creek road and then turned off onto it. We passed the forks of Falls Creek, and the road going to Taylor Saddle was closed, so we went on until we came to the power-line access road. We could follow that road to the Montana state line and then go back to the southwest to Taylor Saddle.

We were only about half way up the power-line road at 6:00 a.m. when, as we came around a corner, I thought I saw a big bear jump over the road bank into the heavy brush. However, when we rounded the next turn there was a cow and calf moose trotting up the middle of the road. It wasn't far before we approached a switchback in the road the moose jumped off into the heavy alders lining the road. It is always exciting to see game even if you're not hunting.

We had gone all the way through to the Montana state line where a road goes down to Trout Creek, Montana, and the other fork goes back to the west to Taylor Saddle. We were about half way out to the saddle when as we passed through some old growth hemlock trees and a grouse flew off the road edge into a tree. We stopped and, after looking for quite a spell, I finally saw the grouse sitting on a limb 100 feet up one of those big trees. I had to crawl down the road bank to where I could get a rest alongside another tree to make the shot. You just don't shoot a grouse any place with a .22 rifle. The perfect shot is right behind the eye, through the head. I made the shot but after the grouse tumbled out of the tree, bouncing from branch to branch, it was a good sixty yards down the steep embankment when it finally hit the ground.

Karen could hear it fluttering around on the ground so I put the rifle back in the truck and started after it. Finally I found a trail of feathers where the grouse had tumbled down the steep mountainside. I was successful in finding a nice fat Franklin grouse (or foolhen as they are called locally). After climbing back up to the road and dressing the bird out, it was 6:45 a.m. We always clean our birds immediately so they cool out fast and because it also causes the meat to be better flavored and tender. I put the grouse into the ice box and got a couple of sodas to quench my thirst after climbing back up that steep hillside to the truck.

After getting to the saddle we proceeded up towards Bloom Peak, watching for game as we drove slowly along the old CCC road. When we reached the summit of Bloom Peak we stopped to listen for elk bugles. Karen said she could hear a bull bugling but it was a long way off. I started glassing the brush-fields for elk, and as I followed and elk trail through the alders I spotted the yellow butt of an elk going into the brush. I didn't see the elk long enough to determine whether it was a cow or a bull, but assumed it was the bull Karen had heard. We then drove on down towards Eagle Creek, stopping to glass and listen several times. As we approached Nocelly Saddle we saw a coyote cross the road ahead of the pickup. By 8:00 a.m. we were in the bottom of Prichard

Creek so I suggested that we drive up West Eagle Creek and try and get some ruffed grouse.

We were just past the last house going up West Eagle Creek when I saw three grouse scurry across the road and go into the tall grass. Finally, I was able to spot a grouse head sticking up above the grass so I kneeled down and shot. The head-shot grouse towered straight up about twenty feet, then hooked off into the trees. I was trying to spot another bird so didn't mark the location of the bird I'd just shot, which would prove to be a mistake. I walked along the line the bird had taken going into the cedar thicket, trying to find it, but would spend thirty minutes looking without locating the bird. Karen said she saw another coyote cross the road while I was in the thicket. Maybe he was hunting grouse, too, and I had interrupted his hunt.

We were only up the creek between the first and second bridges when I happened to look up onto a rockslide above the road and there sat a bear looking down at me. I told Karen about the bear so she suggested that I take its picture as we had a camera along. I stopped the truck and reached down between the seats and pulled out my .44 Ruger Magnum that I always pack in case a wolf attacks me while I'm out in the wilds. I hurried out of the truck and scrambled up the road bank and through a fringe of brush below the rockslide. The bear was still sitting there, looking down at the road where he had seen the truck pass. I hadn't wanted to shoot a bear but now was possessed with the thought of harvesting a bear with my pistol.

The bear was perfectly broadside with its front feet up on a log so I took aim and shot it right behind the foreleg. The bear lurched over the log and tumbled down though the rocks of the slide. In a heartbeat it was back on its feet, trying to go across the slide, so I shot it again in the same spot and it tumbled down within ten yards of me before regaining it feet and started climbing straight up the slide rock. This time I shot it between the shoulders, through the back, and that stopped its struggling. The bear was only a yearling sow but it still took three 240 grain .44 Magnum hollow point bullets before expiring.

Karen was just aghast when I dragged the bear down to the road. She said, "It scared me half to death when I heard that pistol go off because I thought you had the camera and were just going to take the bear's picture."

It was getting pretty warm at the stream bottom so I hurried to get the bear field dressed and into the truck box, laying the carcass across

Fred's bear, 2009.

the spare tire so it could catch the breeze and cool out. When I dressed it we found the stomach so full of berries it was as hard as a basketball. Maybe that was why she didn't run off. I appeased Karen by telling her it would be a good sausage bear. The warm weather subsequently shortened our scouting trip as we had to get the bear to a cooler and skinned out.

When my friends started teasing me about shooting such a small bear, I told them that she had charged me and that was why I shot her in the back! What a rewarding way to cap sixty years of bear hunting by harvesting a bear with my pistol.

Chapter Sixty-three

A LIFETIME IN THE OUTDOORS

I think our parents were typical of the times, migrating to Idaho during the Depression of the "Thirties" from the ranch country of South Dakota in 1936. The farm and ranching industry was the hardest hit because of the drought. I remember my father saying that he was working on a ranch for $1.00 dollar per day, and paying his own board and room out of that dollar!

When they got to Idaho my dad went to work at the Jack Waite Mine where day's wages were $3.25 per eight-hour shift. They rented a company house where the rent was $5.00 per month and that included electricity and water inside the house. This was quite a change from the ranch where they used a coal oil lamp for lights and packed water from a well for household use and drinking water was collected in a barrel that caught rainwater from the roof. At Jack Waite they also had and indoor flush toilet, where on the ranch it had been the old two-hole outside toilet over in the draw.

We were always an outdoor family, going on picnics where we spent the day fishing, hiking, berry picking, and sometimes shooting gophers with an old single-shot .22 caliber rifle. If we went for an overnight trip, Mom stayed home because she had had all the wind and discomfort she wanted on the ranch.

Our territory in those early years was usually within ten miles of home because people just used the family sedan for transportation, and everyone had a utility trailer that was pulled behind the family sedan for extra equipment or hauling of any kind. The Forest Service trails built by the Civilian Conservation Corps went up almost every major drainage for fishing, or along the ridge-tops for hunting. All of these trails were maintained by the U.S. Forest Service for fire protection. That was the main rule, at the time, that was drummed into us: "Be Careful With Fire."

The fishing was phenomenal back then every; stream was full of native fish. As I remember, back before the 1950's the only stream open

249

for fishing was the main North Fork of the Coeur d'Alene River. The tributaries were closed for spawning habitat for native trout.

The main river at that time had about three times the volume of water it has in it now (2009). We had hard winters back then and there was still lots of trees to hold back the runoff. We boys would hike down into Butte Gulch from the headwaters or down to West Eagle Creek to fish, if we were adventuresome. I don't recall that we even knew we were breaking the law. However, I can remember staying on the ranch down on Beaver Creek with old "Uncle Pete," who was no relation of ours. We just called him that out of respect.

Beaver Creek and all of its tributaries were full of native brook trout that you could catch with a bare hook. We used little size 14 gold hooks, usually baited with a worm that we had dug out of Pete's garden. Old George Stout was the game warden back then and we ran him ragged trying to catch us fishing in the closed streams. Upper Beaver Creek had lots of old hollow cedar stumps to hide in, and the brush along the stream was thick enough to discourage a middle-aged man from chasing a bunch of kids in it. I'm not sure uncle Pete condoned our fishing in a closed stream I think he tolerated it to compensate for our vicarious appetites. Even though we youngsters had inexhaustible energy for doing chores, we also had bottomless stomachs like all growing boys of that era. I know if our dad had gotten wind of what we were doing, we would have had a hard time sitting down for a long time. I distinctly remember that before we left home for the real world his parting remark was, "Before you do something stupid and get put in jail, figure out how you are going to get out of jail because I will not be helping you."

My first remembrance of hunting was hanging onto dad's back pockets so he could pull us up the mountain. We were maybe five years old at the time but dad had already started us shooting the old single-shot .22 caliber rifle that we used for forest grouse. If we encountered a grouse, dad would give whoever's turn it was to shoot one shell, and if you missed the bird's head it was someone else's turn to shoot. There were lots of birds back then and I don't recall anyone mentioning there being a limit on how many you could bag. I do remember that a family of nine could put away about six grouse at one sitting.

Back then there were mule deer everywhere. It was no big deal to get your buck any hour of any day. If my memory serves me right, the season ran from the Saturday closest to the first day of October until the end of November. However, as I remember it, most folks hunted black bear starting about the middle of September. I don't think there was a season on bears because they were still considered varmints. I know most of the nonresident hunters back then were after black bear. We boys were quite popular as guides and packers, or you might say draggers. If someone shot a bear down in some hole we would just swarm around it like ants and drag it to the road. We couldn't believe it then, but we even got paid for it more than once.

As I remember it elk hunting didn't open in our territory until the late 1940's or maybe early fifties. I know when dad first started hunting elk they were in only a few drainages along the main river. Dad did most of his hunting on the ridge trail between Butte and Bear Gulches. The trail ran from Maple Peak Lookout down to the mouth of Butte Gulch. I can remember brother Don and me getting several spankings for scaring the elk off with our constant fooling around.

Elk were the only animals that dad really was serious about harvesting. Prior to the season opening in the Coeur d'Alene River drainage dad had always hunted in the Lochsa River country. After the late 1950's elk spread out through the Coeur d'Alene Mountains and we became more successful at harvesting our elk. As I recall, elk hunting was at its best in the late 1960's and 1970's and up into the mid 1980's.

As I said before, our preference had always been with black bear, not that they were that hard to harvest but mainly because that had been our first passion when we stated hunting big game. Deer never were that much of a challenge until the late 1970's. Elk were always one of my favorite game animals because of the prestige that a hunter had if he harvested an elk every year.

As we became more proficient at hunting we expanded our horizons and hunted further away from the Coeur d'Alene Mountains. The Lochsa was our first trip away from the valley, and then the Clearwater, St. Joe, and Salmon river country followed. As boys I remember we read dad's *Field & Stream* and *Outdoor Life* magazines over and over. We dreamed of leading the good life and going on thirty-day pack trips with Jack O' Connor into the wilds of Canada and Alaska. However, I think we had it better than most rich and famous hunters because we could step out the back door and be hunting without the expenditure of thousands of dollars.

Our last stronghold for elk was the Little Lost River Valley in central Idaho. However, then the wonderful "Canadian Wolf" was forced on the residents of Montana, Wyoming, and Idaho, against the protests of residents; the result has been the decimation of our deer and elk herds. The only reason for this travesty was that it was termed "politically correct" and our Fish and Game Departments didn't want to give up any federal dollars or step on any political toes, even though they have always depended upon the sportsmen to fund all of their policies, whether it was for huntable big game or nongame animals. I believe this was done to appease the anti-hunting folks that didn't want to pay for anything, but rather just set the agenda of Fish and Game at the expense of the hunting public.

I say if these folks want the wonderful wolf where they can hear its howl, let them take it into their neighborhoods where they can watch it kill their pets or animals, and, I might add, at their expense and not ours.

I think that time will prove that they have gone too far this time. No matter that hunters have complained about these failed policies, it is still all about the dollars that state game departments can raise to further their own agendas, and to hell with the rest of us.

The year 2009 was the beginning of a focused push to right this wrong. Fish and Game dollars from sportsmen are on the decline, and protest are becoming focused on the responsible parties. Time will tell, but I believe that Fish and Game is going to have to answer to the sporting public, or lose their jobs to someone who will.

2009 was the first ever hunting season that I can remember where we didn't get at least one opportunity to harvest an elk. There were folks that were lucky and harvested elk, most of them being mature bulls. I have always kept a record of animals seen throughout the year and for the past several years I have watched cow-calf ratio decline, as well as cow-bull ratios.

Idaho is not the only state experiencing these declines in deer and elk numbers. This past 2009 elk season I never saw one bull elk after the season opened, and not that many spike or younger elk throughout the year. Our elk herds are not twenty-five percent of what they once were, but Fish and Game says it all about HABITAT! But let me ask Fish and Game, and all of the so-called sportsman's groups, what they are doing about habitat enhancement?

I guess I will end this by saying that in 2009 I hunted harder and saw less game than in any season in recent memory. However, even though I am in my late sixties, I am ever grateful that I can still participate in the great sport of hunting and fishing. However, I don't think those that follow will be able to make that claim.

Back in the day fishing and hunting were the common man's recreation, most all common families would spend their yearly vacation doing one or the other as a family. That is why it saddens me to see this opportunity taken away from the average sportsman because they are unable to pay the high fees to participate. Nowadays we have Super Hunts, Governor Tags, Controlled Hunt Tags, the only catch being that you must pay hundreds of dollars to participate, and apply in multiple states to have a chance at one of these trophy tags. So the hunt has turned in to a lottery where only the rich and famous can participate. You can be the judge but I don't like this system, and I think sportsmen need to take back control of their government agencies so everyone is represented, not just the precious few

Muzzleloader deer and elk camp on the North Fork of the St. Joe River in the fall of 2009.

Our cover photo is of Upper Glidden Lake, which is located right up against the Idaho-Montana state line in the headwaters of Canyon Creek. It was taken by Jay Van Kuiken of Wallace, Idaho.

LISTING OF BOOKS

Additional copies of *Reflections From the Golden Era of Hunting* by Fred S. Scott and many other of Stoneydale Press' books on outdoor recreation, big game hunting, or historical reminisces centered around the Northern Rocky Mountain region, are available at many book stores and sporting goods stores, or direct from Stoneydale Press. If you'd like more information, you can contact us by calling a Toll Free Number, 1-800-735-7006, by writing to the address at the bottom of the page, or contacting us on the Web at www.stoneydale.com. Here's a partial listing of some of the books that are available.

Historical, Hunting Reminisces

Memories of Hunting Idaho's Golden Era, By Fred S. Scott. Experience, through the stories of this book by one of Idaho's most revered big game hunters and master storytellers the saga of a lifetime spent in quest of elk, deer, bear and other game species over a lifetime spent in the wilds of Idaho. 64 chapter, many photographs, 256 pages, 6x9-inch format. Softcover.

From Cottontails to Kudu, By Mitch Rohlfs, Ph.d. The tradition of a life being shaped by the rigors, challenges and joys of hunting looms large in this book, which details the transformation of a young boy on his first rabbit hunt into an international big game hunter and accomplished upland bird hunter. 6x9-inch format, hardcover, 256 pages, dozens of photographs.

The Trail of a Sportsman, By Duane Bernard. Follow the author on a life-long quest to hunt big game across the world and to achieve what is called Oregon's "Super Slam" on a working man's budget. Go with him on adventures to Montana, Idaho, British Columbia, New Mexico, Alaska, Quebec, South Africa, Zimbabwe and Namibka, as well as in his native Oregon. 6x9-inch format, 154 pages, many photographs.

Cow Range and Hunting Trail, By Malcolm S. Mackay. An expanded new edition of the early-day Montana classic first issued in 1925 written by legendary rancher-outdoorsman Malcolm S. Mackay and illustrated by famed cowboy artist Charles M. Russell. 256 pages, 35 photographs, a new long-lost chapter added to marvelous stories of ranching and big game hunting in the West, this book is a reprint of a national best-seller from 75 years ago.

Copenhaver Country, By Howard Copenhaver, the latest collection of humorous stories. Contains rich humor and studied observations of a land Howard loves and the people he met along the way in a lifetime spent in the wilds. 160 pages, many photographs.

They Left Their Tracks, By Howard Copenhaver, Recollections of Sixty Years as a Wilderness Outfitter, 192 pages, clothbound or softcover editions (One of our all-time most popular books.)

More Tracks, By Howard Copenhaver, 78 Years of Mountains, People & Happiness, 180 pages, clothbound or softcover editions.

Mule Tracks: The Last of The Story, By Howard Copenhaver. As one of Montana's most revered storytellers and honored outfitters, Howard spent years leading his mule packstrings through the Bob Marshall Wilderness. Read here of his adventures, misadventures and other wild tales of mules in the wild country. 176 pages, hardcover and softcover editions.

Indian Trails & Grizzly Tales, By Bud Cheff Sr. A wonderful collection of stories taken from a lifetime outfitting in Montana's Bob Marshall and Mission Mountain Wilderness areas, by a master woodsman. 232 pages, available in clothbound and softcover editions.

Colter's Run, By Stephen T. Gough. A big, stirring novel based on the life and times of the most famous of the mountain men who ever plied the trade in the mountains and plains of Montana, John Colter. One learns that Colter was as big as, if not bigger, than his legend as the ultimate mountain man. 392 pages, 6x9-inch format, softcover..

Montana Ghost Towns and Gold Camps, By William W. Whitfield. Explores Montana's rich gold rush era'shistory of more than 71 historical sites. 240 pages, 450-plus photographs.

Hunting Books

The Packer's Field Manual, By Bob Hoverson. Featuring use of the Decker Pack Saddle, this manual written by one of the top experts in the country will literally provide you with every detail necessary to successfully pack with the Decker Pack Saddle. 6x9-inch softcover format, 192 pages, many photographs and illustrations by Roger Inghram.

Hunting Chukar, By Richard O'Toole. This authoritative and detailed guide to hunting the West's most elusive game bird, the chukar, provides both experience and knowledge taken from 35-plus years of experience. Chapters on locating birds, tactics used in hunting them, gear, the choice and use of dogs, and many photographs. 6x9-inch format, softcover, 12 chapters and an appendix.

Solving Elk Hunting Problems, By Mike Lapinski. Subtitled "Simple Solutions to The Elk Hunting Riddle," this book, in 15 chapters and more than 80 photographs tells you now to cope with specific problems you'll encounter in the field – a hung-up bull, changes in elk behavior under heavy hunting pressure, peak rut activity, and so on. 6x9-inch format, both softcover and hardcover editions.

High Pressure Elk Hunting, By Mike Lapinski. The latest book available on hunting elk that have become educated to the presence of more hunters working them. Lots of info on hunting these elk.192 pages, many photographs, hardcover or softcover.

Bugling for Elk, By Dwight Schuh, the bible on hunting early-season elk. A recognized classic, 164 pages, softcover edition only.

A Hunt For the Great Northern, By Herb Neils. This acclaimed new novel utilizes the drama of a hunting camp as the setting for a novel of intrigue, mystery, adventure and great challenge set in the woods of northwestern Montana. 204 pages, softcover.

Ghost of The Wilderness, By James "Mac" Mackee. A dramatic story of the pursuit of the mountain lion, the Ghost of The Wilderness. A tremendous tale of what Jim MacKee went through over several seasons in his quest for a trophy mountain lion in the wilds of Montana. 160 pages, softcover.

The Woodsman And His Hatchet, By Bud Cheff. Subtitled "Eighty Years on Wilderness Survival," this book gives you practical, common sense advice on survival under emergency conditions in the wilderness. Softcover.

STONEYDALE PRESS PUBLISHING COMPANY
523 Main Street • Box 188
Stevensville, Montana 59870
Phone: 406-777-2729
Website: www.stoneydale.com